DIVERSITY

as

RESOURCE

Redefining Cultural Literacy

Edited by Denise E. Murray

Typeset in Palatino and Benguiat by
World Composition Services, Inc., Sterling, Virginia
and printed by
Pantagraph Printing, Bloomington, Illinois

Helen Kornblum *Director of Communications and Marketing*
Marilyn Kupetz *Senior Editor*
Patti Olson *Graphic Designer (Cover)*

Teachers of English to Speakers of Other Languages, Inc.
1600 Cameron Street, Suite 300
Alexandria, Virginia 22314 USA
Tel 703-836-0774 • Fax 703-836-7864

ISBN 0-939791-42-0
Library of Congress Catalog No. 92-061747

*To my students, past, present, and future,
for having opened their worlds to me.*

Contents

Contents

Acknowledgments

Many people have participated in the development of this collection—I am grateful for their help and contributions. I would like to thank the NCTE/TESOL Liaison Committee for giving me the opportunity to organize the colloquium that provided the title and several chapters in this volume. I would like to thank especially Helen Kornblum for her enthusiastic support and promotion of this project; Marilyn Kupetz, for her patience, attention to detail, and timeliness; Ann Raimes, Jack Richards, and the TESOL Publications Committee for approving the project; anonymous TESOL reviewers; the chapter contributors for being such a delight to work with; and finally, all of our collective students for inspiring us to share their knowledge and ours.

Foreword

The theme
is as it may prove: asleep, unrecognized
all of a piece, alone
in a wind that does not move the others—
in that way: . . .
. . . a mass of detail
to interrelate on a new ground, difficultly; . . . .

William Carlos Williams, 1946, "The Delineaments of the Giants"

In the Spring of 1960, the director of a Special Education program in southern California was hard at work trying to convince me—a novice substitute teacher in his program—that the students I would be working with were "mentally retarded—without culture, ambition, or a sense of future." At a particular moment, I looked at this dark-skinned man with whom I had spoken Spanish on my first job interview and said quietly, "But you do not believe what you are saying to me." After a long look out the window onto the dusty fields where he could watch the parents of the children in his classes work, I heard him say, almost under his breath, "I must." The pain of his denial of self and of the full human potential of his younger brothers and sisters has never faded for me.

I knew then that anyone who chose to teach those born into families that did not speak English had to relate "on new ground" and with difficulty.

Those who teach English as a second language or dialect and refuse to accept the labels both formal education and the society at large give their students have known for decades that they were delineating new ground for these "giants." They have known also that their counterparts who teach those for whom English is their mother tongue might have difficulty understanding the "mass of details" of the many terrains one must cover to learn something of the cultural backgrounds of students, their home language uses, and their inner strengths for facing a linguistically intolerant society.

It is not possible to teach the spoken and written English forms required in academic life to those for whom these have not been part of mother tongue socialization without dealing with different cultural ways of believing and behaving—their own and those of mainstream society. Long before it became fashionable in the 1980s to challenge the Western canon of literature, many teachers of English as a second language or dialect worked from the texts of those they taught. They led their students to identify, accept, explain, and understand varieties of language forms and uses. Well before scholars traded critical reviews of U.S. education, these teachers opened opportunities with their students to question and explore the "strange ways" of mainstream institutions. Necessity had been in these cases the mother of creation, invention, exploration, and humaneness.

The chapters of this book make clear to all teachers how they might embrace the breadth, promise, and potential of students from diverse linguistic and cultural backgrounds. These chapters provide clear ideological, procedural, and evaluative steps to put in place the practice of a dominant theme in contemporary reform movements in education: restructuring not only roles and relationships of power but also approaches to learning for all players on the stage of formal education. For those teachers who take up ideas from this book, learning must be something they adopt for themselves and not just for their students. Students can teach much to those of us who have worn too long alone the mantle of "the teacher" as the single source of knowledge in classrooms. The messages of the chapters here are "all of a piece"— they do not fall out in simplistic lesson plans drawn up months in advance of the start of a class. They require integration of philosophy, principles, and practices—all of which come together here in the words of teachers who have learned to speak through and with their students and enable us thus to hear the voices of their students.

The winds of change are blowing across all classrooms in U.S. education. We hear voices beginning to express hope and promise rather than fear of diversity. They admit they can learn much from the varieties of language, texts, and cultures in their schools.

Many teachers of English as a second language or dialect have heretofore silently—behind the closed doors of their own classrooms—initiated some of the changes called for in current reforms. But because these teachers have so often been given peripheral and low-status positions within their departments, schools, and districts, their ideas have not been acknowledged as sources or models for contemporary educational changes. In this book, some of these teachers step forward to make themselves heard and to help others respond positively to these current winds of change.

If others join these teachers and persist, we can expect that, someday soon, students such as those who speak out in these pages will be seen as "giants," as worthy exemplars of the promises of the current theme of reform. When such a time comes, the reward will be not only theirs and ours, but also that of the children who will learn and teach in future generations.

Shirley Brice Heath
Stanford University, California

Introduction

This collection grew out of several events, each one a steppingstone toward a more thorough and inclusive view of "diversity as resource." I first learned to consider students as resources from Sandra Nicholls, who spoke at ATESOL's 4th Summer School in Sydney, Australia in 1985. In her talk on bilingual students, she discussed how to empower both teacher and learner. Over time, I expanded my own thinking and practice by reading widely in anthropology and Rogerian psychology (as the latter relates to the teaching of English as a second language [ESL]). As my ideas evolved on how to tap into learners' language and culture, I presented them at numerous conferences; Chapter 11 of this book comprises the basic ideas of my presentations.

My thinking was also challenged by many publications on literacy (such as Heath, 1983; Pattison, 1982; Street, 1984), which helped me and many other scholars learn to view literacy as a social construct. Shirley Brice Heath (1983), for example, discusses *literacy events*: those events that "have social interactional rules which regulate the type and amount of talk about what is written, and define ways in which oral language reinforces, denies, extends, or sets aside the written material" (1983, p. 386).

This new, "ideological view" of literacy (Brian Street's term) expanded the scope of the concept, showing that academic (or high) literacy is merely one of many literacies. In other words, literacy is "defined not as 'high' and literary culture but [as one that] has been democratized to emphasize individual biographies and experiences" (Candlin, 1989).

The publication of E. D. Hirsch's (1987) *Cultural Literacy* brought to public consciousness the issue of the relationship between literacy and culture. He views literacy as a monolithic, single notion and its practice as academic or "cultured." For those of us working with students from different cultures and different literacies, Hirsch's conception is exclusionary and limiting, disempowering nonmainstream uses of language and cultural practices. Hirsch and many others deem non-mainstream students (and their entire speech communities) illiterate and uncultured in that they may have no knowledge or understanding of the items mainstream, high culture values. As this book will demonstrate, however, such students are not illiterate; they merely practice different literacies. Nor are they uncultured; they merely hold different cultural values.

In 1989, I volunteered to arrange a panel presentation for the National Council of Teachers of English (NCTE) Convention in Baltimore, with the theme "Celebrating Diversity." The theme of this panel (reworked as the title of this book), sponsored by the NCTE/TESOL liaison committee, brought together the various issues I had been working with over the past several years: diversity, literacy, culture, and the celebration of what our students bring with them to the classroom. This book includes chapters by the original participants in the NCTE Panel (Dandy, McLaughlin, Nichols, Soter, Walters) as well as several other chapters by scholars working on literacy in different cultural and linguistic settings.

Diversity as Resource focuses particularly on cultural and linguistic diversity. Every contributor recognizes the importance of age, address (rural/urban), gender, and religion. As educators, we need, of course, to be sensitive to all these factors, but our combined expertise lies in culture and language, areas of increasing importance in education. Colleagues and the popular press are constantly drawing our attention to the linguistic and cultural diversity of the U.S. population in general and the school population in particular. Already, for many school districts in California, the majority of students are not native speakers of Standard English. This situation holds true for many other nations, whether as a result of immigration (e.g., Australia) or of traditional linguistic and cultural patterns (e.g., India)—for school-age children and for adults.

We also consider literacy to be socially constructed and culturally embedded (Murray, 1990) and agree with Street's (1984) ideological model of literacy. "Those who subscribe to this model concentrate on the specific social practices of reading and writing. They recognize the ideological and therefore culturally embedded nature of such practices" (p. 2). Further, because literacy is socially constructed, this book focuses on literacy communities (Murray & Nichols, 1992), an expansion of Heath's notion of a literacy event. *Literacy* communities are *speech* communities that share ways of interacting with text; that share types of literacy events; and that share uses of language that entail cognitive, social, and cultural ways of taking from and making meaning of the world, or, in Judith Langer's (1987) terms, literacy communities are "a culturally-based way of thinking" (p. 17). From this perspective, literacy is more than the skills of reading and writing; it is the ability to comprehend, interpret, analyze, respond, and interact with a variety of sources of information. Literate behaviors, then, do not necessarily involve print, but rather ways of taking from and interpreting the world. With such a view of literacy, our discussions are not limited to reading and writing, but to ways of using language.

No collection of articles describing different cultural literacy practices can hope to cover or even touch on the range of literacy practices within one country, let alone throughout the world. Thus, chapters in this book are not comprehensive; rather we have sought to offer a range of different cultural groups using a range of different language and literacy practices. The book includes chapters on dominated cultural groups in the United States—Native Americans (represented here by the Navajo) and African Americans. We have also focused on the largest immigrant group currently in the United States (Mexicanos) as well as recently arrived refugees (Cambodians and Lao). The Mexicanos are recent immigrants, but Christine Pearson Casanave discusses values of a long-established Puerto Rican community in another chapter. Denise E. Murray, Patricia C. Nichols, and Allison Heisch as well as Tamara Lucas deal with a number of different cultural and linguistic groups—Vietnamese, Chinese, Japanese, Puerto Rican, and El Salvadorean. Some chapters (McLaughlin; Vasquez) discuss children; others (Casanave; Johns; Lucas; Murray, Nichols, & Heisch) discuss college students; yet others (Welaratna) discuss families.

By choosing a variety of different literacy experiences, I hope that readers will come to see the complexity of cultural literacy and discover strategies for understanding the literacy practices of their own students. In addition to a range of literacies and cultures, the work included here draws from a number of different research methods—ethnography (Casanave; McLaughlin; Vasquez; Welaratna); case studies (Johns; Soter); and survey (Murray, Nichols, & Heisch).

The book deliberately includes dominated groups, immigrants, and refugees. Although English may be the first language of the Navajo and African Americans, their varieties are not prestigious, and do not allow them access to the corridors of power. In fact, a look at our contemporary immigrant populations enables us to look at existing diversity and see just how fundamental it is. All the groups and individuals discussed in this book have one thing in common—they are language minorities, not because of their actual numerical size, but because they have "relatively less power, [and fewer] rights, and privileges than one or more dominant groups" (Tollefson, 1991, p. 16).

Part I begins by examining definitions of literacy and culture, the assumptions that underlie such definitions, and methods for investigating cultural literacy and diversity. Keith Walters asks the question that guides this book: Whose culture, whose literacy, and whose language are privileged? As all the chapters demonstrate, the language, literacy, and culture of schooling privileges only one way of taking from and making meaning of the world—that of the mainstream middle classes and that of literary tradition and the literary canon. Anna O. Soter goes further by asking what assumptions underlie our understanding of texts and writing practices. By comparing the assumptions of African American college students with those of their college instructors, she demonstrates that different speech communities bring different assumptions to the task of writing—different purposes, audiences, and views of language. Even more importantly, teachers' assumptions (or hidden curricula) may differ from what they overtly teach their students about the nature of text. Part I ends with a language use survey (Murray, Nichols, & Heisch), showing how this methodology can help faculty uncover the language backgrounds of their students, and thereby facilitate curriculum planning.

In Part II, authors focus on particular literacy practices among culturally and linguistically diverse groups. This section does not provide definitive descriptions and explanations of literacy among a particular community, but rather a small window into different uses of language (and, indirectly, on-going efforts to formulate appropriate names for the diverse populations we discuss as well). In this way, we hope to demonstrate the complexity of language use and literacy and direct readers to ways they themselves can explore differences in their classrooms and research. As educators, we must remember that descriptions of cultural patterns represent group configurations and not the specific behavior of any given individual. These chapters, then, provide in-depth pictures of particular uses by particular literacy communities, including African Americans (Dandy), Mexican immigrant children and their families (Vasquez), Khmer refugees (Welaratna), Lao refugees (Johns), journal writers (Lucas), and sociologists (Casanave).

Each chapter in Part II draws on the authors' research and offers some practical applications.

Part III focuses entirely on classrooms. The three chapters may help teachers tap the potential in their linguistically and culturally diverse classrooms by seeing diverse learners as resources, not problems. They suggest practical, hands-on activities and tasks that can be used with children, young people, adults, and teachers-in-training. Daniel McLaughlin discusses the relationship between power, community language use, and curricula. Moving from this broad picture, I focus on specific ways of valuing adult ESL learners' language and culture, and, finally, Patricia C. Nichols suggests ways of tapping the language heritage of any student group.

Each chapter includes a summary, discussion questions, and projects. Teacher educators will be able to assign the questions and projects to their student teachers. Practicing teachers may not wish to undertake the projects themselves, but they can use both the projects and the discussion questions to further explore ways of using students' knowledge in the classroom. Some projects are suited to students in linguistically and culturally diverse classrooms.

We hope that this book will be useful to ESL teachers and teacher educators as well as to language arts teachers and teacher educators with diverse student populations. We have combined theory, research, and practice so that readers can gain insights into and understanding of the language uses of their students; so that they can examine the relationship between power and the language use of speech communities and thus discover ways to empower themselves and their students; and also so that they can find practical activities to use in their classrooms. When teachers learn to integrate the cultural patterns of language minority children and adults into their teaching, schools should be able to better meet the needs of students from these communities.

Denise E. Murray
San José State University, California

Part I

Expanding Assumptions About Literacy and Culture

1

Whose Culture?
Whose Literacy?

Keith Walters
University of Texas at Austin

To be only functionally literate in a hyperliterate society is to live as an oppressed stranger in an overwhelming world. On the other hand, to achieve cultural literacy, as it has been defined by E. D. Hirsch and others, is to live in passive comfort as a tourist in an alien world. In both worlds the literate agent is constructed by an external agency that has as a primary goal its own reproduction.

> Andrea Lunsford, Helene Moglen, & James Slevin, 1990

Before I built a wall I'd ask to know
What I was walling in or walling out,
And to whom I was like to give offense.

> Robert Frost, 1917 [1914], "Mending Wall"

Since the appearance of E. D. Hirsch's (1987) *Cultural Literacy: What Every American Needs to Know*, the notion of cultural literacy has become a sort of cause célèbre. Many educators, politicians, parents, and granting agencies argue that Hirsch has devised and presented a viable, reasonable solution to the problems they see with education in the United States at this moment in our history. Others, however, believe that Hirsch's approach is fundamentally wrong and contend that adopting such a strategy for dealing with educational problems in this country will yield only disastrous results. Still others, including some who disagree with the goals of the program set out in *Cultural Literacy*, believe that Hirsch has done the nation a service by raising these issues for public debate in the way that he and his associates have.

Whatever our individual response to Hirsch and his program of cultural literacy, it seems fair to say that literacy, as he characterizes it, rests largely on the mastery of two kinds of knowledge: first, what he terms the *standard grapholect*—or written variety of the language[1]— and, second, a body of facts—cultural knowledge—a version of which appears in *The Dictionary of Cultural Literacy* (Hirsch, Kett, & Trefil, 1988). For example, Hirsch writes:

> As the universal second culture [of Americans], literate culture has become the common currency for social and economic exchange in our democracy, and the only available ticket to full citizenship. Getting one's membership is not tied to class or race. Membership is automatic if one learns the background information and the linguistic conventions that are needed to read, write, and speak effectively. (p. 22)

Such a position contrasts strongly with the experiences of many in this country, especially those not born into the middle- or upper-classes, those not born White, or those born into a home in which a language other than English is spoken. Often, people from such backgrounds have discovered that despite knowledge of the standard grapholect or the kind of information included in Hirsch's *Dictionary*, their membership card was revoked, delayed, or, most frequently, never delivered. In short, they have learned that in spite of the sorts of promises made by people like Hirsch, issues of gender, color, class, national origin, and native language make a difference in the academic marketplace and the society at large.

More distressing is the situation of those who—whether because of choice, social pressure, or lack of opportunity—have not mastered what Hirsch terms the standard grapholect or the body of knowledge he and like-minded colleagues have collected. What is to become of the "disadvantaged children," as Hirsch (e.g, 1988, p. xiv) often refers to the many whose language and cultural knowledge differ markedly from those consulted as the *Dictionary* was put together? Although Hirsch writes of the culture he claims to represent as "the universal second culture [of Americans]," on the one hand, and "what literate

Americans know," on the other, the students many of us find in our classrooms hail from languages and cultures notably distant from the first or second culture of the authors of the *Dictionary*. Consequently, we educators are left to ask whose language, whose culture, and whose literacy we should be teaching and why.

As the editors of the collection *The Right to Literacy* remind us:

> Literacy workers in all contexts do well to refrain from jumping on the literacy bandwagon without first questioning the motives of both those who are driving it and those who are funding its operations. It is necessary to ask what kind of literacy we want to support: literacy to serve which purposes and on behalf of whose interests. Since the teaching of reading and writing can never be innocent, literacy workers must choose pedagogical methods with care, mindful of the theoretical assumptions with which those methods are informed.
>
> (Lunsford, Moglen, & Slevin, 1990, p. 2)

Rather than offering a detailed criticism of Hirsch and his program in this essay,[2] I wish to discuss alternatives to what I see as the narrowly focused monoculturalism[3] of Hirsch and many others. The growing diversity I find in the classrooms I enter leads me to seek, instead, a notion of culture, literacy, and language broad enough to encompass the reality of the mosaic we think of as the United States, one constructed by generations of immigrants as well as those who have come, studied, or worked here and returned home. First, relying largely on two essays by the late Raymond Williams, British literary critic and novelist, I will consider how we might think about alternatives to the view of culture found in the work of Hirsch. Then, I will look at the findings of research on literacy across cultures conducted by scholars in several fields, demonstrating their concern with how spoken and written language are used in particular communities. Finally, I will return to a discussion of the view of language found in the work of Hirsch and traditionally promulgated in the schools of this country, offer alternative ways of conceptualizing language, and consider implications of these alternatives for the classroom.

Whose Idea of Culture?

Two essays by Raymond Williams, "Culture Is Ordinary" (1989a [1958]) and "The Idea of a Common Culture" (1989b [1968]), may help us define the term *culture* in positive terms corresponding to the social reality we face each day in our classrooms. Were Williams to read Hirsch's *Cultural Literacy* or the writings of many who support Hirsch's program, he would contend that these scholars are not concerned with a common culture; rather, their goal is a *culture in common*. For Williams, such a culture in common is "a received minority culture" (1989b, p. 33), "received" much as Received Pronunciation (RP) is the prestige accent of British English received or accepted at the royal court and "minority" because it belongs to only a privileged minority on the upper rungs of the social ladder. This conception of culture seeks "a situation in which all people mean the same thing, value the same thing, or, in that usual abstraction of culture, have an equal possession of so much cultural property" (p. 37). As Williams points out, those who value this conception of culture in common constantly fear it will become diluted through contact with the masses. However, they grudgingly make exceptions for "the *deserving* poor" (1989a, p. 7, emphasis his), who, because of their academic achievement and willingness to abandon their roots, show proper respect for the "trivial differences of behaviour" and the "trivial variations of speech habit" characterizing those who possess this minority culture, often as birth-right (p. 5).

These attitudes are precisely those Hirsch espouses in *Cultural Literacy*. Like many, he is very upset because students graduating from high school or college today cannot talk to him about the things he deems important. The things they know are different from the things he knows and values. Further, current graduates cannot qualify as what Hirsch (1988) terms "common reader[s]," whom he defines as "[those] who know the things known by other literate persons in the culture" (e.g., p. 13). A simple exercise in seeking the source and explicating the meaning of this phrase—"common reader"—illustrates several problems with Hirsch's approach to the issues of knowledge and culture. Perhaps this phrase recalls two volumes of Virginia Woolf's (1948 [1925 and 1932]) essays collected earlier this century under the title *The Common Reader*, although the reader assumed by Woolf was anything but common. Not a literary scholar, he or she was well educated in certain subjects, most notably the humanities, at a time when and in a society where such education and a concern with belles lettres were markers of class. As Andrea Lunsford (personal communication, November 26, 1991) has pointed out, the allusion may be to Richard Altick's (1957) *The English Common Reader*, a social history of the 19th century British reading public. Or perhaps the allusion hearkens back to Samuel Johnson's use of the phrase, which was the source of Woolf's title and most likely Altick's. In fact, Woolf (1948) explicitly acknowledged her source for the phrase by quoting Johnson in the preface to the first series of *The Common Reader*: "I rejoice to concur with the common reader; for by the common sense of readers, uncorrupted by literary prejudices, after all the refinements of subtlety and the dogmatism of learning, must be finally decided all claim to poetical honours" (p. 11). Or perhaps by his use of the phrase "common reader," Hirsch intends no allusion or an allusion I cannot identify.

Whatever Hirsch's source, this exercise in tracking sources demonstrates two problems with his approach to facts and knowledge as well as with his goal of a culture in common. First, the webs of interconnected meanings that common and not-so-common readers create and actively use as they read cannot be reduced to the short, memorizable, and, hence, testable entries of the *Dictionary*. Instead, they are characterized by richness and indeterminacy. Second, expeditions devoted to discovering the sources of allusions sometimes have unforeseen consequences, especially when they uncover unexpected and perhaps unintended parallels. Dr. Johnson's sentiments, for example, express a populism that permeates Hirsch's work, but this populism is, in fact, a false one. Despite what Johnson learned about the futility of prescriptivism while creating his famous dictionary, he was a product of the 18th century, and one can easily argue that he continued to believe in the value of "literary prejudice" and "the dogmatism of learning" (cf. Baugh & Cable, 1978, Chapter 9; Finegan, 1980, Chapter 2; and Johnson, 1963 [1755] for information on 18th century attitudes toward language).

Hirsch places himself in a similar situation. Rather than seeking to define descriptively what kinds of knowledge members of this culture who use literacy in their daily lives possess or share, Hirsch has set the goal of inscribing the culture of those he terms common readers: people who cherish and perpetuate the values and knowledge he has chosen to cherish and perpetuate. A consequence of Hirsch's definition of literacy as a body of knowledge and the exclusivity it entails can be seen in his reference to his collaborator James Trefil as "a highly literate scientist who is well known both for his experimental work and for his ability to communicate technical information to the general public" (1988, p. 135). Neither Professor Joseph Kett, "a historian with a special interest in the history of American education" (p. 135), nor Hirsch, "[whose] field is the humanities" (p. 135), needs to be labeled "literate." Such a virtue is assumed for scholars in the humanities but not for scientists, who apparently may or may not be "literate" despite their years of schooling, daily use of the written language, mastery of a body of abstract knowledge and principles, and achievements in their professional lives.

Nearly 40 years ago in his analysis of culture, Williams examined this kind of exclusivity from a personal perspective. He had grown up in a rural community, one with agricultural and industrial roots, and attended university at Cambridge, where he later taught. As someone whose first culture was distant from the culture of the academy, he understood quite well the difficulties and conflicts faced by a person seeking to negotiate life between two cultures, one of which often proclaimed its superiority over the other. Interestingly, Williams writes that he never felt "oppressed" by Cambridge; rather, he saw direct parallels between his home community and Cambridge. For example, he notes that his family did not perceive learning as "some strange eccentricity": "Learning was ordinary; we learned where we could" (1989a, p. 5), much as scholars at the university would contend that they had learned where they could. In contrast to such parallels, which eased the transition from home to university community, was the oppression Williams felt in the teashops of Cambridge. There, he perceived that cultivated people made a point of congratulating themselves on the culture they alone possessed and on their largesse for sharing it with those few from the lower classes who they believed exhibited sufficient aptitude and motivation. In response, Williams noted, "I was in no mood, as I walked about Cambridge, to feel glad that I had been thought deserving; I was no better and no worse than the people I came from" (p. 7). Commenting on Clive Bell, the author of *Civilisation*, a member of the Bloomsbury group, and someone whose attitude represented those found in the teashops, Williams inquires, "What kind of life can it be, I wonder, to produce this extraordinary fussiness, this extraordinary decision to call certain things culture and then separate them, as with a park wall, from ordinary people and ordinary work?" (p. 5).

In fact, during his career as novelist and as social and literary critic, Williams sought to overcome prevailing notions of culture that denigrated or ignored the value of his home community. In contrast to the confines of a narrow "culture in common," Williams juxtaposed "a common culture" (1989b, pp. 34–38). He contended that culture was "ordinary," possessed by every society, created and passed on in the form of "common meanings and directions" that themselves underwent change as they were tested, recreated, and reformed by individuals (1989a, p. 4). Thus, for him, *culture* had two meanings: first, "a whole way of life—the common meanings" of a society and, second, "the arts and learning—the special processes of discovery and creative effort" (p. 4). As Williams saw it, he was trying to use the notion of community, that is, "the common element of the culture," in an attempt to critique and ultimately to reform the "divided and fragmented culture" that existed in Britain in the 1950s (1989b, p. 35). For Williams, a major problem with culture of the dominant social groups in Britain was their suppression of "the meanings and values of whole groups" and their failure "to extend to these groups the possibility of articulating and communicating those meanings [that constituted their cultures]" (p. 35). These words, although written more than 20 years ago, summarize the very charges made by members of groups in the United States who do not see themselves, their language, their culture, or their history included in school curricula and who do not believe the prospect for exploring or expressing the meanings of their cultures exists.

Williams's writings clearly proscribe replacing a curriculum that focuses on the received, minority culture of the highest social class with another based uniquely on the culture of some other social, ethnic, sexual, or regional minority. On the contrary, his common culture

> is not the general extension of what a minority mean and believe, but the creation of a condition in which the people as a whole participate in the articulation of meanings and values, and in the consequent decisions between this meaning and that, this value and that. (1989b, p. 36)

Thus, Williams was concerned with more than curriculum; he was likewise interested in how education and society interact. He saw a common culture as a process, not a possession. In fact, he defines a common culture as "the idea of an *educated and participating democracy*" (p. 37, emphasis his) in which education is not limited to information gained from canonized texts of a distant past, participation is not mere assent, and democracy is not a completed achievement. A curriculum favoring culture as process, rather than possession, would value highly the insights offered by many groups—especially those represented in the classroom and the community—so as to profit from their many perspectives on the past, present, and future.

In contrast to Williams, Hirsch limits culture to simple product, rather than process and product. His goal is a kind of cultural patrimony, which he seeks to preserve; however, defining this inheritance and perpetuating it raise problems. On the one hand, Hirsch argues that a culture and its intellectuals consciously construct language and culture (e.g., Chapter 3); on the other, he contends that received culture changes exceedingly slowly and that educators have a responsibility not to tamper with it, but to pass it on (e.g., Chapter 6). Additionally, Hirsch argues that the failure of our culture to realize its ostensible goal of participatory democracy is due to the lack of the shared body of information that he has labeled *cultural literacy*: If the product were distributed to all, the process of participation would inevitably take place.

In *Cultural Literacy*, Hirsch explicitly describes his program for "putting cultural literacy to work" (pp. 139 ff.). Although school districts in the United States would necessarily retain the right to determine curricula, educators and publishers should devise "an *extensive* curriculum based on the national vocabulary and arranged in a definite sequence" (p. 139, emphasis his). Reading materials at all levels should be changed to include "a much stronger base in factual information and traditional lore" rather than maintaining their current focus on what Hirsch characterizes as stories or literary abridgements and "essays about human feelings" (p. 140). Finally, Hirsch encourages the development of "general knowledge tests for three different stages of schooling, each based upon an agreed-upon body of information" (p. 141), rather than on what he terms the undefined vocabulary of the current SAT (Scholastic Aptitude Tests) tests (p. 142). He suggests testing at the 5th, 8th, and 12th grades. Thus, Hirsch supports the position that if the educational system in this country maintained its general methods of teaching and objective testing while altering the material taught and tested, illiteracy would disappear and democracy bloom in the soil of a culture in common.

In contrast, many of us who teach find ourselves trying to escape the literacy training that we, like Hirsch, received and the assumptions it fosters (cf. Walters, Daniell, & Trachsel, 1987). Rather than perpetuating current methods of teaching and testing, we wish to develop something that might result in Williams's common culture. We hope to build such a culture by beginning with the abilities and skills each student brings to the classroom and using them to help the student communicate his or her perspective on the world to varied audiences, including those whose lives and hence perspectives differ from theirs. Such a common culture will not dwell on blindly glorifying the past but on studying it, analyzing it, and critiquing it so that students can use it to build for a future neither they nor we can imagine.

Teaching for this common culture and for an educated and participating democracy requires that we tear down some of the park walls our own educations have helped erect. It also requires that we explore new territories and learn firsthand, for example, about flora and fauna that we have previously known only through picture books or television specials. Unlike Hirsch's common reader or culturally literate person—"a tourist in an alien world" (Lunsford et al., 1990, p. 3)— we cannot be content to know that an elm tree and a birch tree differ (Hirsch, 1988, pp. 15–16) or to rationalize our inability to distinguish between them because we trust that experts who can distinguish between the two exist should the need arise. Instead, we find that we, ourselves, must appreciate the differences between the two. More importantly, however, we must come to see the distinction, which may not matter to us initially, through the eyes of someone else for whom it is significant for reasons of religion, cultural history, or daily practice. Teaching for Williams's common culture is quite different from teaching for Hirsch's culture in common. Classroom practice that fosters a common culture forces us and our students to see ourselves among others (Geertz, 1983, p. 16) rather than to assume that the perspectives of our native culture or group are the ones that matter most or that our perspectives offer fair and complete characterizations of other groups.

Whose Idea of Literacy?

Having considered how culture might be redefined to serve us in meeting the needs of our students, let us now consider the nature of literacy and how it is usually conceived. As I have noted elsewhere (Walters, 1989, 1990; Walters, Daniell, & Trachsel, 1987; Witte, Trachsel, & Walters, 1986), literacy has been defined in many ways by researchers, yet nearly all of these putative definitions posit (or more often assume) a relationship between language, logic, and literacy. Further, nearly all of these definitions can be seen as either the refinement or the rejection of ideas put forth in Jack Goody and Ian Watt's (1968 [1963]) seminal essay "The Consequences of Literacy." Goody and Watt argue that alphabetic literacy of the sort found in ancient Greece acted as a causal factor in the development of our ability to reason abstractly; similarly, they focus on the mastery of

11

forms of reasoning—the syllogism, in particular—much as later writers focus on the formal characteristics of the essay (Olson, 1977a) or of the variety of language a person uses (Farrell, 1983; Hirsch, 1988). Although Goody has long contended (cf., e.g., Goody, 1987; Goody & Watt, 1968) that he and Watt wished to avoid earlier dichotomous ways of categorizing peoples as found in the work of, say, Lucien Lévy-Bruhl (1985 [1910/1926]), their essay gave rise to what have often been termed *Great Leap* or *Great Divide* theories of literacy. According to such theories, the advent of alphabetic literacy marks a sharp discontinuity between human abilities before and after its coming; in short, adherents to these theories believe that alphabetic literacy caused people to think logically (e.g., Ong, 1982).

As Goody (1987) himself has recently acknowledged, the early view of literacy that he and Watt put forth was far too mechanistic and Eurocentric to reflect what probably happened in ancient Greece. Yet many influential scholars, including David Olson (1977a), Father Walter Ong (1982), and Thomas Farrell (1983), have explicitly or implicitly accepted some version of the usual interpretation of Goody and Watt's (1968 [1963]) essay as the foundation for their own writings about literacy, literate language, and literate behavior, and they continue to do so. In their discussions, these researchers fall back on recurring strings of dichotomies: "literate" is contrasted with "aliterate," "preliterate," or "illiterate"; written language is contrasted with oral language; and "abstract," "logical," or "linear" ways of reasoning are contrasted with "concrete," "affective," or "associative" ways of reasoning. Regardless of these writers' stated intention,[4] readers have equated the first element of each dichotomy with themselves and their own ways of using literacy and the second element of each dichotomy with the Other—people from other social classes, ethnic groups, cultures, places, or times. In doing so, these writers and their readers have often reinforced a view of themselves as developed and advanced and other groups as backward and lacking. Consequently, those who have accepted and advanced many of the ideas often associated with Goody and Watt's essay have, I contend, taught us less about the nature of literacy than they have about our culture's ideology of literacy, that is, the unstated assumptions the hyperliterate (Perfetti, 1987) in this culture use when evaluating the behavior of those with different assumptions about literacy. Hirsch makes no reference to the works of Goody and Watt, Olson, Ong, or Farrell, but he is clearly working within such a paradigm. By defining literacy as the "vocabulary" or knowledge of a particular group, the one to which he belongs, he falls prey to many of the faulty assumptions of those associated with Great Leap theories of literacy.

In contrast, scholars and writers rejecting the approach to literacy engendered by Goody and Watt's essay have sought to reformulate the terms of the debate in several ways. First, they have questioned and usually rejected the sort of polarized thinking fostered by Great Leap dichotomies as the major axes for defining or describing individuals or groups. Second, these researchers have demonstrated repeatedly that literacy involves special community- and context-specific ways of taking from texts rather than merely knowledge of certain discrete facts. These "ways of taking" (Heath, 1982; Howard, 1974) are themselves deeply rooted in historical contexts, in the functions and uses of communication—whether spoken or written language or nonverbal communication—in the community, and in the situations in which literacy is acquired, fostered, used, and sometimes lost. Similarly, these ways of taking are themselves tools that can be used in novel contexts as well as symbols that mark boundaries of individual and group identity. Scholars taking this approach to the study of literacy have looked across diverse communities with the goals of helping us understand not what someone's notion of what literacy *should* be, but what it is and how it functions in the lives of those who are literate. Shirley Brice Heath (1983), for example, spent nearly a decade studying blue-collar and middle-class African Americans and Whites in the Piedmont Carolinas and continues to study socialization into language and literacy among the descendants of these communities (1989, 1990). Amy Shuman (1986) observed White, Hispanic, and African American adolescents in Philadelphia over a period of 2 years. Beverly Moss (in press) analyzed the spoken and written language of ministers in three African American churches in Chicago and the complex ways in which literacy is embedded in the services of those churches. Andrea Fishman (1988) studied literacy among the Amish. Sylvia Scribner and Michael Cole (1981) ushered in new ways of thinking about literacy in its cultural context with ground-breaking research on Liberians who could neither read nor write and those literate in Vai (an indigenous language), Arabic, English, or some combination of these languages. Recently, Rosalind Thomas (1989) has offered a reanalysis of the texts of 5th century B.C. Athens that encourages us to re-examine many of the conclusions that have been drawn about literacy in that culture, the basis for many of Goody and Watt's original claims. The work of such scholars also questions traditionally simplistic ways of thinking about spoken and written language and how they

13

interact; Shuman, in particular, makes a point of questioning this boundary and many of the others fostered by the dichotomies of the Great Leap theory.

Many researchers working in this tradition enumerate the discontinuities or even direct conflicts between school-based ways of using and fostering literacy and those found in many nonmiddle-class communities. Heath (1983), for example, points out that in Trackton, the working-class African American community she studied, literacy events tended to be cooperative ventures during which many parties discussed their perspectives on a text, relating what they knew about the world to what they found in the text. In Roadville, the working-class White community in her study, literacy and its uses were tied in particular ways to the strong, fundamentalist religious beliefs of the community. Both the literate practice of Trackton and the purposes for literacy in Roadville contrasted with the practices and purposes valued by the middle-class community and the school establishment, which was an extension of middle-class life.

Sarah Michaels (1986) found similar conflicting cultural assumptions in her work in the Berkeley, California school system. Contrasting the storytelling style of African American first graders with that of their middle-class White teacher, Michaels demonstrates how these differences led to miscommunication between teacher and student and to negative evaluation of students' abilities. Her work, along with that of other researchers included in *The Social Construction of Literacy*, describes ways in which such patterns of miscommunication can have repercussions that extend far beyond first-grade sharing time to reading and writing instruction in later grades.

Finally, Patricia Nichols (1989) has looked at the differences in storytelling traditions and practices between children of African and European heritage in coastal South Carolina. As she notes, "continuity between oral and written texts within a given cultural tradition is more significant than the difference between orality and literacy" (p. 232). Nichols challenges educators "to ensure that our classrooms honor and respect the living literacies that children bring to them from diverse perspectives and traditions" (p. 243). In order to achieve such a goal, educators must come to see the limitations of the perspectives they—as a result of their own identity, training, and heritage—bring to the classroom and to learn to valorize other ways of "understanding and shaping the world" (p. 232).

We are only beginning to learn about the nature of literacy across monolingual English-speaking communities in this culture, and our knowledge of the functions and uses of literacy in non-English-speaking or bilingual communities is even scantier. From the picture that is emerging, however, we can easily begin to appreciate the great mismatch that so often exists between the attitudes about literacy and the literacy-related skills our students bring to our classes, on the one hand, and the ways in which literacy is taught and evaluated by school as an institution, on the other. At the same time, this research demonstrates the strengths students from various cultural or linguistic groups might possess, strengths to be used as the starting point for our pedagogy and shared with classmates so that all can learn from one another.

Whose Idea of Language?

As I have noted, assumptions about language figure prominently in the texts of those who write about literacy. Researchers who reject Great Leap theories of literacy usually state these assumptions fairly explicitly, probably because these writers find themselves investigating ways of using language that differ, often markedly, from the ways of using language familiar to many middle-class members of this society. Consequently, these researchers must, of necessity, describe views of language found in the communities they investigate and implicitly or explicitly contrast these with the assumptions their readers hold. Researchers who subscribe to Great Leap theories or the tenets of such theories, however, find themselves with a different rhetorical problem. Unless they explicitly state assumptions about language different from those generally held by educated members of this culture, their readers "fill in the blanks" by ascribing to them our culture's ideology of language (cf. Moss & Walters, in press), much as they do when reading what these researchers have written about literacy. Rather than fostering critical examination of our assumptions about language, these writers and their readers unquestioningly permit their assumptions to become dogma. Within this context, let us examine certain of Hirsch's assumptions about language, particularly the relationship between speaking and writing.

Although Hirsch focuses on mastery of the standard grapholect, he often writes about reading, writing, and speaking effectively. In so doing, he makes certain assumptions about the relationship between the way individuals speak and their knowledge of linguistic conventions for using written language. He appears to assume, for example,

15

that the written language is the standard by which spoken language should be judged:

> Although standard written English has no intrinsic superiority to other languages and dialects, its stable written forms have now standardized the oral forms of the language spoken by educated Americans. The chief function of literacy is to make us masters of this standard instrument of knowledge and communication, thereby enabling us to give and receive complex information orally and in writing over time and space. (1988, p. 3)

Similarly, his use of the term *dialect* vacillates between linguists' value-neutral use of the term to mean variety of a language and what Ives Goddard (1990) has characterized as the "derogatory," "popular meaning 'inferior variety of language used by illiterate or uneducated people (p. 14).'" Such assumptions are widespread among educated speakers of American English, who are quick to correct or make fun of speakers who say "warsh" or "Warshington" as they point out that there is no *r* in these words. Ironically, these same Americans rarely notice pronunciations like "sherbert" for *sherbet* in their own speech or that of others.

Of course, in the United States, unlike in Britain, no single accepted accent, or way of pronouncing the language, exists. Regional accents are tolerated and even cultivated in certain areas as evidence of local pride. As in Britain and many other societies, however, there is generally far less tolerance in the United States for class or ethnic dialects than for regional dialects (cf. Trudgill, 1983a). Additionally, radio and television in this country clearly encourage the use of spoken varieties bleached of characteristics that might give away the regional, ethnic, or social origin of the speaker. Many speakers, especially those in the Midwest, believe, first, that this network English constitutes the standard and, second, that they speak this variety. Students I taught at Ohio State, for example, argued that they "sound just like Peter Jennings" when they talk. They were especially troubled when they found out that Jennings was born in Canada and when classmates from other parts of the country pointed out ways in which the speech of Ohioans differs from that of Jennings or other media commentators. The Ohio natives in the class were even more disturbed to discover that Jennings had never completed high school, thereby revealing assumptions they held about accent, education, and class. When told that he had dropped out of an elite, private high school, they relaxed a bit until they realized that they had acknowledged that class, not education, might be the crucial difference in determining accent and success.

In contrast to the situation with accent, we find less tolerance in this country for differences in dialect, or grammatical system; in this case, our norms appear to be far more focused, or clearly defined (cf. Le Page, 1978). Regional variation, however, continues to exist across social strata. Southerners are sometimes bemused when recent immigrants to the Sun Belt do not understand constructions like *It's fixin' to rain* or *You might should see a doctor*. Similarly, college students in parts of Pennsylvania and Ohio are surprised to learn that constructions such as *The house needs renovated* and *Groceries are expensive anymore* are regionalisms stigmatized outside those areas. Of course, what makes such constructions regional is the very fact that they have limited, rather than national, currency, a fact that speakers cannot know unless they have experiences with those who speak differently or unless their educations provide them with basic knowledge about language in general and English in particular.

Norms for using the written language, especially in public contexts, are more highly focused than norms for dialects of spoken American English although, even here, differences exist according to audience and context. Style sheets and some academics continue to insist that *none* takes only singular agreement despite the fact that some professors of English and many writers and editors for the *New York Times* use plural verbs with *none*. In a tradition that has been around at least since ancient Rome and that developed for English during the 18th century, these norms are defined (and taught) in terms of things *not* to do. Thus, educated speakers and writers have been taught to eschew *ain't*, avoid double negatives—and evaluate negatively people who do not. Despite occasional protestations to the contrary (e.g., 1988, p. 3), Hirsch subscribes to a prescriptive view of language resembling this one, which privileges a single variety of the language, Standard English, as the only one of any true worth and the one that must be preserved from contamination. Like many others, Hirsch ascribes to the users of Standard English attributes like intelligence, logicality, seriousness, morality, and perhaps even wisdom. Outside this very bounded variety, labeled "the standard," chaos reigns: regional dialects, social dialects, ethnic dialects, unemployment, immorality, illogicality, illiteracy, illegitimacy, and a host of other social ills.

Schools in the United States, with rare exception, promulgate a view of language quite like the one assumed by Hirsch. Language that

17

is "right" or "correct" is Standard English, and everything else is "wrong" or "incorrect." Consequently, any construction or any word not part of Standard English gets labeled "substandard" or "nonstandard." More importantly, use of the standard language is associated with certain moral values. "Good" people and especially "good" students use the standard language or at least what they perceive it to be. Here, the message is that the standard language is the only language of value and that it should be employed in all contexts all of the time by all speakers or at least by those who wish to better themselves.

Such a view of language soon gives rise to problems. Students, and not merely the good ones, find passages in books—especially literature books—in which writers have used dialect forms in order to achieve a particular effect: to set the tone for a story or to contribute to characterization. One does not have to be too astute to notice that the great writers did exactly the things the teacher said not to do but got famous for doing so. In addition to undermining the credibility of teachers, this unrealistic and inaccurate view of language questions the value of students' home culture and language rather than encouraging them to take pride in their family and heritage and to realize that different varieties of language are used in different contexts for different purposes. Frequently, for example, narrators in autobiographical accounts of growing up outside the middle class recount how they mocked or corrected parents whose language did not match that recommended by the school, frequently alienating themselves from their families and their home communities.

A larger problem, one that has often gone unnoticed, is the inconsistency with which the standard is presented, described, or enforced and the ways in which the standard comes to be defined as "the way I talk or write." I offer two examples from my early education in northern South Carolina, a community quite near and in many ways similar to Heath's Roadville. My fourth-grade teacher made great fun of the two or three students in our class who occasionally used *hit* as the third person singular inanimate pronoun in such utterances as "Hit's on the table." She even encouraged class members to hit these students—albeit gently—when they used such forms. What she never told us and what she may well not have known is that *hit* is the older form, predating *it* by some centuries. Rather than using the "wrong" form, the users of *hit* were merely keeping the historically correct form; the rest of us, who had grown up using *it*, were using a newer form, one that, for a variety of historical, but not linguistic, reasons, had become the standard.

My fifth-grade teacher also had a list of shibboleths. She complained bitterly when students pronounced *pen* and *pin* in the same way, noting that educated people distinguished between the two. Yet she never commented when *ten* and *tin* sounded alike, no doubt because such pronunciations could only cause confusion during a spelling test. Later in the year when explaining the difference between *immigrant* and *emigrant*, she noted that context had to disambiguate the two because they sounded the same. What the teacher had not learned was that before the nasal consonants, /n/, /m/, and /ŋ/, speakers of Southern and Midland dialects of American English consistently neutralize the distinction between /ɛ/ and /ɪ/. Had these teachers known a bit more about the history of the English language or the nature of regional dialects, they might have presented these issues as such, rather than as issues of right or wrong.

Because they did not and because the curriculum did nothing to encourage them to present these issues differently, they presented language use as a forced choice, offering students the option of choosing between education and ignorance. Choosing the standard language and the way "educated" people did things made little sense in light of their life experience. For example, these students learned early that many blue-collar workers in the community earned far more than college-educated school teachers, and their community, like most in this country, saw the purpose of education as ultimately helping one make decent wages. The students' other option, adherence to local ways of using language, represented a rejection of schooling, its value, and its values. In my fairly rural, working-class community, many students understandably chose to remain "ignorant." After all, whom did they wish to be like: their teachers, whose biggest worry seemed to be whether someone said *hit* instead of *it* or pronounced *pin* and *pen* in the same way, or the other members of their home community, including family and friends?

One fact that we can exploit as we teach is that our students know a great deal about language and how it can be used to achieve particular goals in different settings. College students, whether they commute to school or live on campus, for example, realize that they speak differently at school from the way they do in their home communities. All know that a person talks differently to his or her friends, parents, and instructors about last weekend's date. Every speaker of every language engages in this kind of situationally based style-shifting. As students learn to use language in new contexts for new purposes, they are merely supplementing skills they already have by increasing their linguistic repertoires. Moving from home to school, some students find that they have to make few adjustments; others, however, find that they have to switch dialects or even languages as they negotiate the linguistic requirements of their daily lives. Not surprisingly, the task for those who have learned to switch dialects or languages differs from that of those who can shift toward the standard with minor modification. On the other hand, because of the often clear differences between certain regional and social dialects and the standard, those forced to switch sometimes find their task simplified. As an African American student of mine explained to her classmates last year, she has two ways of talking: one for her home community and the other for outside her home community. Continuing, she noted that one was not better than the other but that they were simply different, useful in different situations for different purposes. Interestingly, however, this student was among the finest writers in a class of 50. Certainly, a factor contributing to her skill was her awareness of different varieties of language and the appropriate context for using each. Equally important was the fact that in acquiring and using the standard variety, she had not been forced to perceive her behavior as a deracinating choice.

How might educators talk about language seen from this perspective? First, talking about "right" and "wrong" becomes suddenly meaningless, and talking about "appropriate" and "inappropriate" becomes necessary. Should people eat fried chicken with their fingers, a fork and knife, or chopsticks? The best answer is that it depends on how the chicken is cut and where the meal occurs. A similar answer usually works well for questions about language and language use. Is a particular form correct? Might we not ask our students whether it is appropriate for the task at hand? If that task is writing for most school tasks, the appropriate form will probably be the standard one—or something approaching it. At the same time, we, as educators, must admit to ourselves and to our students that school is not the only context for language use, acknowledging, however, that it is the context most often associated with additional education and ultimately the workplace. We also have to admit that many contexts, especially those involving the use of the spoken language, will not require the use of the standard language and that using it in those contexts might be inappropriate.

Teachers of English as a second language (ESL) have often had no choice but to be conscious of these issues because ESL students frequently bring to class linguistic forms, lexical items, or expressions they have picked up from their face-to-face interactions with native speakers of English. Students frequently use these spoken, informal forms in writing, and teachers must help them learn to appreciate the subtle and complex differences between spoken and written English. A challenge for ESL students as they acquire the language is to learn to distinguish among the registers of English used in speaking, whether informal or formal, and those used in academic writing. This situation differs in important—but largely unexplored—ways from the situation of native speakers, especially ones who speak a socially stigmatized dialect and who must learn spoken and written registers to supplement the spoken variety they acquired growing up in a particular speech community. Certainly, appropriate pedagogies for these two groups of learners would differ, but most traditional pedagogical practice in the language arts has not prepared us to teach language-related skills to students coming from such diverse backgrounds. Especially at the university level, however, teachers increasingly find diverse populations represented in a single class: native speakers whose first dialect contains few stigmatized markers of class, region, or ethnicity; native speakers whose first dialect contains many such stigmatized features; bilinguals who grew up in this society, often speaking stigmatized varieties of two languages; recent immigrants who were immersed in the public education system at some stage and continue to learn English; and international students who are here to obtain academic credentials and may or may not return home. Few teaching in any program or department have had formal training that might help them meet the challenge of teaching effectively members of these many groups. Additionally, as noted, many of us now see the training we received as woefully inadequate because of its focus on something like Hirsch's narrowly defined culture in common rather than Williams's common culture.

A good starting point for developing appropriate pedagogies for diverse populations will be rethinking our own understanding of language as a social phenomenon intimately tied to a speaker's or writer's identity. R. B. Le Page and Andrée Tabouret-Keller (1985) provide such a perspective. Based on years of fieldwork studying creole-speaking communities in Central America, they offer the hypothesis that "the individual creates for himself the patterns of his linguistic behavior so as to resemble those of the group or groups with which from time to time he wishes to be identified or so as to be unlike those from whom he wishes to be distinguished" (p. 181). However, such efforts are not always completely successful. Consequently, Le

Page and Tabouret-Keller attach four riders to their hypothesis, noting that as individuals,

> we can only behave according to the behavioural patterns of groups we find it desirable to identify with to the extent that:
>
> (i) we can identify the groups
>
> (ii) we have both adequate access to the groups and ability to analyse their behavioural patterns
>
> (iii) the motivation to join the groups is sufficiently powerful, and is either reinforced or reversed by feedback from the groups
>
> (iv) we have the ability to modify our behaviour. (p. 182)

This way of thinking about language seems an especially appropriate starting point for educators in this country as we seek to prepare ourselves and our students to live and work in an increasingly diverse society. Rider iii is of particular importance for educators because the ways we present information about the linguistic behavior of various groups certainly affects the extent to which students will be motivated to take that group—or the group(s) to which we belong—as a model to imitate. Additionally, we might expect different patterns of response from what John Ogbu (1987b) has termed autonomous, voluntary, and caste-like minorities.[5] In our efforts to redefine cultural literacy and to find a common culture, we must take care to present students with information about language that will permit and encourage them to make informed linguistic choices so that they create the futures they envision—becoming contributing members of society at large—while maintaining loyalties to the groups that provide them with support in ways school never can.

However, educating our students and re-educating ourselves about the nature of language, especially the relationship between the standard variety and regional, social, and ethnic dialects, cannot be the end of our task. We must also remember that an appreciation of the differences between the language of everyday life and the language of schooling must be based on two kinds of knowledge: an understanding of the varieties of language and ways of using those varieties that students bring to the classroom with them, on the one hand, and an understanding of the particular ways of using language associated with education and schooling, on the other. Additionally, we must come to realize that despite the great variation we find across speech communities with respect to patterns of language use, the ultimate goals—creating an identity appropriate within the context of the home community and behaving so as to maintain one's own face and the face of significant others—remain constant across cultures or communities (Brown & Levinson, 1987). In addition to the academic works listed in the bibliographies of chapters in this book, other important sources of information about patterns of language use and what we might term world view in diverse communities are short stories and novels written by members of these communities. Interestingly, nearly all such literary works comment directly or indirectly on patterns of language use within the community and the ways in which they contrast with those outside the community in institutions such as school.

As important as understanding the language students bring to our classes is understanding the language we use and expect to be used there. A growing body of research demonstrates the existence of a register of language that we might term academic discourse, which is used in most educational settings. Rather than being a universal, value-free, neutral channel for transmitting information or fostering learning, it is the product of many historical and social forces, and its implicit assumptions are often not transparent to those who do not already share them (Soter, this book; Stubbs 1990; Walters, in press).

Finally, as educators, we must ask ourselves why—especially in a society that lauds its democratic way of life—basic information about the nature of language, accents, and dialects does not constitute part of language arts instruction from kindergarten through college in classes for both native and nonnative speakers. No doubt one of the first steps in coming to appreciate diversity in the classroom and to use it as a resource is to help students begin to understand the nature of language (cf. Stubbs, 1980, 1990; Trudgill, 1975, 1983a, 1983b) and linguistic diversity in our own society (e.g., Conklin & Lourie, 1983; Lourie & Conklin, 1978; McKay & Wong, 1988; Wolfram, 1991).

Conclusion

In his provocative essay entitled "Teach the Conflicts," literary theorist Gerald Graff (1988) encourages teachers to seek novel ways of teaching and learning, ways "that do not efface the relations and differences among subjects, theories, ideologies, contexts, and methods, but bring them into focus" (p. 107). He suggests "collective models" in which teachers learn to see past the narrowly focused confines of their disciplines by interacting with teachers of other subjects in order to appreciate other ways of thinking about what they teach and how they teach it. Such practice, he contends, will more effectively achieve Hirsch's goals of cultural literacy than Hirsch's own educational program because "cultural literacy would then be treated not as a neutral body of 'background information' to be processed but as something itself open to interrogation and dispute" (pp. 108–109). In short, such teaching would create Williams's common culture, "in which the people as a whole participate in the articulation of meanings and values" (Williams, 1989, p. 36).

To Graff's list of things not to be effaced, we might surely add the linguistic and cultural diversity students bring to our classrooms. By coming to respect and appreciate other ways of speaking and being, we find ourselves involved in *collective* teaching because we are comparing our perspectives not with those of colleagues but with those of our students. In so doing, we often find that we must alter our own ways of teaching. We give up the false self-image of one who knows everything of importance and disseminates it in order to learn from and with our students. Similarly, we begin to acknowledge differences of opinion, language, and culture. Rather than seeking to eradicate them, we celebrate them, finding in them logical places for teaching and learning. Ultimately, we find ourselves contributing to a common culture and a common literacy, and we help realize the process of an educated and participatory democracy, one in which no one is walled out because of language or culture.

Summary

Rather than imposing a culture in common, in which all students possess and value the same knowledge, teachers can meet the challenges of today's classrooms and tomorrow's society only if they create a common culture, one in which each group contributes to the pool of knowledge to be mastered as well as the ways of knowing used in gaining that mastery. Creating such a learning environment means renegotiating traditional notions of authority in the classroom. Instead of privileging our own ways of using language and literacy by assigning them universal status, we must constantly seek to understand the diversity of ways in which members of our culture use spoken and written language and find ways in which we and our students can learn from one another. As our society continues to acknowledge its diversity, this challenge faces all who teach language in this country: teachers of language arts at the elementary and middle school level, high school teachers of English, university professors who require any writing in their courses, and ESL teachers at all levels.

Acknowledgments

Preparation of this essay was made possible in part by a research grant from the College of Humanities, Ohio State University.

The author wishes to thank Beth Daniell, Marilyn Kupetz, Andrea Lunsford, Beverly Moss, and Denise E. Murray for comments on earlier drafts of this essay. Perhaps the text would be more readable if he had taken more of their advice.

Discussion Topics and Projects

1. One of the most interesting facts about our culture's ideology of literacy is the way in which we often limit discussions of literacy to school-based tasks that involve reading and writing to understand or produce extended texts. In order to investigate the validity of this notion, keep a diary in which you record for 1 week all of the ways you and your family members use literacy in your daily lives. Such uses will possibly include reading stop signs or other traffic signs; writing notes to yourself, family members, or friends; and reading instructions for preparing food in a microwave oven. Other common uses may involve consulting an instruction manual in order to repair a car or appliance, reading a local newspaper or *TV Guide* in order to find out what is on television, using the telephone directory, or writing grocery lists. If you or members of your family are literate in two languages, note the language in which the reading or writing takes place. (If you or members of your family are bilingual but use only one language for reading and writing, you may wish to consider why.)

Once you have completed your diary, categorize these uses of literacy by asking yourself the main purpose of each use of reading and writing. After you have finished categorizing these uses, compare your responses with those of your classmates. You may also want to compare them with the functions and uses of literacy described by Heath (1980) in Trackton and Roadville, an African American and a White working-class community in the Carolina Piedmont, respectively.

When you have finished this exercise, try to answer the following questions:

a. What are the major purposes for which members of your community use reading and writing in their daily lives? Why?

b. Do the purposes for which members of your community use reading and writing change across a lifetime? How? Why?

c. What is the range of differences you discovered when you compared the findings from your home community with your classmates' findings? What does this comparison teach us about the nature of reading and writing in our society?

2. Do some detective work on the history of your community. What groups lived there before and after the arrival of European settlers? What languages have been or continue to be spoken there? What accounts for any shifts in language use that might have taken place? Divide into groups, with each group responsible for one of the ethnic communities that has resided in your area. Try to discover as much as you can about their uses of language—spoken or written. If the ethnic group used writing, try to find out about the institutions in which they used it: school, home, business, religion, etc. Did (or does) the group make any special efforts to use and preserve the language? What kinds of efforts are these? How successful are they? Why?

Good sources for this information include grandparents, who often enjoy being interviewed, or other elderly natives of the area. (Audiotape the interview if you can, labeling the tape with the interviewee's name, his or her age, and the date and location of the interview. Write a summary of the interview to be stored with the tape.) Other excellent resources might be the local library, historical society, house of worship, or any other community-based organization that keeps written records.

After your group has found all of the information available, draft a report, and share your findings with your classmates. Be sure to document carefully all of your sources of information so that students in future classes can use your reports as a starting point for additional research. You may wish to compare your findings with those of Walters et al. (in press), who surveyed ethnic communities that used a language in addition to English in Columbus, Ohio.

3. This essay recounts Raymond Williams's encounter with Cambridge University and with those who spent time in the teashops in the surrounding town. Williams was comfortable at the University, but he was very uncomfortable with the students who frequented the teashops because of their attitudes and assumptions about people who were not like them, people who were, instead, like Williams and members of his family back in Wales. For many of us, Williams's experience rings true because on at least one occasion in our lives, either while speaking our native language or dialect or while trying to speak another language, we have felt insulted or violated by someone with whom we were trying to communicate, often because of his or her assumptions about the language we used or the way in which we

communicated something. In a short essay, recount one such event, analyzing why you think it occurred and how it influenced you.

4. A major thesis of this essay is its contention that the models of language promulgated by schools in general and teachers of language in particular are inadequate. Take a language textbook that you commonly teach (or one that you might teach, if you are not teaching now) and examine it carefully, looking for the unstated assumptions about language, the standard language, and other varieties of language. What picture of language does the book put forth? Does it discuss the differences between spoken and written language and the appropriate contexts of use for each? If so, how valid are its claims? Does it acknowledge that different communities use language in different ways for different purposes? If not, why do you think not? How might you supplement the text in class, calling students' attention to the limitations of the text? Textbooks written for native and nonnative speakers differ in this regard; in general, they will fail in different ways although both tend to assume a brittle view of language.

5. Another major contention of this essay has been the claim that teachers need to learn a great deal about the ways of using language their students bring to class as well as their own preferred ways of using language. How might we get this information? As noted in the text and in the Further Reading section, we can read research about other cultures, and we can read literary texts written by writers from cultures other than our own. Finally, and perhaps most importantly, we can talk about these issues with students, acknowledging that differences exist and seeking to learn from one another about the nature of these differences. Design a series of assignments that would require you and your students to gather and analyze information about the different ways in which language is used in your home communities (cf. 1 and 2 above) and to share it with one another.

Further Reading

In addition to references noted in the text and the other chapters in this book, see Henry Trueba (1987, 1989) on the problems associated with and prospects of educating children from communities in which a language other than English is spoken. The last 5 years have seen a great deal of research devoted to the complex interaction between the ways specific groups use language and literacy in their home communities and ways school encourages—or even requires—that they be used. Nancy Smith-Hefner (1990) and Gail Weinstein-Shr (in press) consider the Khmer and the Hmong, two groups of Southeast Asian immigrants. Mark W. Dewalt and Bonnie K. Troxell (1989) and Andrea Fishman (1988) provide information about language, literacy, and culture among the Old Order Mennonites and the Amish, both autonomous minorities (Ogbu, 1987b). Daniel McLaughlin (1989) presents information about literacy on a Navajo reservation. Jonathan Tamez (1989) analyzes the attitudes toward language, literacy, and education among adult undocumented workers from Mexico, considering the relationship between these attitudes and performance in ESL classes mandated by the Immigration Reform and Control Act of 1986. Ralph Cintron (1989), Marcia Farr (in press), and Juan Guerra (1990) discuss literacy in Hispanic communities in Chicago. Finally, Madeline Maxwell (1985, in press) offers information about literacy in the deaf community.

Journals that regularly publish articles dealing with these and related topics include *Anthropology and Education Quarterly, Language in Society, Linguistics and Education,* and *Written Communication.*

2

Whose Shared Assumptions?

Making the Implicit Explicit

Anna O. Soter
The Ohio State University

What do academics consider "good writing"? Equally significant to this question is its corollary: How does one produce "good writing"? Underlying both questions are many assumptions, some shared and others not, by writing teachers and their students. In this chapter, I will explore the degree to which assumptions about good or effective academic discourse are shared by writing teachers and students from nonmainstream cultures both generally and through specific examples drawn from an ongoing study of the perceptions of writing by young African American writers in their first year of college. Particularly relevant to a discussion of the nature of these assumptions is Louise Rosenblatt's (1988) suggestion that reading and writing in academic contexts include, among other things, the internationalization of norms for interpretation and for interaction specific to each academic discipline. The extent to which individuals wishing to enter a variety of academic discourse communities have internalized the expectations of those communities is a problem that concerns all teachers, especially those working with English as a second language (ESL) and other nonmainstream students. Progress has been made in ESL composition instruction toward helping ESL college students become familiar with patterns of organization and rhetorical criteria for writing within particular academic disciplines (Shih, 1986; Spack, 1988). However, as Terry Santos (1988) and Ann Johns (1991a, this book) have indicated, college professors within their disciplines rarely provide either ESL or other minority students with explicit and detailed models of desirable writing within those disciplines. This lack of direct modeling suggests that students ought to know (i.e., have internalized) the rules of discourse within their academic disciplines and that their errors represent misapplications of those rules rather than a lack of internalization of those rules. I will argue throughout this chapter that a pedagogical focus on the surface errors of students' papers does not result in their knowing the rules. My focus on African American student writers is one example of how we must help instructors of all nonmainstream students find bridges to enable them to make the transition from where they are to where teachers want them to go. (See McLaughlin, this book.) As we discover what cultural and linguistic resources nonmainstream students such as those discussed in this chapter bring with them to academic writing, we also discover to what extent our assumptions about written text match or do not those of our students. Furthermore, and perhaps more significantly, we discover the extent to which we have internalized and accepted our assumptions about written text and what constitutes good writing such that we cannot see the potentially misinformative signals we give to the students we teach.

Assumptions About Written Text

Many writing instructors believe that becoming an effective writer means having control over a range of linguistic and rhetorical resources from which we select according to a range of contexts, purposes, and audiences. Being able to make such selections assumes what I would like to term *insider knowledge* of the rhetorical communities we wish to enter. To have such knowledge is critical, given that, as Donald Murray (1985) and others have long attested, teachers may seem to base grades on editorial proofreading although real problems related to information, structure, voice, and style make up our unstated agendas and influence the grades we assign. As members of academic communities, we have not only mastered their discourse codes but have so assimilated these codes that they are no longer a separate part of us. Therefore, when we approach any act of reading, we do so as highly literate readers and have, as a result, developed high expectations of what should characterize well-written text. These expectations are present even when we read texts written by novices; their impact is perhaps even greater when we approach texts written by students from different social and cultural backgrounds who may or may not share them.

Any reading of the research and scholarship on the evaluation of writing reveals that although terms used to develop scoring categories may differ, there is, in the vast majority of assessment scales developed within the United States, a high degree of agreement as to which features characterize top-, middle-, and bottom-ranking writing samples. Grades and their criteria, scoring schemes, and teachers' corrections and comments are the windows through which we see our assumptions at work. Although variations in criteria are related to specific genres and modes, most schemes indicate that the following features should appear in good writing: The ideas should be interesting, logical and original; the work should be coherent, clear and well-developed; paragraphs should contain controlling ideas and supporting details; the work should reveal conviction and an authentic voice; the language used should be fresh and original; sentences should vary in structure and length; transitions from sentence to sentence and paragraph to paragraph should be smooth; writers should avoid fragments and run-ons; the work should be free of usage, punctuation, and spelling errors. Teachers frequently use these terms in feedback to students, yet when faced with the task of explaining to students, especially those outside the mainstream culture, the meaning of terms such as *coherence, logic, well-developed,* they are not able to be as explicit as we might expect. The problem is that as experienced readers, we have developed an intuitive understanding of what these terms represent but may experience real difficulty in explaining them to students so that they might achieve these desirable characteristics in their own writing. Christine Pearson Casanave's (this book) description of the absorption of the fundamental values and practices as "disciplinary socialization" highlights the difficulties nonmainstream students have in knowing these ground rules for effective discourse because they have not been native members of the communities in which "these values and practices have accumulated over many years and generations."

Such criteria reflect what C. H. Knoblauch and Lil Brannon (1984) have described as a belief that "to write is to display ideas" and that "writers proceed by choosing forms—syntactic, rhetorical and logical"

32

(p. 14). In consequence, writing instruction as well as writing evaluation is founded on skill inventories, and the predominant purpose of having students sit in writing classes is to master these skills. Teachers' commentaries, as Knoblauch and Brannon (1984) and others have described, are the tools by which teachers point out to students "the difference between what they have done and what they should have done" (p. 14). This was certainly the scenario in traditional writing classrooms. Teachers are now gradually adopting the more open and active classroom emerging under the auspices of modern rhetorical instruction, based as it is on the beliefs that writing is a manifestation of thinking and that the act of writing involves an ongoing creation and re-creation of meaning in our attempts to give articulation to our thoughts. However, mixed messages are given to students when, despite implementing classroom practices that focus on writing as an exploration of students' own experiences and knowledge, teachers nevertheless apply purely formalist criteria to evaluating the writing that students generate. Until teachers adopt response and evaluation measures that acknowledge the value of students' thinking for themselves and working through the articulation of their ideas for genuine audiences, students will continue to strive to give us what they perceive we really want (i.e., as perceived through our actual responses to their writing) while at the same time trying to give us what we say we want (as perceived through our statements in our classes and our directions when setting assignments).

Why do such discrepancies between practices and stated beliefs occur? Knoblauch and Brannon (1984) have thoroughly explored this question, but for the purposes of this chapter, I will briefly refer to their three major contentions: Because of their training, traditionally in English departments as students of literature, writing teachers typically "rely on a mixture of literary ideas and folklore about writing" (p. 3). Teachers also lack theoretical sophistication in their understanding and beliefs about writing because the study of classical rhetoric has mostly disappeared from the standard academic curriculum. Last, writing textbooks offer a monolithic view of rhetoric that results in a focus on form at the expense of content. Thus, even when teachers embrace notions derived from modern rhetorical theories, such as "writing to learn," "the composing process," "revision as the heart of writing," and so on, they often cannot see that when responding to and evaluating student writing, they must also incorporate these notions. At the very least, students would have the opportunity to respond to one another's texts in terms of how these texts come across to real readers. Teachers' comments would focus on responding to both content and form in a manner that invites writers to think of alternative ways of expressing their intended meanings. Finally, provision would be made for acknowledging and recording growth as well as recording how written products are perceived.

I do not believe that there is so much a mismatch in perceptions of what is required in good writing as a lack of articulation by teachers as to how best to achieve such a goal. Thus, students practice what they believe will help them write better papers, yet somehow they still do not make the grades they expect. In other words, the information they actually receive from teachers through comments and grades on their papers does not get to the heart of the matter, which is that there is indeed a close connection between language and thought and discourse and knowledge. What teachers leave unsaid relates to these latter dimensions, what teachers themselves have osmotically absorbed as a result of their experiences as readers: how texts come to have the shapes they do, how texts are composed, how writers develop expertise over time and often what criteria are to be used to judge the effectiveness of the written product.

This book explores cultural diversity as a resource rather than a liability. However, it can only be considered a resource if teachers and students from culturally diverse backgrounds as well as those in the mainstream perceive it as such. If, on the other hand, students from culturally diverse backgrounds perceive themselves as those who have much to learn rather than having much to offer, diversity is, as it has historically been, a liability (Ogbu, 1987a; Sledd, 1984; Trueba, 1988). This is especially so given that successful performance in academic literacy is measured most frequently against rigid norms and conventions governing usage and discourse. The students represented in my study have found that deviation from those norms, whether at the level of usage or at the level of discourse, is not typically rewarded. And, however supportive a Basic Writing instructor may be, students are still in a "context in which the power relations are such that they have no influence on problem or task formulation or upon the criteria for judging solutions" (Lave, Murtagh, & de la Rocha, 1984).

Assumptions About African American Student Writers

Although the studies on African American writers have contributed enormously to our knowledge of how we might describe the written

34

texts they generate, very few have examined what young African American writers know of the more subtle levels of information needed to perform appropriately in academic contexts. We need to know how home discourse and language influence the written product as well as what young African American writers actually know about academic discourse and, essentially, whether they know what is required to crack the code of successful academic writing. At the same time, in recognizing that people from diverse cultural and linguistic backgrounds bring with them knowledge and experiences that significantly influence how they read and write in another cultural context, we must face a challenge: Can we, legitimately, continue to measure performance in writing and reading according to norms that reflect one culture but not another?

Broadly, studies and scholarly writing that concern themselves with the writing of African American students may be grouped as follows: those with a linguistic focus, primarily concerned with the appearance of Black English Vernacular (BEV) features in the written products of students; those that examine cultural and social influences in the discourse of African American student writers; those that focus on strategies used by African American student writers in the act of writing; those that examine the impact of standard measures of writing performance on African American student writers; and those that identify factors related to successful literacy performance.

A review of studies in each of these domains is beyond the scope of this chapter. Rather, a brief account of the impact of the findings of studies with direct relevance to the concerns of this chapter follows and will, I hope, illustrate how little attention to date has been given to examining what African American student writers think about academic writing. Because research has focused almost exclusively on the products of these writers, we have remained outsiders looking in, with at best, circumstantial evidence of what is going on in the minds of young African American students writing academic prose.

Studies of African American student writers in the 1960s and 1970s focused on language use, with an emphasis on oral rather than written language. Researchers such as William Labov (1969), Johanna DeStefano (1972), Marilyn Sternglass (1973), Barbara Gray (1975), and Michael Linn (1975) sought to identify features of BEV in student written samples and to determine to what extent these features could account for the failure of these students to succeed as writers. Later studies examined discourse and stylistic features of African American student writing (Cronnell, 1984; Morrow, 1989; Nembhard, 1983), and others investigated differences in the oral and written language of African

American students (Demarest, 1969; Smitherman, 1969; Wolfram & Whiteman, 1971). These studies were significant in establishing that BEV contains regular linguistic features enabling us to identify it as a legitimate dialect. Therefore, we could argue that the language of African American English writers is not error-ridden Standard American English but rather, contains linguistic and stylistic features that are directly attributable to a systematic BEV. It is not surprising, therefore, that sociolinguists and anthropologists in the 1970s and 1980s began investigating how much BEV African American students' written products reflected relationships between language and social and cultural experiences (Heath, 1983; Cook-Gumperz, 1986, 1987; King & McKenzie, 1988). Researchers argued that because language and sociocultural experiences are closely related, we must become familiar with social and cultural factors influencing particular uses of language (Cooper, 1977; Couch, 1978; Farr & Daniels, 1986; Linn, 1975; Michaels, 1981; Noonan-Wagner, 1980).

More recently, attention has turned toward investigating the writing processes of African American student writers (Bernhardt, 1988; Fowler, 1985; Jeremiah, 1987) although no studies have yet emerged on high school students. Margaret Grant (1987) found that the African American freshman students in her study appeared to function as writers based on prior school experiences emphasizing rote drill and isolated learning. Similarly, Catherine Gutierrez (1987) found in her study of ethnic minority (but not African American) and low-achieving, academically underprepared students that their writing processes were shaped by their prior knowledge, socialization to an academic culture, rhetorical knowledge, and skills. Others (e.g., McLean, 1990) have stressed the need for teachers to become more culturally sensitive in their instructional approaches and have identified strategies they believe will be effective with African American student writers. The conclusion emerging from these studies is that we can no longer simply focus on the products of such writers but must, instead, explore relationships between their written products and the sociocultural experiences shaping them. If, as Barbara Mellix (1989) argues, in order to write White, African American students must think White, we are faced with not only the challenge of assisting African American students to become bidialectal but also bicognitive (i.e., to develop a second style of thinking). At the very least, we must understand how African American student writers currently think about writing.

In examining the assumptions about writing held by one group of African American students, I have attempted to go beyond the knowledge about writing these students gleaned from their years of writing in high school courses. I have found, when discussing their responses with them, that the bases upon which their assumptions rest are not ones they have developed themselves but are the results of their interpretations of what they believe teachers have been telling them or have implied in response to their written products. From the data collected, we can see clear concordance between the students' beliefs about what is required for their products to qualify as good writing and their teacher's grades and comments on their products.

Yet the students are, nevertheless, placed in a Basic Writing class, a clear indication that they are not perceived as proficient academic writers but, rather, in need of remediation. In other words, a gap exists between belief and practice—the students know what is expected, believe they know the criteria by which their writing will be judged and believe that they can deliver the desired products if only they do what is expected of them. However, as their written responses in a questionnaire reveal (see Appendix 2A), they do not appear to know how to bridge the gap between belief, knowledge, and practice (i.e., to write as effectively as their teachers expect). The problems appear to lie in the domain of articulating their ideas into acceptable academic written form. I would like to argue that what remains unstated and undemonstrated is how to proceed with the conversion implied in transforming ideas into well-articulated prose—as one student expressed it in a written response to a questionnaire used in the study: "It would be much easier for me if he were to explain in detail how he wants the paper to be written." The students in this classroom do receive feedback praising their ideas but they also receive comments such as: "Sentence structure needs work."

As will emerge in the subsequent discussion of the students in this classroom, their teacher emphasizes process approaches to writing instruction and has created an encouraging, supportive environment so that the students are not only comfortable with him but also highly respectful of his efforts to help them become effective academic writers. Yet Lisa Delpit (1988) argues that the shift in emphasis from product to process creates powerful barriers to success in academic contexts because students' experiences become emphasized at the expense of the demands of the academic rhetorical community. Similarly, Ann Murphy (1989) asserts that when writing teachers in the basic freshman composition class (often containing a high ratio of African American student writers) adopt a role that enacts nurturing, positive feedback to students and validation of the students' own

37

experiences, beliefs, attitudes and language, they actually do students a disservice by protecting them from the realities of the world outside the Basic Writing classroom.

John Ogbu (1987a) has already extensively discussed barriers toward effective literacy acquisition by students from African American backgrounds. Implicit in his discussion of these barriers is the lack of identification with the language, discourse, and, according to Mellix (1989), thinking style of someone who writes White. Murphy (1989) argues that the current progressive approach to teaching writing in Basic Writing programs in colleges can, in fact, be counterproductive for minority students. In creating a nurturing environment in which personal, expressive writing functions as a primary means for releasing an inhibiting leash on the writer's pen, teachers unwittingly make students more dependent on them; in stressing ideas (content) rather than form, teachers, again unwittingly, give students the false message that there is little relationship between form and content. The real message, though, is delivered time and again in feedback that focuses on errors of structure and form and through less than satisfactory grades on final products.

This leads me to present insights from a preliminary investigation into the perceptions of writing held by one group of African American freshmen who had just begun their first quarter in a Basic Writing course. Outcomes of this investigation center on ways in which writing instruction for African American students can be made more meaningful and relevant and ways in which we can help nonmainstream students learn the close connections between academic discourse and culture.

Missing Links

Late in the Fall of 1989, a group of 19 freshmen in a traditionally African American college met with me to discuss their responses to a questionnaire on their perceptions of writing in academic contexts. (See Appendix 2A.) I selected African American freshman writers beginning their first writing course because I wished to investigate not only what these students were able to do as writers by the time they took their first college class but also to explore the attitudes they had developed toward writing during their school lives.

The questionnaire about the students' writing preferences and about their views on academic writing was distributed to the students

during the second week of the quarter by their teacher. The questionnaire was built into the course in order to help the students reflect on
writing and on themselves as writers. We believed this would result
in responses reflecting the students' actual perceptions and practices.
The instructor also collected two writing samples from the students'
regular writing for the course—a personal narrative and a review of
an autobiography or biography selected by the students. Because the
samples were part of their writing for the course, students submitted
drafts they had chosen to revise. I also gathered information about
their college entrance scores based on standardized tests created by
their college on vocabulary, grammar, reading/comprehension and
holistically scored essays.

The data collection itself was challenging. According to their instructor, my presence would be intrusive in the early stages of data
collection. The students had become sensitive to outsiders gathering
information from them and possibly using it to embarrass them. Consequently, the instructor acted as my intermediary, explaining the
project, its purpose, and the method for collecting data. During the
quarter, however, I was invited to talk with the class about their
responses to the questionnaire; a report of this discussion is included
to help explain why students responded as they did.

Responses to the Writing Questionnaire and Links to the Students' Writing

The questionnaire asked students to describe their habits as writers,
their perceptions of writing, and what is required of them as writers
in school and college.

A list of the questions I asked the students is provided at the end
of this chapter. Of these, I have chosen to discuss responses that
reflect the extent to which students have really understood what is
required of them to write effectively and that have a direct bearing on
their final products.

Throughout their high school lives (recall that these students were
first-quarter freshmen) the students had, to varying degrees, learned
that writing was a skill they needed to master, but as their responses
to the questionnaire revealed, very few had made a personal commitment to it. To them, it was a means to an end—a successful career,
better job opportunities, and upward social mobility. The debriefing
discussion later in the quarter, however, revealed that the students

were often frustrated because their efforts with writing did not usually meet with success. Many were very dependent on their instructors for determining if their final products were successful. Much remained a mystery and the mystery could only be unraveled by the expert, their teacher, as these questionnaire responses revealed:

> Chris[1]: When I had to write about my childhood and I didn't understand the project, I got a "C."

> Pat: Teachers should explain to us what we are writing and why.

According to these students, writing was what Knoblauch and Brannon (1984) describe as "the natural tendency to explore, to progress from what is known to what is not yet known (p. 72). For most, it was, when self-initiated, a source of comfort, a means of letting off steam or something very private. Yet little self-initiated writing occurred. The students reported that in the rare instances when they did write for their own purposes, they did so mainly in the form of personal letters and notes to friends. Some students indicated that writing for them was a means of self-expression with a communicative goal, a way of exploring what they knew about life and their attitudes to it. Most, however, perceived school writing quite differently—that is, as a means of fulfilling requirements and thus quite different from self-initiated writing:

> Tracy: It's a "have-to" (cause of concern in assigned writing).
> None (in response to concerns in self-initiated writing).

> Casey: The grades (assigned writing).
> I take more care in the interest I have (self-initiated writing).

Every student viewed writing as something to be mastered, a skill to be taught and learned and as an activity that required everyone to do the same thing in the same way. For example, almost all students (70%) indicated that they revised at least on some occasions. More than one third (37%) stated that they always revised. Yet when we examined the drafts they submitted with their finished products, their revision was restricted to minimal editing. None had reconceptualized their pieces or reordered chunks of text where appropriate. At most, we saw correction of errors circled by the instructor in an earlier draft. Revisions were not made in response to instructor comments such as "weak ending," "Watch sentence structure," "This is not clear," "You need paragraphs," "awkward wording," or "Is this what you want to say?" According to their instructor, little substantive revision occurred in this class, even after more detailed conferencing with the student. However, the students believed that they were carrying out what had been requested of them, based on the instructor's feedback. To go further appeared to be running against a locked door, but their later discussions with me revealed that feedback often required movement of chunks of text and, at times, adding substantially to the original draft. The feedback, however, did not help them understand why they needed to restructure a piece, watch their wording, or unravel confusing sentences. One student's responses to four questions on the questionnaire indicated their inability to connect the implications of their perceptions across the different categories:

> *Pat:* I stick to my topic; give proof behind my statements (how student perceived own strength).
>
> Leaving a statement and topic; I stop writing about the same thing (how student perceived own weakness).
>
> Order; good supportive sentences (how student perceived teacher's perceptions of strengths).
>
> Punctuation (how student perceived teacher's perceptions of weaknesses).
>
> Teachers should explain what we are writing and why (student's advice to writing teachers).

This student's responses are typical of most others. We see agreement between the student and teacher in their perceptions of the student's strengths but not in their perceived weaknesses. However, the student's own perceived problem with punctuation was not the critical factor in his difficulties with meeting requirements—the most telling response was in his advice to writing teachers.

Most students perceived their main challenges in writing well as centering around knowing what the teachers wanted, their lack of past experience as writers ("To write more often than I used to"), and being able to find topics for papers ("Coming up with subjects to write about"). Yet their perceptions of their limitations as writers were more diverse in focus, ranging from using appropriate and correct language ("I have trouble expressing myself without using too much slang"), to problems with mechanics ("weak punctuation") and word choice ("I can't always find the simplest words to explain what I am talking about"), to starting their writing ("I don't always know how to start so that it doesn't sound boring"). Their perceptions of their teacher's perceptions of their weaknesses focused much more centrally on structure and mechanics:

D. J.: Writing clearly.

Bobby: Run-on sentences, clarity, too much detail.

Casey: Body, structure, conclusion.

When we examine, as noted earlier, the instructor's comments on many of their papers, these perceptions appear to be accurate portrayals of what they believed was required, most of their teacher's comments having focused on grammatical correctness, clarity, and organization.

Yet despite their understanding of the requirements as stated in the feedback on their papers, and despite the accuracy of their perceptions and their attempts to do as requested, they did not make the kind of progress we might have expected from such a clear understanding of the requirements. The students also did not achieve the rewards in the form of improved grades for the strengths they believed they had as writers:

D. J.: My ability to think well; creativity; developing my English skills.

Tracy: My strengths lie with ideas.

Chris: I don't give up easily; I like to impress myself and others.

Jean: When I'm given a topic I can come up with quick ideas about the subject.

Terry: I have a broad imagination and seldom have problems writing down my thoughts.

In the debriefing discussion that occurred later in the quarter, students were eager to talk about the nature of writing as an activity and to understand its effects upon them when they undertook it. They were stunned to discover that they, as writers, experienced writing in quite diverse ways. Some of them wrote more freely at different hours of the day; some had writer's block on one task and not another; some shared difficulties such as grammar and structure; but all experienced a range of difficulties at various times; many procrastinated at one time or other. Once the ice was broken and students began to ask questions in which they had personal and obviously vested interest, my intuitions were confirmed: Discrepancies existed between what the students believed was successful in writing and how they actually performed in the academic context. Although the students acknowledged that they had some problems with formal writing, they believed on the whole that they knew what was required and that they were receiving the kind of instructional support that would help them improve their writing. However, as they revealed in the questionnaire, they would have liked more explicit information on how to improve their writing. Furthermore, as their written products indicated, they appeared not to have cracked the hidden code implied in the instructor's responses to their essays:

Final Comment on D. J.: Try to bring discussion into tighter focus.

Final Comment on Bobby: Some good narration here, but discussion needs to be controlled.

Although the students in this group enjoyed the encouragement of a very supportive instructor, they were not lulled into a false sense of complacency. Their perceived main challenges to writing well in college (described earlier) indicate that they suspected only too well that having good ideas was not enough to perform satisfactorily. Tension existed between what they perceived they needed for effective results and what they perceived writing teachers should do in order to bring about those results:

D. J.: Teachers should understand people before criticizing them.

Bobby: Teachers should let students write however they want to—using slang and their own expressions.

Kim: We should talk and communicate like we would with our own friends.

Kelly: Slow down and make it meaningful. Get suggestions on what we would like to write on.

As noted earlier, other students preferred the teacher to be more explicit in explaining what was required, but the general tenor of the responses in answer to the question of what they would suggest to their writing teacher for improved instruction was that they felt a nurturing, student-centered environment would meet their needs. These discrepancies between responses suggest that the students did not really know what would help them become more effective writers. In fact, students are "encouraged to talk about their daily experiences, to discuss emotional and contentious matters, to express their own ideas and experiences rather than to reproduce styles appropriate for academic writing, they are caught between divergent goals and practices which are, nevertheless, normative though for perhaps different ends" (de Castell & Luke, 1988, p. 169). The intentions of student-centered instructional approaches attending to individual differences are grounded in well-intentioned and sensible sociopsychological perspectives on learning as being a process of discovery. However, the reality of the marketplace as well as the college classroom is that development proceeding at an individual, natural pace is not conducive to the goals of a system that seeks to universalize skills and regards as desirable adherence to forms that can be measured in standardized ways. As de Castell and Luke (1988) assert, "technocratic literacy systems posit an imaginary 'every-student' . . . and by attempting to address everyone . . . this literacy model actively militates against the development of full communicative competence" (p. 172).

The questionnaire responses revealed that the students were certainly intuitively aware that their best writing was produced when they were allowed topic choices, when they wrote on subjects reflecting personal experience and knowledge, and when they wrote to self-selected audiences:

> *Charlie:* I like writing to my family and friends. But when I write something for school I get nervous and start writing fast.
>
> *Kelly:* I like to write things that interest me. I do my best writing when I am alone.
>
> *Evelyn:* When I use humour—to make stories or reports interesting.

We could argue that two of the missing elements in their instructional contexts were an intrinsic motivation to write and a definable audience with whom they wished to communicate. We could speculate further and investigate in future research if the lack of a self-initiated motivation for writing and the lack of a definable, familiar audience was at the root of problems such as those exhibited in their own writing and in the writer described by Marcia Farr and Mary Ann Janda (1985). They argued that their writer did indeed pay attention to appropriate form but lacked a functional attempt to communicate with a reader. That is, their writer did not write as he did through dialect interference or through ignorance of conventions governing Standard American English. He exhibited adequate skills in style shifting appropriate for diverse oral and written contexts but was not regarded by his teachers as sufficiently skilled to escape the Basic Writing classroom. They also admit that they had no positive answers to explain why he wrote as he did.

Features of Student Writing

The personal narrative essays collected during the course of the first quarter reveal the types of problems all students in Basic Writing programs share: the usual array of usage and mechanical (spelling and punctuation) errors, weak conclusions, lack of supporting detail, assumptions that the reader shares the same perceptions as the writer, problems with organization and logical structure according to conventions governing formal informational writing, and the use of extraneous or irrelevant material. Because the topic was a familiar one (the impact of a particular event or person on the life of the writer), we might expect to see some commonalities across the essays, yet it is clear that the subject itself did not influence the structure of the personal narratives nor their style and tone. The students appear to write according to a formula—an introduction that states the influential event/person; perhaps three or four paragraphs developing and supporting the introduction; and a concluding paragraph stating the impact of the event/person on the writers' lives:

> *Kim:* A great experience for me was when I found I had gotten excepted to "X" College. I was at home, it was morning when the mailman came. I wasn't thinking of anything when I seen the letter from "X" College. . . .

> *Evelyn:* My story is about me & my father. It started when I was six years old. My father was taking me to school, and a man who very scared of my father, ran upbehind him and shot him six times in the neck. With me being so young & scared at the time, I put my sweater under his head and ran & asked a lady could she call the cops. . . .

Cecil: One of my greatest experiences is when I got my frist car. At that time I had a job and it was really to get a car. So we were looking around and we just counldfind anything. So one of my mother friends call and said that he had a 1979 starfire for sale. So I went and look at it. The 1979 starfire was in good shap. The car was a back [unidentifiable word] and a 4 speed. . . .

The students were carrying out the stated requirements for effective writing—that is, get to the point, identify the topic and provide the reader with a frame of reference for continued reading. However, they failed to fulfill certain implicit expectations behind their instructor's statements, such as "get your reader involved," thereby failing to engage the reader at the affective level. Three of the students in this group did go beyond simple statements of personal fact with, we would argue, more compelling results:

Jamie: Even though I have never really live with my grandmother when, I visit her on the farm it seems like a great experience for me. The feeling begins as soon as I cross the threshhold of the little house and tumble into the arms of my grandmother, aunt and cousins. The sense of welcome overwhelms me. . . .

As a rule, the essays displayed a lack of personal involvement apparent throughout by the voicelessness of the prose, suggesting that the writers had not identified an audience interested in reading their prose. Two experienced readers consistently reported that they perceived the writers as only superficially interested, simply fulfilling the assignment and appearing as detached, impartial reporters, passing on the facts of what happened rather than writing as excited participants.

Some students expressed a strong personal perspective in their narrative—a reflection of the encouragement given by their instructor to take a stance and to focus on voice. At this early stage in the classroom, however, his influence is still competing with what they had learned during 12 years of previous schooling. What the students claimed as concerns in self-initiated writing (i.e., communicating with specific readers for specific purposes) did not appear to play a significant role in their assigned writing. Rather, as the questionnaire responses indicated and as played out in two samples of writing that follow, they appeared to be concerned primarily with the business of "getting it right" according to the criteria they perceived would be used to judge their performance.

In these two essays, we see minimal elaboration, with the reader being expected to know the context for action being described or events identified. The opening paragraphs of Essay 1 indicated, to two experienced readers, that the writer was quite adept at telling the reader what was happening but did not consider, or may not have known, that the reader expected to be drawn into the description of the events empathetically:

Essay 1

During my 8th grade year they held the annual Lucy Mae Wyatt Speech contest. I decided that would be the appropriate time to break out of my shyness.

In preparing for the contest signup sheets were sent to all our home-rooms. My teacher asked if anyone was interested. I gathered up my courage and raised my hand. The look I received from my teacher was full of pride and satisfaction.

As the week proceeded on it was audition time. I stood up and walked on stage. I presented myself and spoke loud and clear. My knees were as weak as a baby fol at birth. My heart bounded hard and continious. My chest seemed to be too small for my heart. Somehow I managed to show no sign of fear. As I listened to everyone else, I felt they were much better than me. The judge sent us back to class without a word.

We can identify this essay as a personal narrative intended to convey an event of considerable significance to the writer through the opening declarative statement. However, we wonder how different the discourse would be, had the writer been invited to orally convey the experience. As is evident in the first paragraph of the essay, we are expected to know who was responsible for conducting the contest. We are also expected to know that the writer has had a history of shyness. Given that the significance of the event was not the contest itself but the impact it had on the shyness of the writer, very little of the most interesting information about the writer was provided.

During the debriefing session with the students, they informed me that they were not certain as to how much personal information was permissible or even desirable in their writing when required to fulfill an assignment. No student in the group was able to identify the stylistic and rhetorical criteria they believed would be used to judge the essay.[2]

Students were less confident and less effective in writing a second task, a review of a book, despite their written assertions that the book affected them deeply. As the following sample illustrates, one of the main difficulties facing students with this type of writing was knowing what to do with the facts they were describing:

Essay 2
Mothers and Daughters Learning to be Friends
by Marie Chapian

This book should be read by every mother and daughter who are having or not having problems with one another.

This book discusses from both the point of view of the mother and daughter and how they are each viewed in each other's eyes.

This book explores the mother-daughter relationship with an eye towards helping mothers and daughters discover the gift that is theirs and theirs alone. No other relationship can be compared to the of mother and daughter: no other bond reaches the space this relationship has in the lives as females.

These two representative essays illustrate the sense we had in reading all of the essays, that the students were not sure what was really required of them. That is, they did not know the hidden curriculum of good writing: Largely driven by the highly literate expectations of experienced readers, it requires writing not only to obey formal linguistic and rhetorical conventions but also to require that the writer engage the reader, an elusive but essential requirement. Both essays reflect the lack of opportunity for the essayists to write for genuine audiences and for genuine communicative purposes. The prose speaks to no one other than, perhaps, the teacher who in this role is not so much a person or a reader but a functionary of the system.

Shirley Brice Heath (1987) describes the consequences of stressing the "importance of learning conventionally literate behaviours" as ones in which "the internal motivation and self-defined goals for communicating which drive us to be successful oral language learners become displaced by externally established goals and criteria. Thus, learning written language casts from the outset an identity-threatening rather than identity-enhancing aura" (p. 92). As sociolinguists and anthropologists (e.g., Halliday, 1978; Heath, 1983; Labov, 1969; Ogbu, 1987a) have long argued, all children intuitively know the discourse

[handwritten margin note: Good point: who is our writing audience?]

rules of their own speech communities before they come to school. Although all children, and ultimately, adults, must adjust and adapt what they know of these discourse rules to suit the school context and to a greater or lesser extent learn a new variety (Standard American English) in order to perform effectively in that context, African American children appear to have a much larger task facing them in mastering the new variety (Farr & Daniels, 1986; Ogbu, 1987a).

Perceptions of the Students' Writing

For an outside, objective evaluation of the perceived writing proficiency of these students who had just exited from high school, I referred to the placement essay score students received on entry to college. On that holistically scored test, students' scores ranged from 2 to 7 with the majority scoring in the 4–6 range, the maximum possible being 12. The student who scored the highest on the essay test (7) ranked in the lower ranges on all other tests, and the student who scored the highest in the vocabulary test and in the grammar test, scored in the lower range (4) in the placement essay test. As these scores indicate, these students were not, initially at least, perceived as proficient writers.

A small number of studies have focused on the evaluation of African American student writing, notably Geneva Smitherman (1983), Hugh Jenrie Scott (1979, 1981), Robert Green and Robert Griffore (1980), and Roscoe Brown (1986). Despite general consensus among these researchers of the test bias against African American student writers, there is little, if any, acknowledgment in either the general public or the academic community that "the discourse conventions of the academic community (and school) are so unfamiliar to nonmembers as to constitute something very much like a foreign language" (Witte, Trachsel, & Walters, 1986, p. 23).

African American and other minority students, however, are still assessed according to the criteria described earlier in this chapter and set by the academic community without regard for the possible lack of familiarity with those criteria by such students. As Smitherman (1983) illustrates in her reanalysis of the National Assessment of Educational Progress (NAEP) Writing Achievement results, even the measures used to evaluate African American students' writing may, in fact, present an inaccurate picture of their writing ability. The difficult question raised by the arguments of those scholars who believe the assessment of African American students is biased, is that if we do not use the criteria of the academic community to evaluate the quality of their writing, what criteria do we use?

Based on the responses of the students' instructor to their papers and reflected in their grades, some correspondence exists between the way others perceive their writing and their own perceptions of their products. Their instructor's comments typically focused on lack of clarity, lack of focus, unresolved conclusions, and usage, although some acknowledgement was given for "good ideas." We will recall that when asked, in the questionnaire, what caused the students most concern in assigned writing, typical responses included "the grade," "the fear I might fail," and "the fear of not doing my best and the teacher knowing it." Yet later in the questionnaire, when given the opportunity to express how they thought writing teachers could better help them improve their writing, only two students stated explicitly that they would have liked more explicit information about how to improve their writing. Their inability to clearly identify the sources of their problems as writers suggests at least two possible causes: First, they may not have been able to identify the exact nature of their difficulties because they had not received the kind of feedback that would have enabled them to do so; second, they may have believed that they had already been told all they needed to know and the problem, essentially, lay with them and not with the instructional context.

Based on their responses to the questionnaire and on the debriefing session with them, I believe that these students were not fully aware of the reality that everything we write in a public context is "governed by attitudes, beliefs and values consistent with a traditional outlook governing the ways in which we write" (Knoblauch & Brannon, 1984, p. 14). An outcome of this lack of awareness is that they wrote in ways that indicated uncertainty not only about the language and rhetorical structure, but also about the context in which the writing would be judged. Furthermore, when students receive feedback on their essays on correct usage and clarity, we continue to deliver the message that they must attend to basic skills. Yet when we read the two essays previously illustrated, it is also clear that the skills and knowledge related to the art of rhetoric and to effective communication in written language in general, encompass a much broader range of rhetorical, linguistic, semantic, and social knowledge than students typically consider when laboring to produce what they perceive we want.

Murphy (1989) argues that they (Basic Writers) "clearly, have no illusions about their "individual autonomy. . . . They already arrive knowing far too well that language is elusive and complex; we need to help them see that it is also accessible and empowering" (p. 180). As is apparent from the students' responses to the questionnaire, they too had "relegated language and expression to a safely mechanical matter of sprinkling commas appropriately across the page" (p. 181). In assigned writing, they ranked usage and mechanics (punctuation especially) more highly than identifying a communicative purpose and engaging potential readers. In essence, they were striving to do as they perceived their instructor requested in his feedback, but the results do not appear to be effective. Their problems are not so much linguistic ones as code-related ones, that is, what to do with the language in a variety of rhetorical modes and for a variety of rhetorical purposes.

One tentative assumption that can be drawn from this small study is that the students' natural, intuitive sense of effective communication (oral or written) was not allowed to function in the school writing context. Possibly, as Farr and Daniels (1986) and others have argued, students' knowledge of what constituted effective communication never had a place in the mainstream writing context. Furthermore, their knowing what constituted "effective communication" needed to be grounded in knowledge of the criteria that particular rhetorical communities use to judge written communication and, more generally, knowledge of the values represented by those criteria.

Concluding Inconclusive Thoughts

Learning to write in ways that are acceptable in academic contexts is obviously a complex task. Types of discourse typically approved of in college and school writing are not regularly used in daily life. Despite some increased tolerance by teachers toward the use of what has come to be termed as "expressive language" (Britton, Burgess, Martin, McLeod, & Rosen, 1975), students ultimately must still master academically preferred codes or perform poorly on writing tests that are assessed according to conventions outside the student's own language. What Vivian Zamel (1987) argues as still being the case for ESL writers also exists for many African American students in schools: that is, conscious memorization of grammatical and rhetorical rules out of the context of writing and a disregard for the students' perceptions and attitudes toward language use and toward writing. Furthermore, writing instructors still perceive themselves as language instructors with an error and correction fixation. Prescriptive principles are still used, despite otherwise supportive contexts, when instructors respond to students' written texts.

well put...

African American students as well as increasing numbers of mainstream students can only benefit from experiences that make writing primarily a communicative act. Such experiences include opportunities for risk-taking; for writing for meaningful purposes and genuine audiences; for observing teachers modeling writing behaviors; for responding to one another's texts as readers engaged in a quest for meaning; for allowing students to utilize rehearsal and invention strategies; and for linking writing with learning in all subjects.

At the very least, African American student writers should be provided with classroom experiences that help them see relationships between form and content and how choices made at the topic level will affect choices at the rhetorical, stylistic, and linguistic levels. Only when such relationships are understood can students begin to crack the code of effective school writing. The communicative styles of a culture are not made explicit in the mainstream culture classroom. By the time students emerge from elementary school and certainly by the time they are in college, most of us (mistakenly or not) assume that they know the rules and if they do not, the fault somehow lies with them. In order to help these writers acquire the rules for written interaction that are characteristic of the mainstream culture, the following suggestions may be helpful:

1. Provide an explicit framework of the expectations and needs of the academic or school audience and of the organizational forms of academic discourse (Raimes, 1983);

2. Provide peer and teacher feedback that includes questions focusing on audience expectations, communicative norms, and questions related to the intent and the writer's stance in relation to audience;

3. Provide model essays and opportunities for extensive reading in order to demonstrate various principles for developing and organizing ideas and illustrating how diverse rhetorical structures relate closely to intention, audience, and topic;

4. Utilize the learner's own discourse particularly in the early phases of writing activity (e.g., brainstorming, early drafting) to allow the student to grapple with ideas and perspectives without

having to juggle a number of constraints related to other aspects of writing (Flower, 1981);

5. Link all discussions of structures and forms to meaning, effects, and intentions;

6. Perceive all writing as an act of thinking and purposeful communication.

I have also argued elsewhere (Soter, 1990) that teacher education must play a role in providing teachers with knowledge about language acquisition and development so that they understand the powerful influences of early language and discourse experiences. Language Arts and English teachers must have a background in sociolinguistics if they are to understand notions such as linguistic variation and relationships between spoken and written language. Furthermore, unless teachers themselves understand the sociocognitive nature of writing, how can we expect them to help their students understand writing as anything other than a skill? Prospective mainstream English teachers in my own classes have echoed findings a decade ago by Laine and Fagan (1980) that the majority of mainstream English teachers feel unable to help students from diverse cultural backgrounds. That this is still so, a decade later, should be great cause for concern—if change does not occur on the campuses generating the research that has informed us, where will it occur?

Delpit (1988) argues, and I strongly agree, that it is not through focusing on either skills or process but through creating classroom environments in which "meaningful communicative endeavours" are explored and in which students learn the arbitrariness of the codes of the culture of power so that they too may understand the power of their use and manipulate them accordingly, that we may finally discover a sensible starting point for literacy instruction not only for African American students but perhaps for all language minority students. Finally, throughout this chapter, I have focused on what non-mainstream students must become aware of as writers in order to become participating members of the various academic communities they wish to enter. In having done so, I have perhaps seemed to imply that we ought to accept the fixed notion of "academic community" suggested in Donald Bartholomae's (1985) essay in "Inventing the University." In it, he states that the "student has to learn to speak our language, to speak as we do, to try on the peculiar ways of knowing, selecting, evaluating, reporting, concluding and arguing that define the discourse of our community (p. 134)." To accept this assertion without question or challenge has not been my intention. I have argued that as educators, we share with our students the explicit assumptions and values of the academic discourse communities we represent. However, at the same time, I share Joseph Harris's (1989) concern about the narrowness of the term *community* as it is often represented in scholarship that supports a social view of writing. The tension (i.e., the notion of community as a dynamic or fixed entity) Harris refers to in his discussion of Bartholomae's definition of the "discourse of our community" (p. 13) is one we all face and must challenge. If we argue that cultural diversity is a resource then we must also face the challenge of redefining the notion of community in academic contexts. For again, in arguing that cultural diversity is a resource, we implicitly accept the corollary that a resource is something to be drawn upon, to be utilized, to be mined, as it were. The results of the study presented in this chapter, however, make it clear that this redefined notion of resource has yet to gain wide acceptance. The real challenge facing us as writing teachers with nonmainstream students may be to help our students "not leave one community to enter another but to reposition themselves in relation to several continuous and conflicting discourses" (Harris, 1989, p. 19).

Summary

In this chapter, I have examined what is meant by good writing and what assumptions underlie such a description. In exploring the concept of good writing and the criteria that support it, I also discussed to what extent good writing reflects hidden agendas of the academic rhetorical community. These hidden agendas in turn, reflect the value judgments held by readers who are highly literate and, I believe, accompany even instructors' readings of texts by novice student writers of diverse social and cultural backgrounds.

Hidden agendas (criteria that govern our tastes as readers as distinct from our own tendencies as evaluators of student-written texts) have been a source of confusion for students: They attempt to practice what they receive in feedback from their writing teachers who typically correct usage, structural errors, and problems related to focus. Teachers' feedback may omit guidance as to how texts come to have the shapes they do, how texts are composed, how writers develop expertise over time, and the criteria readers use to judge the effectiveness of the final written product. Through focusing on one group of African American students, I explored the extent to which they appeared to share assumptions that those in the academic community have about writing in general and about effective writing in particular. We see a gap between belief, knowledge, and practice that is not addressed by feedback such as "sentence structure needs more work." The chapter concludes with suggestions that teachers might use in order to make writing more communicative. Only when students from diverse cultural backgrounds are provided with classroom experiences to help them see relationships between form and content, that is, how choices made at the content level affect choices made at the rhetorical, stylistic, and linguistic levels, will they be able to crack the code of effective school and academic writing.

Acknowledgments

I would like to sincerely thank Ronald Price, who helped me gain access to several classrooms and provided many insights into how his students perceive writing. I also wish to thank Cheryl DoBroka who developed a peer response sheet for narrative writing, enabling us to examine which features of the compositions used in the study reflect "reader awareness" and "writer intention." Her thorough work as an expert reader of the students' essays and her competent assistance in collating questionnaire results is also greatly appreciated.

Discussion Topics and Projects

1. Draw up a list of the criteria you believe teachers use to judge your writing. Share these with your peers, determining features in common or differences. Discuss the sources for criteria and decide which of these were explicitly stated before writing and which you inferred. Explore to what extent the criteria match and discuss if your performance would have been improved by your knowing exactly what was required. Follow this through by creating writing assignments in which you clearly state the criteria by which they will be judged.

2. Interview students or teachers from diverse social and cultural backgrounds. Have them describe what they believe are the criteria for effective oral and written communication in their ethnic groups. Discuss differences, if any, in criteria for oral and written communication. Examine the extent to which students try to use these criteria when they write English academic prose.

3. Identify what you believe is meant by *community* in terms of writing. Follow this activity by identifying and defining discourse communities with which you are familiar in terms of how they influence writing. To what extent are assumptions and values concerning writing shared and not shared, made explicit, or left implicit?

4. Using the group exploration of criteria for effective writing in diverse rhetorical genres and modes, identify cultural values represented by these criteria. Follow this activity by identifying your own expectations and tastes as a reader and to what extent you are conscious of these expectations when you read one anothers' texts. Discuss how linking criteria to cultural values can help students identify audience and audience expectations.

5. Explore your own perceptions of writing by reflecting upon your preferences as a writer (e.g., about time, location, revision, topic choices, etc.). Describe your habits as a writer and investigate what one well-known writer has said about him/herself as a writer. Then write a report about yourself as a writer and what new understandings you have developed about the act of writing from this investigation.

Further Reading

Teachers with African American students in their classrooms will benefit from reading Marcia Farr and Harvey Daniel's (1986) book, *Language Diversity and Writing Instruction,* in which the authors "synthesize the findings of linguistic research on nonstandard dialects and instructional research on composition into specific practices for working with real students" (p. 1). For insight into the composing processes of African American students, teachers would find especially informative R. J. Fowler's (1985) chapter, "The Composing Processes of African American Student Writers" in *Tapping Potential: English Language Arts for the Black Learner* and Barbara Mellix's (1989) "From Outside In," in *Our Times: Readings from Recent Periodicals.*

For an understanding of the issues related to requiring students from diverse cultural and social backgrounds to perform effectively according to criteria established by a dominant culture, Lisa Delpit's (1988) article "The Silenced Dialogue: Power and Pedagogy in Education of Other People's Children," in the *Harvard Educational Review,* and John Ogbu's (1987a) chapter "Opportunity, Structure, Cultural Boundaries and Literacy" in *Language, Literacy and Culture* offer opportunities for teachers to think about the problems of literacy acquisition from the perspectives of their students. Finally, for an excellent discussion of the notion of community as it functions in academic contexts, Joseph Harris's (1989) essay, "The Idea of Community in the Study of Writing," in *College Composition and Communication,* provides a good foundation for exploring the extent to which community embodies commonly shared assumptions and values. This can be followed by a reading of Ann M. Johns' (1991a) article, "Interpreting an English Competency Examination," in *Written Communication,* in which she discusses the values underlying tests and challenges the notion of competency as reflected in many writing tests in academic institutions.

Appendix 2A

Writing Perceptions and Habits Inventory

Please write all of your responses on the questions paper and the extra paper provided for longer responses.

1. Given the time limits you work under, when do you function best as a writer? Please circle one of the following.

    (a) 6 am–noon
    (b) Noon–6 pm
    (c) 6 pm–midnight
    (d) Midnight–6 am

2. What kind of setting do you like best for writing? Please circle one of the following.

    (a) A room of your own
    (b) A library
    (c) Outdoors
    (d) A room with others in it
    (e) Other (please describe)

3. Do you know whether you will revise a paper or just use the first draft before you have written the draft?

    (a) Always
    (b) Never
    (c) Depends on the paper

4. In a typical week indicate how much writing (one, two, three or more pieces) of *your own* you do (i.e., not required by courses, etc.). Please circle as many as apply and indicate as accurately as you can, the number of pieces.

    (a) Personal letters
    (b) Creative writing (prose or scripts, e.g., stories)
    (c) Creative writing (poetry)
    (d) Journal or diary writing (number of entries)
    (e) Notes to yourself/friends (number of notes)
    (f) Letters to friends or others (number)
    (g) Other (please describe and indicate amount)

5. In writing assigned papers (class work) are you a midnight-oil burner or one of those who gets an early start or in-between? Please circle one of the following.

(a) Always last minute (midnight-oil burner)
(b) Always an early start to allow time to revise
(c) Depends on the task and my inclinations
(d) Other (please explain)

6. In self-assigned writing, which of the items in No. 5 accurately reflects your behaviours?

7. Do you have access to a wordprocessor?

(a) Yes
(b) No

8. If you answered *Yes* in No. 7, please answer the following questions:

i. Do you use a wordprocessor regularly in your writing?

ii. What system do you use and what software system (e.g., AppleIIc, MacIntosh, IBM, WordPerfect, etc.)?

iii. Where did you learn to use the wordprocessor?

(a) Through composition classes
(b) In writer's workshop/lab
(c) On your own with help from manuals
(d) Through special classes in wordprocessing

iv. For how long have you been using the wordprocessor?

(a) Less than one year to one year
(b) Two years
(c) Three years
(d) Four or more years

v. Indicate your attitude toward writing as a result of using the wordprocessor.

(a) I used to hate writing and now love it
(b) I used to like writing and now tolerate it
(c) I used to fear writing and now don't
(d) Other _____

vi. Circle any changes in your habits as a writer that have occurred as a result of using the wordprocessor.

(a) No changes
(b) I revise more than I used to
(c) I never revised and now do so
(d) I now don't have trouble getting started
(e) I now don't worry about corrections until I get my ideas down
(f) I now get pieces finished more quickly
(g) I now get pieces finished more slowly
(h) Other _____

9. Describe with as much information as possible what you regard as your principle *strengths* as a writer (e.g., you might consider organization, ideas, grammar, clarity, humour, etc.).

10. Describe with as much information as possible what you regard as your principle *weaknesses* as a writer (e.g., you might consider starting a piece, coming up with ideas, grammar, etc.).

11. Think back as far as you can to all the writing you have done for school/college assignments. What was the most consistent perception or description your teachers had of your writing in terms of

Strengths _____

Weaknesses _____

12. Do you always

(a) have to get a sentence just right before you go on?
(b) find it best to write quickly, then review and/or edit?
(c) vary your pattern according to the task?

13. What causes you to take most care in?

   (a) Assigned writing (e.g., audience, interest, etc.)
   (b) Self-assigned writing (e.g., audience, interest, etc.)

14. Do you like to write?

   (a) Yes
   (b) No

Please explain your answer in as much detail as you can.

_____

15. Do you like to read?

   (a) Yes
   (b) No

Please explain your answer in as much detail as you can.

_____

16. Are you consciously aware of the connections between what you read and write?

   (a) Yes
   (b) No
   (c) Sometimes

17. If you answered _Yes_ or _Sometimes_, how can you see these connections operating in your own reading and writing?

18. Please describe your _best_ and _worst_ writing experiences.

   Best _____

   Worst _____

19. What matters most to you in writing (describe as many factors as are relevant to you; you may consider grammar, ideas, feelings, anything else you can think of)?

20. What matters least to you in writing (describe as many factors as are relevant to you)?

21. Do you feel you have a good command of language in general (i.e., well enough to allow you to communicate your needs and interests)?

(a) Always
(b) Never
(c) Most times
(d) Sometimes

On what basis did you make your decision?

22. Do you feel you have a good command of written language of the kind required from you for school/college?

(a) Always
(b) Never
(c) Most times
(d) Sometimes

On what do you base your response to this question (e.g., grades, teacher comments, self-assessment, etc.)?

23. Can you describe the differences and similarities in the way you communicate in

(a) your daily life?
(b) school/college life?

24. If you were given the chance to tell teachers how you think writing should be taught, what would you say to them that would be most helpful to you?

_____

25. What do you think will be your main challenge in becoming a successful writer in high school?

_____

Note: Students will be given more space in questions which request them to answer in their own words.

3

Identifying the Languages and Cultures of Our Students

Denise E. Murray, Patricia C. Nichols, and Allison Heisch
San José State University, California

In every country where English is the dominant language, we teach-ers face classrooms of students who are different from ourselves. To understand and respond to this diversity among our students, we must inform ourselves about their languages and cultures so that we can answer the questions raised earlier by Keith Walters and Anna Soter: Whose culture? Whose literacy? Whose language? Whose as-sumptions? In this chapter, we will discuss one method, a language use survey, that we have used at San José State University (SJSU) in California to identify the linguistic and cultural backgrounds of the students on our campus. Survey data, like other self-report data, have two limitations: How accurate are the respondents' memories? How often do they say what they think the teacher wants to know? The latter was eliminated as much as possible because of the anonymity of the data collection method in this survey. The former limitation is more difficult to assess and we address this issue in detail towards the end of the chapter.

The SJSU campus, part of the California State University, has 30,000 students. In the past decade, we have seen our campus become increasingly diverse, linguistically and culturally. Our colleagues across campus reported large numbers of English as a second language (ESL) students in their classes during this time, primarily Asian immigrant and refugee students they did not know how to help appropriately. These students exhibited difficulties with written English that were different from those of previous groups of students—international or native English speakers—whose academic English was weak. The university did provide a small ESL composition program, one designed for international students. These classes gradually became filled primarily with recently arrived immigrants or ones who had passed, at least, through U.S. high schools. Increasingly, large numbers of these students found themselves in regular composition classes because the ESL classes were full, or they considered themselves American, not foreign students. Before we could address the concerns of the faculty at large and the composition faculty in particular, we wanted to determine if our perceptions of these students were accurate. To identify our student population and their writing proficiency, we developed a Language Use Survey that focused on students' reading and writing practices and experiences.

We will describe the survey instrument and some of the results. We will then discuss the strengths and weaknesses of this particular survey instrument, making suggestions to refine it as a tool.

Description of Study

Survey Instrument

After piloting a questionnaire in Fall 1986 and adapting it as a survey instrument, in Spring 1987, we administered the revised 45-item questionnaire (see Appendix 3A) consisting of four sections: biographical data (Q 1–13), self-rating of adequacy in language use (Q 14–22), current writing experiences (Q 23–26), and current uses of a language other than English (Q 27–45). The biographical data, in addition to providing a profile of the student population, also identifies variables that might correlate with writing proficiency (e.g., language at age 6). The self-rating of adequacy in language use covers the four language skills of listening, speaking, reading, and writing, and identifies writing requirements affecting students' performance in courses. Questions concerning students' current writing experiences deal with the extent to which specific writing requirements like term papers, as well as the amount of writing done both in and out of class, might affect writing performance. The final section of the questionnaire deals with how frequently a language other than English (LOTE) is used in different settings to determine the effect of this use on writing proficiency.

As a measure of student writing proficiency, we used the pass/fail grade on the university-wide holistic essay. Using such a grade as the sole measure of student writing proficiency has several advantages. It is more reliable than teacher-assigned grades, which consider effort and development, not just writing proficiency. Even more importantly, on our campus, the final essay is part of the normal assessment procedures for all students and is considered to be a major measure of student competence in writing, along with course grades assigned by individual instructors.

The composition program at SJSU offers four levels of composition: basic writing and the required first-, second-, and third-level college courses. Students in each level write a common essay examination on a topic chosen by departmental and university composition committees. Topics are different for each course level, and the essays are written at a set time for each level on a Saturday toward the end of the semester. Not knowing the topic in advance, students have a brief period for prewriting, then from 45 to 60 minutes to write the final essay, depending on the course level. At least two instructors grade the essays holistically on a 6-point scale, without knowing the names of either the student or the instructor.

Administration

In Spring 1987, we directed the administration of the 45-item questionnaire to a sample of the 4,101 students who were taking the four composition classes. Student assistants went to these classes to administer the questionnaire. We trained our assistants to minimize the number of incorrectly recorded responses and to prevent biasing the results by asking them not to discuss the project's major goals. Assistants gave students instructions on how to mark their responses on machine-readable forms, and all students who agreed to participate signed an informed-consent form.

Of the 1,588 questionnaires we collected, 1,363 could be correlated with students' scores on the final holistically graded essay examinations. Approximately 200 surveys could not be used because students incorrectly filled out the forms or because they did not take the final essay examination. Only the data from these 1,363 questionnaires and essay scores are used for the following discussion.

Results

Biographical Data

Because some students either did not respond at all to some questions or marked an invalid column, percentages have been adjusted for the number of cases actually reported; thus not all item totals are 1,363. Results reported below include raw numbers of cases as well as adjusted percentages.

The responses were broken down by the level of composition course in which students were enrolled. (See Table 1.)

Table 1
Comparison of Sample and Total Population

Class	Sample	Total
Basic writing	61 (4.5%)	211 (5.1%)
1st course	207 (15.2%)	531 (12.9%)
2nd course	410 (30.1%)	1,313 (32.0%)
3rd course	682 (50.1%)	2,046 (50.0%)

At each level, our sample represents the total number of students taking the examination in Spring 1987. Our decision to administer the survey to a random cross-section of all composition classes was crucial in assessing the extent of our bilingual population. Approximately 10 percent (10.5% or 140) of our sample was enrolled in ESL composition sections. Yet almost three times the number registered in ESL classes were actually bilingual (27%), based on our conservative criteria: students' use of LOTE as their primary language at age 6, their birthplace outside the United States or Canada, and the birthplace of both parents outside the United States or Canada.

Two factors suggest that 27% is a conservative figure. First, because the majority of SJSU students transfer from community colleges, many students take the required first- and second-level writing courses elsewhere. This is especially true for our bilingual students; thus our data are likely to underestimate the percentage of these students in the university population. Second, SJSU is located in central California, where Spanish was the dominant language for nearly a century before English was introduced (Nichols, 1988). Because our conservative criteria for bilingualism include birth of both parents outside the

United States or Canada, our figures exclude students of Spanish-speaking parents who were born in the United States.

Most students were born in the United States or Canada (67% or 911). Of the one third born outside these two countries, most were from Asia (63% or 284). Almost half of all respondents (46.4%) had at least one parent born outside the United States or Canada. (See Table 2.)

Table 2
Place of Birth

Country	Number	%
United States/Canada	911	67.0
Mexico/Central America	30	2.2
South America	15	1.1
Asia	284	20.9
Africa	7	0.5
Europe	36	2.6
Indian Subcontinent	20	1.5
Pacific Islands	44	3.2
Other	12	0.9

$n = 1,359$

Figures on how long the nonnative students have lived in the United States (Table 3) indicate that we are not looking at recent arrivals, but at students educated in U.S. high schools.

Table 3
Years in United States for Those Not Born in United States

Time (Yrs)	Number	%
<1	9	1.7
1–2	23	4.4
3–5	104	19.9
6–9	149	28.5
10–20	156	29.9
>20	79	15.1

$n = 522$

Of those born elsewhere, the majority (73.6% or 384) have lived here for more than 5 years; more than 93.5% (488) have been here for 3 or more years. Although we were not surprised by the raw numbers of non-U.S.-born students, we were surprised that so many had received their high school education here in the United States. This result raises concern about the sort of instruction in academic English that ESL students receive in their K–12 education.

The number of writing courses our students had taken prior to the one during which the survey was conducted indicated their considerable difficulty with college-level written English. At the time the survey was administered, students would normally have completed no more than two college-level composition classes, either at SJSU or elsewhere. The usual sequence is first-, second-, and third-level classes. So we would expect students in the third-level course to have completed two courses prior to the administration of the survey, those in the second-level course to have completed one, those in the first-level to have completed none. Although SJSU does offer basic writing classes, these are not part of the expected sequence and are taken only by those students with poor academic writing skills. Yet we found that 40.8% (554) of our students had already completed three or more college-level writing classes. Clearly, a large number of students had difficulty with academic writing, resulting in their taking more than the required number of college-level composition classes.

Almost one third (31.5% or 427) of all our respondents stated that they did not speak English as their main language at age 6. The largest non-English-speaking groups reported were Chinese (9.1% or 150), Vietnamese (7.2% or 119), and Spanish (5% or 71). We chose age 6 as representative of the time when many children the world over must acquire a public language in addition to the language of the home, as part of their formal schooling. This figure probably includes students who have native-born Spanish-speaking parents, and, as such, is likely a more accurate measure of bilingualism in our student body than the figure of 27% cited earlier.

Along with more usual questions on biographical data, we included a question on how often students had been read to as children. Recent research (e.g., Heath, 1983) has shown that children who are read to develop better literacy skills so long as the activity includes approaches for decontextualizing the text (see Introduction; and Walters, this book) similar to those used in school settings. Because of the nature of our questionnaire, we could not determine what type of reading had been done in the homes of our students, or even the language used for reading. Even with this limitation, however, answers to Question 13, "How often did someone older read to you as a child?"

provide intriguing information for further investigation, which we will address again later. Almost two thirds of all the respondents (63.5% or 861) either were not read to at all or were seldom read to, and only 11.4% (154) were read to every day.

Language Use

All students.   We asked all students to indicate their current writing experiences, asking them how many papers and essay exams they wrote (other than in their composition classes) and how much they wrote in English for noncollege purposes. As we had anticipated, many students were not required to write in their college classes and were not required to take essay exams. Whereas half the students wrote three or more papers (other than for composition classes), 17% (213) wrote no papers at all and 25% took no essay exams (except for composition). More than half (51.3%) the students did very little or no writing in English that was unrelated to college assignments. The more students did write outside school, the better they did on the final essay test. A closer examination of the data shows that this relationship was due primarily to the writing practices of students in the second- and third-level classes. In other words, writing outside of class had a more beneficial effect on advanced students than on beginning ones.

Another use of language that correlated positively with academic writing proficiency in English for bilingual and monolingual students alike was having listened to an adult read to them as children—the more students were read to as children, the better their academic writing. As indicated earlier, we have no information on the language used for this activity or on the manner in which it was done; nevertheless, this activity in childhood was significant for the subsequent development of writing proficiency.

Students using a language other than English (LOTE).   Almost half our students (48.6% or 655) stated that they used a LOTE. This figure undoubtedly includes a number of students bilingual in Spanish and English, who did not consider Spanish their primary language at age 6 but who nevertheless are active speakers of this language. Almost one-third of all students used a LOTE with family members and at work. Of those classified as bilingual, about half used it almost always when speaking with parents (304) and with grandparents (316). The majority of the bilingual speakers used a LOTE at least sometimes when speaking with parents, siblings, and grandparents as well as at work and on campus. Exactly half of the bilingual speakers watched television in a language other than English at least some of the time. Figures for the use of a LOTE in specific contexts are given in Table 4, both for the total population surveyed as well as for bilingual students as a group.

Table 4
Use of LOTE in Specific Contexts

Setting	% Total population who use currently	% Bilingual speakers who use currently
Listening	40.6	78.6
Parents	39.9	72.4
Siblings	33.5	62.7
Work*	32.1	60.2
Grandparents	30.1	56.3
On campus	28.4	53.4
Television	26.6	50.0
Community/Campus events	25.7	48.0
Read books	23.9	44.7
Read magazines	23.5	43.8
Shopping	22.5	41.9
Restaurants	22.4	41.2
Read newspapers	21.3	39.1
For lecture notes	19.6	37.0
Business letters	8.8	16.5
Personal letters	8.3	15.6

$n = 733, 1,347$
*Most who used it at work said they used it "sometimes."

As Table 4 indicates, fewer than half of the LOTE speakers used it for reading books, magazines, and newspapers; for shopping and dining out; or for writing lecture notes, business letters, and personal letters. Some of these uses, however, correlated with proficiency in academic written English.

As Table 5 shows, more formal uses of a LOTE entailed in reading books and newspapers and in writing business letters correlated with proficiency in written English, as measured by scores on the essay examination. Table 5 shows a summary of the results of the chi-square analysis of the data. Table 6, which gives the complete chi-square analysis for reading, is given in full to show how we obtained the summary. A less formal use of a LOTE than entailed in listening to television also correlated strongly with proficiency in written English. Bilingual students who read books, wrote formal letters, and watched television extensively in a LOTE at the time they were enrolled in a university using English as the language of instruction did not become proficient in written English. We speculate that the amount of time they spent engaged in such activities using a LOTE, rather than the use of the LOTE itself, is the important factor here. In a university environment requiring extensive use of formal English almost daily, some students may well have been using the LOTE at the expense of English for the activities listed in the table.

Table 5
LOTE Students' Uses of Other Languages by Proficiency
(Essay Pass/Fail)

Use	N	Chi-Square	df	p
With parents	619	1.4291	4	.9391
With grandparents	637	.5235	4	.9712
On campus	637	4.9775	4	.2896
At work	637	5.9769	4	.2009
For business letters	636	10.0052	4	.0403
For lecture notes	638	2.6702	4	.6144
Reading books	632	17.4188	4	.0016
Reading newspapers	632	9.1855	4	.0566
Watching TV	635	13.5280	4	.0090
Personal letters	633	6.6676	4	.1545

Examining the specific uses of a LOTE proved to be more informative than a more simplistic look at the use/non-use of a LOTE. Only responses from the beginning composition students (basic writing and first-level) showed a strong correlation between general use of a LOTE and writing proficiency in English ($X^2 = 8$, p = .02; $X^2 = 8.7$, p = .003 respectively). The more these beginning writers used a LOTE, the less adequate their writing. There was no significant correlation between use of a LOTE and writing proficiency for more advanced composition students. We speculate that, although any use of a LOTE adversely affected beginning college students, only specific uses of a LOTE adversely affected more advanced students.

Table 6

Cross-tabulation of Holistic Essay by Frequency of Reading Books in a LOTE (n = 731)

Read books	Almost always	Frequently	Sometimes	Never	Not any more	Raw total
Pass	21	55	199	301	28	604
Fail	11	12	29	61	14	127
Column Total	32	67	228	363	42	731

Chi-Square	df	p	Min E.F.	Cells with E.F. < 5
17.4188	4	.0016	5.560	None

Self-evaluation. Student self-evaluations in all questions except vocabulary were unreliable. For example, we found that the more writing classes students had taken, the more their self-rating of their own writing proficiency correlated with the holistic essay score. It seems then, that students learned to evaluate themselves according to the way they were measured by faculty in their writing classes. In other words, their perceptions resulted from teacher assessment rather than from their own writing experiences. For all writing levels, there was a strong correlation between their perceived adequacy of vocabulary and their measured writing proficiency. A comparison of bilingual and monolingual students shows that bilingual students experienced greater "difficulty in finding the right word when writing an essay" [Question 2].

Recent research on university professors' reactions to student writing (Santos, 1988) found that this important audience for students' writing rated lexical errors as the most serious kind of error, and this research pointed to the need for greater emphasis on vocabulary improvement and lexical selection for bilingual college students.

Conclusion

This study indicates both the difficulty and the importance of ascertaining the extent of bilingualism within contemporary educational settings (in this case, a university) in an English-dominant society. When bilingual students are recognized as a significant component of a student body, their special needs can be addressed. Having identified major language backgrounds and patterns of language use associated with academic English writing proficiency, we have only begun to explore these needs with this initial survey. In a population in which roughly 10% identified themselves as bilingual by enrolling in ESL composition classes, probably one third could be classified as active bilinguals. For beginning students, any use of a LOTE negatively affected their academic writing proficiency in English, but for advanced students only uses of a LOTE in reading books, writing business letters, and watching television correlated negatively with academic English writing proficiency. The more they read, wrote business letters, and watched television in a LOTE, the less their writing proficiency. Students' self-evaluations suggest that inadequate vocabulary in English detracted from writing academic English, while having been read to as children in any language positively affected writing academic English.

Implications for Teaching

Our results have important implications for the education of bilingual students, and our survey instrument demonstrates how educators can try to identify the diversity in their institutions.

Our Findings

In many major universities, teachers run across bilingual students in all classes at every level. Many bilingual students will take longer than their monolingual English peers to attain college-level proficiency in academic written English. Instructors can best help bilingual students develop their language development by encouraging extensive reading, writing, and listening in English and by placing more emphasis on the vocabulary needed in academic settings. Because so many students, both monolingual and bilingual, are not read to as children and because this experience seems to impede their writing skills, classroom activities might provide listening experiences that foster acquisition of the rhetorical patterns of written English. These patterns are, of course, culturally grounded in experiences and traditions of the English-speaking world. Where they differ from a student's native-language patterns, English rhetorical patterns might be presented as an addition rather than a substitution—much like vocabulary.

Survey Instrument

Although this survey was designed specifically for our own campus, it is typical of those used in other educational settings such as K–12 districts, adult education programs, community colleges, and individual classrooms. These gross findings are useful for instruction, but we must remember that our students are individuals with varying language experiences (see Lucas, this book). We have already noted that our survey did not differentiate among the ways children are read to. Our recent case studies of language use and academic writing success (Murray & Nichols, 1992) have shown us just how complex an issue this is. We found that many students just did not recall whether they were read to; others recalled sitting on a parent's knee while the parent read the newspaper aloud, and gradually learning to read for themselves; others recalled reading the newspaper aloud for grandparents, even though they did not understand what they were reading; others claimed they did not need to be read to because they could read for themselves; still others claimed they were not read to as children and yet recounted that they read the newspaper aloud to grandparents. We have no way of knowing how these case study students with such experiences would respond to our survey question about being read to as a child. We did find, however, that those early experiences with literacy often helped students develop a love of reading and writing in their first language, a love that drove them to read and write in English.

We also noted that students' perceptions of their own writing ability are so conditioned by their teachers' evaluations that they are unreliable as an independent measure of their writing proficiency. In our case studies as well, we found that students' perceptions were affected by the way teachers and others responded to their writing. One student, a poet in his native language, was successful in academic writing in English largely because he used humor to express voice and touch the reader. Interestingly, this student also claimed that he was a good writer because he knew English grammar so well. Yet his writing was as grammatically flawed as that of other students who had found less success in academic written English. Clearly teachers focus on correct grammar as a sign of good writing (see Soter, this book). This student did not realize that his writing worked, despite the grammatical weaknesses, because he was able to organize his thoughts and speak to the reader.

Thus, we would encourage experimenting with language use surveys to identify the extent of bilingualism in a particular educational setting and to examine some of the relationships between language

74

use and academic writing in English. However, we would caution against using any but the biographical data as definitive. The very nature of a quantitative survey collapses the data; individual differences get lost. It is only with in-depth case studies or ethnographies such as those advocated by Walters (this book) and presented by Christine Pearson Casanave, Tamara Lucas, and Olga Vasquez (separate chapters, this book) that specific uses of language can be uncovered. A survey does, however, enable educators to determine numbers of bilingual students and raise questions for follow-up case studies. Thus, we can investigate ways these students add to our linguistic and cultural heritage, at the same time identifying strategies that have helped students become part of an academic community.

Summary

The study reported here investigated the self-reported language use of 1,363 composition students and correlated it with their performance on a holistically graded essay examination. Only 10% (140) of the students were enrolled in ESL composition classes although at least 27% (371) of the students could be classified as bilingual based on their country of origin and that of their parents. For beginning students, any use of a language other than English (LOTE) correlated with their performance on the written essay. For advanced students, only specific uses of a LOTE correlated with their performance: reading books or newspapers, listening to television, and writing business letters. Factors that correlated with students' academic writing proficiency were ones reflecting extensive exposure to written English: writing in nonacademic settings and in classes other than composition classes; studying in a particular field; having an inadequate vocabulary; and listening to someone read to them when they were children. The final variable, being read to as a child, was the only variable that correlated significantly with writing proficiency for monolingual and bilingual students.

Acknowledgments

We would like to thank Bruce Wilson and Zeljko Pavic in the SJSU Testing Office for their guidance at various stages of this study. Without the meticulous administration of the survey by Neal Lerner, we would not have had such extensive and reliable data.

Discussion Topics and Projects

1. Administer the survey in Appendix 3A to several native English and nonnative English speakers. Compare and contrast your findings with those reported here.

2. Administer the survey in the Appendix to one native English speaker and one nonnative English speaker. Administer the survey face-to-face, walking through each question with your respondents. Have them tell you questions they don't understand, questions to which they cannot respond adequately, and questions that were not asked. Using this input, adapt the questionnaire. Test your new questionnaire on two more respondents.

3. Interview five people about being read to as a child. Ask them for types of texts used, what the older person did in addition to actually reading the text (e.g., asking questions about the text or pictures, extrapolating from the text), how the child and adult were seated, and if this was an enjoyable experience for the child.

4. The survey results reported here indicate that using a LOTE may negatively affect acquisition of academic written English. These results seem to contradict those found in other studies of bilinguals (e.g. Cummins, 1982). Such studies (see Collier, 1989, for a summary of such studies) indicate that literacy in the first language facilitates literacy in the second language. How can these two apparently contradictory findings be reconciled?

5. The results of the survey reported here indicate that students' perceptions of their own writing come largely from the way their teachers evaluate writing in class. How can researchers probe for what else students feel about their own writing? How can teachers help shape students' perceptions in more positive ways?

Further Reading

For further reading on academic literacy, see chapters by Dandy, Casanave, Soter, and Walters in this book. For research on the writing of ESL students, see Ann Raimes (1985) and Vivian Zamel (1983,

1985). For methods and approaches for teaching writing to bilingual students, see Donna Johnson and Duane Roen (1989) and Susan Goldman and Henry T. Trueba (1987). For an overview of the research on vocabulary development and a discussion of two major approaches to vocabulary instruction, see Moran (1984)

Appendix 3A

Language Use Survey—1987 (revised)
Undergraduate Studies—San José State University
(SJSU)

Please respond to these items on the scantron sheet. *Enter your name & social security no. in appropriate place.* Use only a number 2 pencil and make all your marks heavy and black. Choose only one response for each item; if you erase, do so completely.

A. Biographical data:

1. English course currently enrolled in:

   (1) 1A
   (2) 1B
   (3) 100W
   (4) 2L
   (5) 3A
   (6) 3B

2. Are you enrolled in an "F" section of this course?

   (1) Yes
   (2) No

3. Age:

   (1) 15–20
   (2) 21–25
   (3) 26–30
   (4) 31–35
   (5) 36–40
   (6) 41–45
   (7) 46–50
   (8) 51+

4. Sex:

   (1) Male
   (2) Female

5. Place of birth:

   (1) U.S. or Canada

    (2) Mexico or Central America
    (3) South America
    (4) Asia
    (5) Africa
    (6) Europe
    (7) Indian subcontinent
    (8) Middle East
    (9) Pacific Islands
  (10) Other

6. Place of your mother's birth:
(Use same scale as in item 4)

7. Place of your father's birth:
(Use same scale as in item 4)

8. If your place of birth was *not* the U.S., number of years here:

    (1) More than 20 years
    (2) 10–20 years
    (3) 6–9 years
    (4) 3–5 years
    (5) 1–2 years
    (6) Less than 1 year

9. Your main language at age 6:

    (1) English
    (2) Spanish
    (3) Vietnamese
    (4) A Filipino language
    (5) Korean
    (6) A Chinese language
    (7) Persian
    (8) Arabic
    (9) An Indian subcontinent language
  (10) Other

10. Number of college composition courses (any level) completed:

    (1) Less than 1
    (2) 1–2
    (3) 3–4
    (4) 4+

11. Years at SJSU:

    (1) Less than 1
    (2) 1–2
    (3) 3–4
    (4) 4+

12. Area of study at SJSU:

    (1) Business
    (2) Engineering
    (3) Humanities and the Arts
        (art, liberal studies, English, foreign languages, etc.)
    (4) Science
        (math, computer science, biology, etc.)
    (5) Social Science
        (psychology, political science, anthropology, social science, etc.)
    (6) Applied Arts and Sciences
        (industrial technology, aerospace studies, nursing, occupational technology, journalism, advertising, etc.)
    (7) Other

13. How often did someone older read to you as a child?

    (1) Almost every night/day
    (2) Frequently
    (3) Sometimes
    (4) Never

B. Self-rating for adequacy in English:
   For items 14 through 18, use the scale below to rate your competency (as compared to that of your classmates) for the following language tasks:

    (1) Not competent at all
    (2) Barely competent
    (3) Competent
    (4) Very competent

14. Speaking

15. Listening

16. Reading

17. Writing

18. Writing term papers

19. I do better in courses if I don't have to write essays.

    (1) Strongly agree
    (2) Agree
    (3) Disagree
    (4) Strongly disagree

20. I would rather take a scantron exam than write an essay exam. (Use same scale as in item 19)

21. I do better on essays when the professor grades for content and not for grammar or punctuation. (Use same scale as in item 19)

22. When I write an essay in class, I have trouble finding the right words to express my meaning. (Use same scale as in item 19)

C. Current writing experiences

23. What's the total number of papers you will write for classes this semester?

    (1) 5+
    (2) 3–4
    (3) 1–2
    (4) None
    (5) Do not know

24. How many other papers will you write this semester for classes *other than* composition class? (Use same scale as in item 19)

25. Have you had (or will you have) essay exams in any class besides composition?

    (1) Yes
    (2) No
    (3) Do not know

26. How often do you do writing in English that is unrelated to college classes?

    (1) Every day

(2) Frequently
(3) Sometimes
(4) Never

D. Use of language other than English

27. Do you use a language other than English for any purpose?

(1) Yes
(2) No

If you answered *No*, stop. Thanks for filling out this survey.
If you answered *Yes*, continue. Please choose only *one* response to each question.

Use the following scale to rate how often you use a language other than English in the following situations:

(1) Almost always
(2) Frequently
(3) Sometimes
(4) Never

28. With parents

29. With grandparents

30. With sisters or brothers

31. Shopping in the U.S.

32. At community or campus events (fairs, sports, picnics, parties, church or temple)

33. Reading a newspaper

34. Reading magazines

35. Reading books

36. Watching television in the U.S.

37. Traveling outside the U.S.

38. Writing letters to friends/family

39. Writing business letters

40. Writing lecture notes in SJSU classes
41. As a student in a language classroom
42. On campus (outside class)
43. Eating out in a restaurant in the U.S.

Part II

Specific Literacies and Uses of Language

4

Sensitizing Teachers to Cultural Differences

An African American Perspective

Evelyn Baker Dandy
Armstrong State College, Georgia

The high rate of discipline problems for minority students involves behaviors related to cultural and communication issues (Foster, 1986; Hale-Benson, 1986; Kunjufu, 1986; Nelson-Barber & Meier, 1990; Taylor, 1987). Of the behaviors punished, more than half are related to those concerns, including challenging the teacher's authority, not listening quietly when the teacher is presenting a lesson, interrupting another student, responding in a loud voice, socializing in class, and using physical means to settle a conflict (Taylor, 1987). Such punishments are not surprising because educational institutions often do little to prepare teachers for the differences between their cultures and those of the students they will be teaching (Pine & Hilliard, 1990).

According to recent reports, the majority of discipline problems occur with African American males. All adolescents search for self-identity, to clarify who they are and what their role in society will be; for African American males this search takes the form of developing their self-confidence and asserting their masculinity as they leave the world of childhood and seek acceptance into adulthood. During this transition period, the peer group exerts significant influence on how they talk, how they dress, and how they interact with others (Mussen,

87

Conger, & Kagan, 1956). Their manner of talking, walking and dressing is deeply embedded in African American culture.

European American women comprise 80% of the current teaching force in the United States (Chira, 1990). Because the first direct contact teachers may have with African American males is in the classroom, teachers need to study and experience the African American culture in order to be sensitized to its many subtleties. Communication between two individuals from different cultures can fail simply because of the culturally oriented assumptions the speakers make about one another's responses. For example, speaking loudly and wearing a hat indoors are considered impolite in some middle-class school cultures. Other cultures consider the hat a part of an outfit and requests to remove it for class might be regarded as offensive. Students who take offense by responding in a loud voice to such a request could then be interpreted as challenging the teacher's authority. The goal of this chapter is to help teachers become more aware of African American language and its use so they can communicate more effectively and build on their students' cultural strengths.[1]

The Status of Black Language

Many urban working-class African American males have distinct ways of communicating that differ significantly from those of their teachers and school administrators. The manner in which they use language is a reflection of their culture, and its development is an essential ingredient in the socialization process for males as they pass from boyhood to manhood.

Many names for the language variety exist: Black English, Black English Vernacular, Nonstandard English, Black Dialect, Ebonics, Negro Nonstandard English, broken English, Black Street Speech, Black Language, and dialect. Most of these terms are pejorative and reflect the low status the language has in the United States today. Orlando Taylor (in Dandy, 1991) describes that status:

> All too often [the language of African Americans] is degraded or simply dismissed by individuals from both inside and outside the racial group as being uneducated, illiterate, undignified or simply non-standard. In this regard, the language of African Americans is unique in relation to virtually all other groups of Americans in general and groups of of color in particular. Most of the other groups of color are at least given credit

for having a legitimate language heritage, even if they are denied full access to American life. Who, for example, considers Spanish to be an ill-formed language, or Japanese to be an undignified language, or Chinese to be a non-standard language? (p. ii)

Mary Rhodes Hoover (1985) suggests using the term "Black Communications," (pp. 2–3) which predicates that this language system is more than just speech and more than just English. For her, Black Communications comprises

1. A *speech code* with grammar, phonology, lexicon, intonation, and semantics;

2. *Verbal strategies* or *speech acts*, such as *testifying, sounding, woofing, signifying, rapping,* and *playing the dozens;*

3. *Style*, which includes call-response, dramatic repetition, and improvisation;

4. *Nonverbal behavior*, such as silence in response to a ridiculous question, kinesics or side-by-side stance in conversation, and oculesics (eye rolling);

5. *Sociolinguistic rules for speaking*, such as not using *boy* for man, *girl* for woman, or *you people* for African Americans (pp. 9–23);

6. *Personal talk*, which involves special speaking behaviors used by those who are familiar and trust one another (Abrahams, 1972); and

7. *Moral teachings* through proverbs and sayings, such as "What goes around comes around." (See Figure 1.)

This chapter will examine one broad feature of Black Communications: verbal strategies as they are used by African American males aged 6 through 14. I have chosen to focus on males for several reasons:

1. Historically, African American males have been noted for using a particular kind of stylized talk;

2. Learning how to use this talk is an essential part of passage from boyhood to manhood;

3. Those who are successful at using this talk are often misinterpreted and subsequently punished by schools;

89

Figure 1
Components of Black Communications

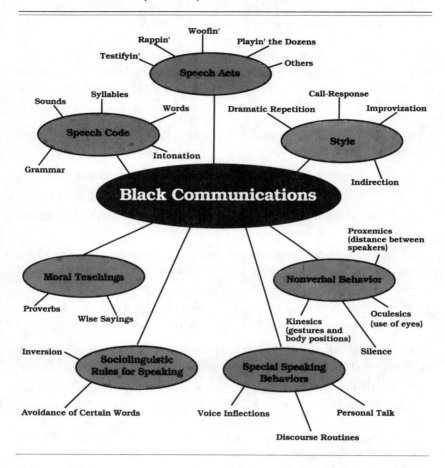

4. Most teachers are unfamiliar with the rules, purpose, and intent of this stylized talk;

5. Significantly large numbers of African American males are achieving below potential and are placed in classes for the mentally retarded, behavior disordered; and

6. African American male students lead the nation in being placed in the corners of classrooms, sent to the principal's office, suspended or expelled from school, and in dropping out of school.

Joseph Johnson (1990) has described African American males as an endangered species: they are at the bottom of the social totem pole—below African American females, White females, and White males—on every scale (test achievement, school behavior, remediation, dropout, employment, crime, imprisonment, and death by natural causes); more African American males are in prison than enrolled in college.

Society has painted a deviant picture of African American males through its television and newspaper portrayals of them selling drugs, committing crime against other people of color, getting arrested and filling prison cells. George Bush's 1989 presidential campaign legitimized the media's negative emphasis by showing pictures of Willie Horton, the African American criminal Michael Dukakis was supposed to have released from jail. A vote for Dukakis was perceived as a vote for Willie Horton. Those who voted for Bush were expected to infer that Michael Dukakis would allow such criminals to walk the streets freely.

I want to sensitize teachers to the ways many African American males use words. It is my hope that teachers will listen more intently to these young men and search for ways they can capitalize on their students' communicative competence to improve communication between themselves and their students. What are in fact cultural strengths can be utilized for positive teaching and learning experiences as teachers devise creative and constructive ways of integrating orality and literacy.

The Oral and Literate Traditions of Black Communications

Black Communications had its roots in the indigenous languages of Africa (Asante, 1987; Turner, 1949; Vass, 1979). It was carried here in the hearts and minds of enslaved Africans, who were brought by force to the Americas. Only the strongest and most determined survived the passage, bringing no mementos or luggage, only the clothes on their backs.

The new land was hostile to them: Members of the same village were forbidden to talk with one another under penalty of death. So they devised covert ways of communicating and disguised them in their talk, their music, and their actions. Although they were forced to learn new words to respond to their captors, they retained the basic grammar, idiom, and deep structure of their native languages. They also maintained their basic views of the world.

The Language Derived from the African World View

Essential to the African American world view was belief in God as the creator and sustainer of all things, both spiritual and material. This view maintained a fundamental unity between the spiritual and the material. Religion and nature were one, with Africans always seeking a balance and rhythm in this unity (Nobles, 1980). Robert Farris Thompson (1981) also found evidence of this overriding theme in his investigation of the art of African tribes. Melville Herskovits (1941) confirmed this unity in his descriptions of the integration of song and dance in Dahomean and Gold Coast choruses, the Shango cult songs of Trinidad, and the Brazilian Negro melodies. Across their diaspora, wherever large groups of Africans reside, evidence of the theme of unity, balance, and rhythm survives. In the African kinship system, the tribe or village gave identity to the individual. The individual was part of the collective unity, a participant in collective responsibility. Whatever happened to the individual happened to the tribe. Solidarity and community life were esteemed. African self-concept derived from the belief that "I am because we are and because we are, therefore I am" (Nobles, 1980, p. 29). The African world view emphasized survival of the village, oneness with nature, cooperation, commonality, groupness, and interdependence. In sharp contrast, the European world view emphasized survival of the fittest, control over nature, competition, differences, individuality and independence (Nobles, 1980).

Oral Tradition Rooted in Written Word

The language of Africans had strong literate beginnings (Asante, 1987; Sy, 1989; Van Sertima, 1989; and Vass, 1979). Thousands of years before Christ, bushmen of southern Africa wrote in stone about their daily activities. Egyptian mythology recorded on papyrus the deeds of ancient ancestors. As early as 3100 BC, inscriptions on sacred texts, tombs, monuments, paintings, and pottery used all genre of literature to depict the culture of ancient Kemet (Egypt) (Hilliard, 1985). Although the ancient Africans were prolific writers, oral language was also important.

The spoken word, called *nommo* by the Africans, held magic power (Asante, 1987) for them. Sy (1989) calls it the "primordial Verb" (p. 277):

> All activities of men, and all the movements in nature, rest on the word, on the productive power of the word, which is water and heat and seed and Nommo, that is, life force itself. . . . The force, responsibility, and commitment of the word, and the awareness the word alone alters the world. . . ." (Smitherman, 1977, p. 78)

The names of newborn children did not take on meaning until their fathers whispered the new names in their children's ears. In African oral tradition, words accompanied medicine, death rites, and work; words preceded and sometimes accompanied battle. The songs, histories, and traditions were the very soul of the village and were enshrined in the oral language (Tarynor, 1976).

In his epic novel, *Roots*, Alex Haley (1976) described the *griots*, men who could recite generations and generations of history in an effort to keep alive great deeds of ancient kings. Urban and rural streetwise men from Bermuda and the Caribbean could also relate family stories for hours on end—all as a means of maintaining their reputation as verbal performers. African languages and cultural forms were carried on intact in Brazil and the Caribbean with later generations reciting church rituals in secret languages (Alleyne, 1980, p. 17).[2]

Reinforcement of Oral Tradition in the New World

In the American Colonies and later in the United States, New World Africans were isolated from the rest of society, resulting in the maintenance of their culture. Further, because Africans were forbidden by law to read and write, orality, or word of mouth, became the primary mode of maintaining the culture, a mode that came directly from the African tradition.

Today the African American community places high value upon

the ability to verbalize. This value is especially significant among African American males. Every time a speaker opens his mouth, he is further establishing his reputation. Language is a means of survival, helping the user acquire status, leadership, and success. It symbolizes toughness, bravery, and masculinity. Orality can make the difference between

> having or not having food to eat, a place to live, clothes to wear, being accepted or rejected by one's peers, and being personally and emotionally secure or risking a complete loss of ego. Therefore, for a member of street culture, language is not only a communicative device but also a mechanism of control and power. (Abrahams & Gay, 1975, p. 159)

Roger Abrahams and Geneva Gay's (1975) description reflects the magic power of the word—*nommo*. Verbal strategies are part of the skills African American males must learn in order to pass from boyhood to manhood. They are an integral part of the culture shared by males within the African American community. Muriel Saville-Troike (1989) describes similar uses of verbal play by children from China, East Java, Korea, Samoa, Saudi Arabia, Turkey, and Venezuela.

Verbal Strategies

How well an African American male survives in his peer group depends upon his adeptness at using a variety of verbal strategies, the highly stylized use of words and gestures to impress, persuade, or control an audience. Names for the strategies vary according to the location and the time period. For instance, informants who live in San Diego, California report that *basin'* is the same as *playin' the dozens*; in Savannah, Georgia, it is called *checkin'*; in Washington, D.C., *jonin'*. See Figure 2 for names that describe various strategies (Smith, 1974).

These names are in a constant state of flux. New words are always being developed in an effort to maintain a secret code that only the African American peer group understands. Although the names for the verbal strategies vary, the functions remain the same, attesting to the important position these strategies occupy in the African American community. The appropriate use of verbal strategies is an integral part of the communicative competence of African American males, a

Figure 2
Names for Verbal Strategies

basin'	fat mouthin'	markin'
buggin'	gum beatin'	mockin'
bulldozin'	harpin'	playin' the dozens
bustin'	hoorahin'	rappin'
cappin'	humbuggin'	shuckin'
checkin'	jeffin'	signifyin'
coppin' a plea	jibbin'	soundin'
crackin'	jonin'	sweetmouthin'
dissin'	lollygaggin'	talkin' smack
dozin'	loud mouthin'	testifyin'
droppin' lugs	luggin'	woofin'

competence that involves gaining the skills that will prepare them for manhood: purpose, control, self-discipline, and independence.

Verbal strategies involve the words as well as how the voice and body are used in saying the words, how the utterances are used in social settings and how others interpret their use. In this chapter, I discuss three verbal strategies: *rapping, woofing,* and *playing* a game called *the dozens* as well as the verbal interaction termed *call-response*— a mode of communication rather than a strategy.

Call-Response

Call-response reflects the African world view of unity and interdependence, a view that seeks to bring together the speaker and the listener in a unified movement. It is a "spontaneous verbal and nonverbal interaction between speaker and listener in which all the speaker's statements (calls) are punctuated by expressions (responses) from the listener" (Smitherman, 1977, p. 104).[3]

In call-response, both parties talk and both parties listen, creating an emotional synergism. Speakers give one another constant feedback so they both can assess the effectiveness of their performance. The speaker has the responsibility to issue the call, and the listener has the obligation to respond in some overt way by smiling, laughing, nodding, rocking side to side, hitting the desk or saying something like *Amen* or *Uh-huh* to confirm agreement or disagreement. The only wrong response is no response.

95

Contemporary jazz, popular music, rock, and rap all have many instances of the call-response common in the slaves' songs. In the traditional African American church, in fact, the reputation of the minister is determined by how adept he is at issuing the call and receiving responses. The same holds true for African American males in terms of their peer groups. Group status is based upon the youth's adeptness at eliciting responses from his audience.

The European world view contrasts sharply: A listener sits quietly, looks at the speaker, and may only rarely display an outward sign or response. Depending on the specific cultures, it may be impolite to talk when someone else is talking. According to Thomas Kochman (1981), Whites often consider continuous feedback in conversation as interruption.

Cross-cultural miscommunication can occur when European and African Americans interact without knowing the cultural obligations of the speaker and the listener. Because the African American perspective assumes that the listener must react in some overt way, when this does not happen, the speaker may assume the listener is uninterested or just does not care. Thus, students may mistrust a teacher who displays what they perceive to be an uncaring attitude.

Rapping

Although it is enjoying a popular resurgence, rapping, or rappin', as a verbal strategy is an old tradition. Originally, rappin' was employed in male-female relationships as an introduction device. A male who was interested in pursuing a relationship with a female would "rap to" her to test her receptiveness (Abrahams & Gay, 1975). Rappin' is "a colorful or distinctive style of talking into which the speaker injects his personality so as to make a favorable impression" (Burling, 1973, p. 84). Its most recent uses blend the traditional with the new. Today, African American males rap to exercise their verbal ability and sharpen their wit.

Kochman (1981) lists three common uses of rap:

1. To provide information to someone (e.g., *runnin' somethin' down*);

2. To convince or persuade someone to do something (e.g., *whuppin' the game*);

3. To introduce oneself (e.g., rappin' to a woman to win her affections) (pp. 76–88);

96

Nowadays, we must add a fourth:

4. To entertain through music and bring a message that is played to a definite beat with the lyrics chanted rather than sung.

Any rap is highly stylized, exaggerated, and flamboyant, accompanied by a performance—the use of gestures, movement of the head from side to side, or leaning one way or another. The performance/rap is good if it brings a response: a smile, a handshake (e.g., *giving skin*), applause, consent, wild laughter, or some other overt reaction. This strategy assumes call-response. The intent of the rap is to put the speaker in the position of control and to impress the listener.

The rapper is successful if he can absorb the audience in his conversation. As he performs his rap, he may change the pitch, volume, rhythm of his voice, place stress on an unusual syllable, or use a range of vocal effects, such as rasp, growl, falsetto, and whine. The rapper uses active verb forms in his efforts to *throw a rap* or *run it down*. His rap is filled with slang, colorful hyperbole, and exaggerated comparisons.

White culture generally views as negative African American students' efforts to control authority figures, and their bragging and boasting mark such students as show-offs. Muhammed Ali, for example, endured a negative image in his efforts to prove that he was "The Greatest", and the media tends to disparage athletes who seem cocky.

Some middle-class African Americans and Whites are very fearful of rappers, especially if they are unfamiliar with the strategy. Groups of loud-talking, boisterous, gesturing, shoving adolescents walking down a hall may frighten teachers, and their fear may lead them to react negatively by confronting the students or reporting them for possible suspension. Teachers can usually get the rappers to settle down, however, by making a culturally and professionally appropriate request as the following excerpt shows:

> One morning I was working in my office, and one of our students came in and started moving up and down and said he had to go to the lavatory. I listened, kept working, sort of ignored him, but watched him out of the corner of one eye. Finally, after a few minutes, I turned to him and said, "No, you can't go. Your rap is weak." He laughed and said, "Ok, see you later." And he tipped on back to class. (Foster, 1986, p. 210)

The teacher's reaction was appropriate for that individual. He basically communicated with the student without embarrassing him. Had he blown up the issue by openly chastising the student, he might have interrupted instructional time and embarrassed the rapper unnecessarily. The teacher also might have alienated the rapper, causing subsequent retaliation and no-win situations. Peer groups are very important in the evaluation of the rap, for they are the rapper's audience; they must assess the success of his performance, which includes the reactions of the rapper's instructors.

Another form of rap, the love rap, allows an African American male to approach a female he does not know. It is a means of introducing himself, and winning the heart, affections, and mind of the female. (For example, performers Issac Hayes and Barry White use this kind of rap in their vocal music.) Geneva Smitherman (1977) offered an example of a love rap written nearly 100 years ago. Even today it has only to be uttered aloud by a convincing African American male to bring a reaction from a female, who smiles to indicate that she is interested or frowns and turns her head away to show that she does not care to talk to the suitor: "My dear kin' miss, has you any objections to me drawing my cher to yer side and revolvin' de wheel of my conversation around de axle of your understandin'?" (*Southern Workman Hampton Institute Folklore Collection*, 1895, p. 83, in Smitherman, 1977). Current rap music, in fact, is a kind of folk music, prevalent on radio, television, and in some school hallways and schoolyards today. Young people can recite detailed, meaningful rhymes that carry a message with no apparent preparation and deliver them at speeds up to 200 to 250 words per minute, without missing a beat. This verbal strategy has been assimilated into the advertising and entertainment industry so that even the Pillsbury Doughboy has a rap—along with comedian Bob Hope and McDonalds. An organization called Stop the Violence (Gray, 1989) has succeeded in combatting the negative influence of some rap groups, dedicating their profits to using rap in positive ways to inspire young people.[4]

Pat Pike (1987) has also used this cultural strength to create a supplemental reading program designed to help students who have severe problems with decoding skills. *Wordbuster Reading Rap* (1987) covers long and short vowels, the consonants /c/ and /g/, syllables, vowel digraphs (*ai, ea, ee*), and silent *e* through a catchy rap and accompanying written and motivational activities. Pike provides step by step directions and music for creating additional raps and coordinating poetry writing and articulation drills through cooperative learning. She has capitalized on a strength of many students who are not succeeding in school. Used in this very positive way, rap coordinates a holistic view of language that is thought about, spoken, written, and read. Profiting from this cultural difference, the teacher uses the strengths of students who can compose rhyme, write down, memorize, and perform it for an audience. For some students a very natural process, rapping, can be converted into what Shirley Brice Heath (1983) calls a literacy event: a piece of writing that revolves around talk.

Woofing

Selling *woof (or wolf) tickets* refers to any kind of strong language that is purely idle boasting, a form of bragging that is nearly always taken for the real thing by an outsider from another culture. Woofing, or woofin', can be a kind of rap. It is "a ritual wherein anger and hostility can be sustained at the verbal level *without* violence. Through woofin', a player can maintain an image of being fearless and tough with the hope that once that image is achieved, he won't have to prove it" (Hale-Benson, 1986, p. 171, emphasis author's). Woofin' is also called *dogin', bogardin', loud mouthin', loud talkin', soundin',* or *runnin' a strong rap.*

There are usually two people involved in woofin' although there can also be an audience. To accept a challenge to fight is to accept a *woof ticket.* The intent of woofin' is intimidation. In the school setting, woofin' can take these forms:

1. Standing in the hall and blocking the teacher;

2. Standing in front of a teacher or walking down the hall with a belt opened;

3. Yelling and moving one's body in a menacing way while arguing about a grade;

4. Just standing and staring at the teacher (Kunjufu, 1986, calls this the *Showdown*; Cooke, 1980, labels it the *silent rap* (p. 149);

5. Almost any nonverbal, verbal or physical form of intimidation (Foster, 1986, p. 192).

Whether at one another or at the teacher, students have to be on the offensive to woof. The general rule for woofin' is that you do not woof on someone you cannot beat, frighten, or intimidate. For woofin' to work, the person woofed on must be on the defensive, and the one selling woof tickets on the offensive. The woofer has an I'm-bad-and-I-know-I'm-bad attitude where *bad* means excellent. Students generally agree about which teachers they can *get over on* by woofin' them: weak teachers who don't understand this verbal strategy. Abrahams and Gay (1975) report that

> students themselves testify to the effectiveness of their use of language as a means of exerting power and control over the teacher and the classroom situation. Black kids claim that the middle-class teacher is 'stupid', 'lacks common sense', 'dumb', 'naive', and that she will 'believe anything'. Her vulnerability and ignorance about black life and how black students function makes her an easy prey for students. They are so easy to 'run a game on' that the exercise is hardly worth the effort. (p. 164)

For a middle-class female teacher having her first direct contact with African American males, woofin' can be terrifying. In Showdown during which the student just stands with his arms folded and stares at the teacher, the student has the advantage. He chooses the battlefield, the strategy, and the weapons, all of which involve the use of words. His skill at 'keeping cool' is so well developed that it is hard to shake or surpass. The teacher tells him to do something and he does it, but in a way that unnerves the teacher so that he has the upper hand throughout the situation, as in the following example. To illustrate my point about female teachers, I have altered the dialogue in the following account, replacing "brother" in "Right on, brother" with "teacher":

> On this particular day the students have decided not to do anything in class. The teacher enters and instructs the students to begin work. No one says or does anything. Then one student begins to sing softly to himself. The teacher asks the singer to be quiet and return to his regularly assigned seat. The student responds with "Right on, [teacher], I'm gonna move," and he does. The teacher says something else and the student answers, "Right on, [teacher]." The teacher, very much irritated says "Shut up." The student answers very softly."Right on, [teacher]." The teacher says, "I don't like your attitude today and if you don't be quiet I'm gonna put you out." The student, more forceful this time says, "Right on, [teacher]". The teacher answers with "Get out," and the student responds, "Right on [teacher]", as he slowly walks out of the door. (Abrahams & Gay, 1975, p. 165)

The student saw the teacher as incompetent, so he won that game. The students in that class lost respect for the teacher, confirming their supposition that she was a pushover. Now, they could run that same game on her again whenever they decided to do so.

Herbert Foster (1986) describes this next woofin' scenario as Reality 58, or a Showdown:

> A new teacher was walking in the hall when a few boys approached her from the opposite direction. One of the boys peeled off from the group, and as he and the teacher came face to face, he moved his hand out in front of the teacher, placed his palm against the wall, and looked at the teacher. (p. 194)

What options would the teacher have in reacting to this attempt at woofin'?

1. She could stop, turn the other way and run. If she flees, however, the student has won. He loses respect for her and will not listen to another thing she says. He sold the woof ticket and she bought it.

2. The teacher could become visibly upset and preach to the student about the value of respect, telling him she will report him to the office if he doesn't move. The student, as in the previous scenario, would probably show no visible sign, ignore the teacher, and aggravate her even more. The student might even push the teacher into hitting him by simply outstaring, laughing, or sneering in the teacher's face. If the teacher hits him, the teacher has lost again. He'll probably hit the teacher back. Remember, he's selling tickets in front of an audience and they will encourage him not to lose face.

3. The teacher could sell some woof tickets of her own. She could outstare him with a look that is "badder" than his and say emphatically "Move!" Or the teacher could quickly snap his arm at the pressure point and move him out of the way. The teacher wins his respect by not yielding to his efforts to frighten her. Any time teachers touch a student, however, they open themselves to possible physical or legal repercussions, so this decision must be weighed seriously.

4. The teacher could reproduce a supply of woof tickets and hand one out to the student who runs the game on her. This tactic would

acknowledge the student's adeptness and confirm the teacher's understanding and appreciation of his attempt to intimidate her. This might disarm the student because the objective of woofin' is to avoid physical confrontation through effective intimidation. The teacher could hand out the ticket quickly and move on to her destination and still maintain control over the situation without antagonizing the student (Foster, 1986).

5. The teacher could observe how African American teachers who understand the verbal strategies respond in their classes.

Kochman (1981) found that verbally aggressive behavior such as woofin' is regarded very differently in African American and White communities. As with woofin', African Americans hold that angry verbal disputes do not have to escalate to actual physical fighting. According to Kochman, "Insults and threats can be maintained by blacks at the verbal level *without* violence necessarily resulting," whereas, "Whites tend to see the public expression of hostility. . .as a clear warning of intent to act upon that threat" (pp. 48–49, emphasis his). So from a White cultural perspective, woofin' is regarded as a prelude to a fight, not an attempt to avoid a fight—the latter being the actual intent of this verbal strategy.

It is quite possible, then, for insensitive teachers to report woofin' to the office and label frequent woofers as "overly aggressive discipline problems." African American males who continually exercise their adeptness at woofin' are often placed in in-house suspension or in programs for the "behaviorally disordered," responses that are inappropriate to this verbal strategy.

Playing the Dozens

Playing, or playin', the dozens, which may begin as early as age 6, is considered a rite of manhood (Abrahams, 1963; Cooke, 1980; Hannerz, 1977; Kunjufu, 1988; Nobles, 1980; Schulz, 1977). It is a game in which two opponents dual verbally, making derogatory remarks about each others' family members, usually the mother or other females in the family. The basis for this game is call-response. Each player is appreciated and judged by the group, whose responsibility it is to urge the players on. The rules include avoidance of talk about deceased family members, never playing the game with a stranger, and using inaccurate statements of reality to defame one another's mothers.

The winner of the game is determined by the audience, who judges both players' reactions to one another's comments. The cultural hero is the player who hurls the most linguistically derogatory comments and still maintains his composure.

The slurs can be in the form of a rhyme: "I saw yo momma on the railroad track, looked at her and said 'Oooh, git back'" (Kunjufu, 1986, p. 16). Or the slur can just be the words "yo momma" or "your mother."[5]

Smitherman (1977) reports that the original verses of the dozens included 12 sex acts, each one given in words that rhymed with the numbers from 1 to 12. She describes the game as "a competitive oral test of linguistic ingenuity and verbal fluency." References to sex acts are what distinguish the dirty dozens from the dozens.

Ample evidence shows that the origins of this game are in Africa. Nathan and Julia Hare (1985) report that playing the dozens might be a re-creation of *trickstering*, a Nigerian rite during which the boy verbally puts down his father. Wade Nobles (1980), in his treatise on African philosophy, notes that such traditions were handed down from father to son. He describes ritualized orations and dance ceremonies used to release suppressed emotions and instances during which the spoken word was used to make the individual feel better psychologically. Foster (1986) also reports on African origins of the dozens.

The Ashanti, for example, sang *opo* verses and were known for devising verbal and nonverbal insults about ancestors. There are also references to the Trinidadian game *mamaguy;* the African Giguku taboo that infuriates a man when someone mentions his mother's name in an indecent way; the Dahomean joking relationship; and African songs of recrimination. An example of how this game was used during slavery times is found in *Ossie: The Autobiography of a Black Woman* (in Foster, 1988):

> They (slaves) wasn't just playing for fun. They was playing to teach themselves and their sons how to stay alive. The whole idea was to learn to take whatever the master said to you without answering back or hitting him, 'cause that was the way a slave had to be, so's he could go on living. (pp. 228–229)

Other names for the dozens include *checkin', crackin', getting down on the crib, getting on the kitchen folks, getting on moms, going to the kitchen, giving a man the spoke, joaning (jonin'), playing, putting a man on the wheel, signifying (siggin'),* and *sounding.* Although rubrics vary from city to city and region to region, every male I have interviewed, from school superintendents and college presidents to cab drivers and students, knows about the dozens and admits to having played the game himself or having heard it played. Most have related a specific humorous incident that stood out in their minds. Some, however, have stated outright "I don't play that" or "That's a dangerous game."

It is interesting to note additional historical accounts of cultures that used ritual insults to precede a battle and even to avoid it. In the Bible, when David slays Goliath, a similar dialogue ensues as the two warriors hurl verbal insults before combat. The events of this book occur in approximately 1020 BC:

> And the Philistine said to David, Come to me, and I will give thy flesh unto the fowls of the air, and to the beasts of the field.
>
> Then said David to the Philistine, Thou comest to me with a sword, and a spear, and with a shield; but I come to thee in the name of the Lord of hosts, the God of the armies of Israel, whom thou has defied.
>
> This day will the Lord deliver thee unto mine hand; and I will smite thee, and take thine head from thee; and I will give the carcases of the host of the Philistines this day unto the fowls of the air, and to the wild beast of the earth; that all the earth may know that there is a God in Israel. (King James Version, I Samuel, Chapter 17, verses 43–46)

During the 1990–1991 war in the Middle East, an ancient Semitic tradition was revived when Saudi television aired ritual insults in rhyme written by Saudi poets. The Iraqi army retorted with poets who could quote from ancient verse in the verbal war that preceded the physical war:

> And given the possibility that the trading gibes could turn out to be the full extent of the war, the question of who is better at it takes on considerable importance. Whose barbs have been more devastating? Whose poets have produced more quotable quotes? These questions occupy Arab viewers almost as much as the issue of who enjoys better odds on the battlefield, and few will deny that Saudis are winning the verbal war hands down. (Ya'ari & Friedman, 1991, p. 26)

Verbal dueling is also used by Turkish boys, East Javanese and Chinese children; preschool boys and girls of Saudi Arabia engage in competitive individual and group recitation with adult approval.

A good dozens player demonstrates the following competencies:

1. He must control his emotions. In the presence of friends, terribly derogatory statements are made about his mother or other female family member who is dear to him.

2. He must begin to search for his masculine identity as he pulls away from the strong influence of his mother by withstanding derogatory comments.

3. He must develop the ability to make words rhyme and utter them spontaneously.

4. He must be able to improvise, think on his feet and counter with an even more clever slur upon his opponent's female relative.

5. He must be brave enough to take the risk of being bested in front of his peers. Losing means disapproval, being proved ineffective at words, being considered effeminate in the eyes of peers.

In the classroom, peers playing the dozens can present a serious problem for teachers, especially if they are unaware of the game and its significance. A typical example of how playing the dozens can disrupt a classroom: The students in a science class are about to do an experiment. All materials have been distributed. The teacher has explained the details for each group. One student loudly accuses the other in his group of talking about his momma. The students face each other as if they might begin to fight. How could a teacher respond to this situation?

1. She could direct the other groups to begin their work, go to the two players, and state clearly that she does not allow the game of the dozens in her classroom (employing, of course, the term for the dozens used in that part of the United States). This would tell the students that she is aware of the game, she understands what the students are doing, but that she will not permit them to play it in her classroom.

2. She could stop the class and talk briefly about the game. An integral part of the game is that the players must be convincing.

Although students can appear angry at one another as they shout slurs, 5 minutes later they are friends again. Therefore, most games can be diffused by simply announcing that the game is over.

3. She could tell the other students to begin their experiments and mediate for the two players: "Just because he talked about your mother, it doesn't mean what he said is true. Now let's move on to the experiment at hand." This game might have started the day before or on the school bus and have been continued throughout the halls prior to this class meeting.

4. She could diffuse the game and move the class to completing the experiment. Set aside a specific time to talk by assembling the class into cooperative groups. Have them brainstorm first about all the positive aspects and then about the negative aspects of the game. Be certain students learn about the history and the purpose of the game: It is designed to let off steam and relieve tension; it is a manhood rite developed to teach the players how to be strong in dangerous or frightening situations and think on their feet. Discuss the competencies of a good dozens player and turn those competencies into advantages by having students match wits about some character in a history lesson or about a scientific concept. Classmates could award points for accuracy and delivery.

5. She could set up debates on the content of topics discussed in class: abortion, teen pregnancies, drugs, AIDS, and others of interest to that particular group. Be certain to channel the best dozens players into leading roles in this debate.

6. Deemphasize the fact that the boys may come to blows. This detracts from instructional time. Howard Hill (1989) recommends that teachers locate a mentor, that is, another teacher in the same school, who is adept at handling boys' use of verbal strategies. Teachers should talk with their mentors about how to handle their students' efforts at self-identity. Most important is to remember that a face-to-face confrontation is an effort to avoid a fight.

Many features of the language of African American males may be incorporated into constructive instructional strategies. Verbal strategies such as rappin', woofin', and playin' the dozens rely on the ability to use words in powerful ways. Teachers can capitalize on this adeptness with words by incorporating verbal interplay as a teaching strategy.

106

Cooperative Learning

Cooperative learning is a teaching strategy that can take advantage of several aspects of African American language features and the African world view: call-response, group self-concept, collective responsibility, the oral tradition, and the power of the word.

This small group process integrates immediate feedback, problem-solving, orality, and literacy and has been used successfully with students of all ages. Cooperative learning involves dividing a given class into heterogeneous groups of three or four and assigning each group a certain amount of time to solve a problem or answer a research question. Group participants offer solutions that are recorded and then reported to the class. The teacher integrates the group solutions by writing responses on a chart or the chalkboard, using the entire class period to reflect on the many solutions, and then having the class set priorities.

Research has documented numerous advantages to this teaching strategy: improved problem-solving skills, increased motivation as well as improvements in achievement, attendance, involvement, and the building of oral and written communicative competence. These skills are developed through intense interaction required within the groups. Each group member has a specified role: to lead discussion, to record notes, or to keep participants on task. All must listen and react to one anothers' suggestions. For every group activity, the individual roles change so that all members must participate and take their turn assuming each role. Students have an opportunity to interact with their peers, to express their ideas, transcribe them into print, compare them to those offered by their peers, and select appropriate actions. With cooperative learning, orality can feed into literacy in creative and constructive ways. (See Heath's, 1983, description of a literacy event; see Slavin, 1987; Pine & Hilliard, 1990, for additional suggestions on cooperative learning.)

Conclusion

In most educational settings, African American males are most frequently placed in the corner in classrooms, sent to the principal's office, suspended, or expelled. African American males comprise the majority in classes for the mentally retarded and behavior disordered. Students recognize that this happens, so they devise strategies for survival—verbal strategies that they can use to maintain some measure of control over a school situation where all the cards seem to be stacked against them. They develop their verbal techniques using those same skills that help them survive in their communities or on the streets.

It is most unfortunate that, for the most part, those African American males who are most adept at rappin', woofin', and playing the dozens are least successful in the school setting. Jawanza Kunjufu (1988) contends that African American males face a serious dilemma in the schools: to be popular or to be smart. If they choose to be popular among their peers, they are ostracized by the majority culture of the school. Being popular entails practicing and perfecting stylized verbal strategies, wearing name brand clothes, walking a special walk, wearing a special haircut, and achieving below their academic ability.

If they choose to be smart, students are more likely to succeed in school. They may be applauded by their teachers and listed on the honor roll. They may become bidialectal, using Standard English in the classroom and Black dialect features when in the company of the peer group. Unless the student has learned to become bidialectal, the choice of being smart, however, means ostracism by the African American peer group and being labeled a nerd, brainiac, or sissy.

It is the responsibility of teachers to learn to communicate with all of the children in their classes. Teachers who are sensitive to the existence, origin, and intent of verbal strategies can watch and listen for them in their classrooms and search for more effective ways to communicate with those who use them.

So-called discipline problems may stem from communicative issues and cross-cultural conflicts. African American males who appear to challenge the teacher's authority may be selling woof tickets. Those who are not listening quietly when the teacher is presenting a lesson may be giving the teacher feedback on the information presented. Those who interrupt another student may be responding to a call that has been issued. Those who are socializing and responding in a loud voice may be searching for their identities, asserting their masculinity, and confirming friendships. Those who seem to be using physical means to settle a conflict may be making their best effort to avoid a fight. Students who are successful at these verbal games must have the same intellectual ability that is needed to become school leaders: quick wit, good memory, and ability to capture the attention of an audience with linguistic ingenuity and verbal fluency.

Teachers handle incidents such as these based on the rapport they have established with their classes and whether or not they have made a serious effort to understand this natural process of moving from boyhood to manhood. Teachers are urged to listen to their students as they confirm their attempts at self-identity and be consistent in their treatment of them. It is the teacher's responsibility to control the teaching-learning situation. Teachers must make a concerted effort to learn more about the cultural differences and similarities between themselves and their students. The significant disparity between the performance of African American males and European American males must be viewed as unacceptable.

Summary

Current (1990s) demographics indicate that only 1 out of 10 teachers will be African American; the other 9 will be White, probably females whose undergraduate education has presented them with little or no knowledge of the cultural orientation of African American males. The chapter attempts to sensitize teachers to three commonly used verbal strategies, their origin, purpose and use in the classroom and provide alternatives for teachers so they can maximize the communicative competence of those African American males who use them.

Communication between individuals from different cultures can fail simply because of the culturally oriented assumptions the speakers make about one another's responses. The higher rate of discipline referrals among African American males involves behaviors that are related to cultural and communicative issues. In an effort to build their communicative competence these adolescents adopt a highly stylized use of words and gestures, many of which can be misinterpreted by those who are unfamiliar with their culture.

Discussion Topics and Projects

1. What reasons might you use to encourage those adolescents using verbal strategies to become bidialectal?

2. Should teachers approach the teaching of language arts to culturally diverse learners any differently from the way they would teach other children? Give reasons for your answers.

3. Should teachers use the same verbal strategies as the students do? Why or why not?

4. View the videotape "American Tongues" and answer the following questions:

   a. How many different dialects exist in the United States?

   b. Cite examples of call-response.

   c. Look for verbal strategies used by other cultures. Are there any examples of what happens when people talk a special way and are ridiculed by authority figures or use standard speech patterns and are ridiculed by peers? Cite specific instances.

5. African American males: Collect oral histories as described by Patricia Nichols (this book) by focusing on the language used by older siblings, fathers, grandfathers, uncles, cousins, and even ministers and church deacons.

6. Watch and listen to how people use language. Conduct a survey of television programs that have adolescent African American males. Make a note of the verbal strategies they use. Although some examples of current television programs have been provided, more recent lists may be offered by students in your class. You may want to set the survey up as follows:

TV Program	*Character*	*Strategy*	*Example*
Fresh Prince of Bel Air			
What's Happening			
Different World			
Family Matters			

7. Interview a group of African American males and have them give you the local names for three strategies described in the article. Have them demonstrate each one. Find out how they feel about using Standard English. Ask them questions such as these: What is Standard English? When would you use it? How might you use Standard English to help you? Give the names of people you know who use both Standard English and Black Communications.

8. Direct a group of students in producing and performing in a rap video that summarizes a book or describes a concept they have learned. Use cooperative learning groups to write the script, design the costumes, select the scenery and the music, and direct the performance. Have the best rappers take a leadership role in each group.

9. African American males: Conduct surveys such as those described by Denise E. Murray (this book) noting when you hear, and where, why, and with whom you hear or use verbal strategies. Use Dell Hymes' (1986) SPEAKING mnemonic to examine the characteristics of such speech events and make comparisons with other cultures.

Further Reading

For an excellent introduction to dialect variety, see Louis Alvarez and Andrew Kolker's (1986) videotape, "American Tongues." The Portland, Oregon Public Schools (1990) has produced *African American Baseline Essays* to provide awareness of the history, culture, and contributions of people of African descent along with lesson plans (by subject and grade level). Taylor (1987) succinctly introduces the cultural aspect of communication and assists teachers with ways to recognize and utilize diversity. Janice Hale-Benson (1982) presents early childhood applications for learning style. See Dandy (1990, 1991),

Smitherman (1977), and Burling (1973) for thorough discussions of Black English with suggestions, resources and activities for teachers. Foster (1986) speaks from a European American perspective, gives clear documentation and provides actual situations during which verbal strategies are used in the classroom. Kunjufu (1987) and Tony Browder (1991) are appropriate for African American males aged 8–13—to inspire and inform them. George Pine and Asa Hilliard (1990) provide suggestions for curricular interventions. Abrahams (1963, 1972, 1975) and William Labov (1972) provide comprehensive coverage of numerous verbal strategies. Saville-Troike (1989) gives examples of speech play and its influence in the development of communicative competence in various cultures. Hill (1989) offers practical suggestions directed to teachers of minority students.

5

A Mexicano Perspective

Reading the World in a Multicultural Setting

Olga A. Vasquez
University of California, San Diego

Reading does not consist merely of decoding the written word or language; rather it is preceded by and intertwined with knowledge of the world. Language and reality are dynamically interconnected. The understanding attained by critical reading of a text implies perceiving the relationship between text and context.

Paulo Freire & Donaldo Macedo, 1987

In immigrant homes across the United States, and in particular in the homes of four working-class Mexicano[1] residents of the east side, an unincorporated sector of Lincoln City in California's San Francisco Bay area, children learn to "read" their world using the language and realities of their multicultural setting. As an ethnographer studying language in the home, I found that the language and knowledge sources of the community, the home, and the school converged in family members' ways of talking about knowledge in the social world.[2] Thus, immigrant children look upon a world full of unpredictable nuances and expectations, relying for its interpretations on the collective construction of reality offered by members of their social networks.[3]

The conversations these Mexicano families conducted in their homes about what they had seen and heard in the larger world revealed the dynamic interrelationships between reality and reading, writing, and oral language. In documenting actual instances in which knowledge of the world both precedes and is interconnected with reading the written word, this chapter strengthens the case for a reconceptualization of literacy that expands the notion of literate oral activities and its undergirding assumptions of a close relation to discrete written text.

The four families participated in a variety of extended discussions that covered every aspect of their daily lives. Some extended discussions involved storytelling and interpreting procedural arrangements with institutions (Vasquez, 1989; Vasquez, Pease-Alvarez, & Shannon, forthcoming). Another type of extended discussion, and the focus of this chapter, involved collaborative encounters in which family members collectively constructed their reality around the signs and symbols that made up their multicultural world.

The exclamation "Hey! Check this out!" for example, called attention to a segment of a *telenovela* [television soap opera]. It invited anyone within earshot to relate background information, contextual clues, and personal commentary to the collective visual experience. These spontaneous conversations socialized children to read and interpret their world in collaboration with other members of their social network who shared relevant knowledge and prior experience. This collective construction of reality was expressed through a discursive pattern I have labeled *Extensions*: collaborative interactions about information in the social sphere of the family.[4]

Analysis of the pattern of Extensions in the four Mexicano families I observed allowed me to achieve two goals. First, I could examine the convergence of the linguistic and cultural resources available in the everyday language of nonnative speakers of English. Second, I could examine more closely the blurring of the boundaries between oral and written language and affirm a connection to literacy in a context where experience with print was not as prominent as it presumably is in middle-class homes and in the classroom. This connection was observable in the oral strategies individuals used to talk about their social and physical reality.

To make a connection to literacy in a discursive context in which children have limited experience with extended written prose begs an explanation of the use of literacy and texts fundamental to this connection. The view of literacy elaborated in the section below expands the notion of texts to include oral, visual, and written materials as alternative sources of literate activity. This way of looking at what makes a literate activity suggests a continuity between analytical oral strategies (i.e., interpreting, extending, and comparing the texts in media events, isolated words, photographs, multidimensional environmental print, and documents) and those literacy-mediated activities conventionally labeled literate (Heath & Hoffman, 1986; Langer, 1987). In this expanded framework, analytical similarities emerged between oral language activities in the homes of Mexican immigrant families and conventional literate activities in the classroom setting.

✳ Literate Oral Language Activities

— Has excellent
inf. For ed.
drama research
uliu ...

The basis for labeling oral language activities as literate lies in distinguishing between *literacy skills* and *literate behaviors* as two individual dimensions of literacy. Most research on literacy has focused primarily on the common dictionary definition of literacy skills as involving reading and writing skills that enable an individual to manipulate written symbols to gain or make meaning. Statistics on literacy rates and assessment of success in schooling use this definition of literacy skills (Langer, 1987). Literacy skills typically focus on surface features of written language such as spelling, pronunciation, syllabication, vocabulary, and rudimentary comprehension exercises. These skills are often emphasized in repetitive, mechanical, and text-based exercises that appear on dittos, in workbooks, or in end-of-chapter questions. Literate behaviors, on the other hand, encompass the ability to talk about the meaning of a literacy-mediated text (Heath & Hoffman, 1986; Langer, 1987).

literacy
skills...

vs

literate
behavior
+
oral
activities

Literate oral activities conjure up images of face-to-face deliberations on the content of a piece of prose such as a storybook. Discussants would engage in analytically dissecting a text, saying what it does and does not mean, and rejecting, criticizing, and extending its propositions. This classic image of classroom language is more broadly applicable than is commonly recognized: My research findings indicate that certain aspects of home-based language display analytical possibilities equivalent to those conventionally considered as literate.

In Eastside, I found that nonnative speakers of English talked about a variety of texts using all the analytical possibilities commonly associ-

↓ ed.
drama
possibilities
tied in
to literacy? — see next
page as
well

115

ated with talk about extended written prose. In this setting, what has been classified as literate was extended to include the ability to talk about environmental print such as the writing on cards, wall hangings, and signs as well as the fragmented, often cryptic language found in billing statements. Literate activity in this context meant the ability to talk about television programs, isolated words, and songs, texts whose written base was once removed from the social situation. Lastly, it meant the ability to decipher and interpret the texts embedded in photographs, brochures, and symbols. In their homes, the individuals I observed analyzed, criticized, rejected, and expanded upon the meanings embodied in these types of alternative texts in much the same way as did individuals displaying literate behaviors, as described by Heath and Hoffman (1986) and Langer (1987).

Expanding the notion of text to include fluid and intangible forms of knowledge opens the possibility of examining the analytical strategies individuals use to talk about information. This approach provides a critical first step in applying the concept of literacy to oral-based settings, a step criticized by scholars who interpret literacy in a much more narrow and conventional manner. Criticism is typically reflected in questions that address the "literateness" of the oral strategies I describe below. Are these strategies not simply a low form of literacy or cognitive ability? Isn't this just emergent literacy? And how can you call this literate when there is no connection to print? In the sections below, I will show how home-based language is a viable source of analytic possibilities and how these analytic possibilities come to resemble literate strategies used in the instructional setting.

Although more research is needed to actually pinpoint the origins of literate activity in the same way that Eduardo Hernandez-Chavez and Jan Curtis (1984) and Emelia Ferreiro and Ana Teberosky (1982) have identified the conceptualization of print, the present study strongly suggests that the uses of language attributed to literacy-mediated activities are not restricted to extended written prose. Individuals in the east side had ample opportunities to interpret and articulate the meaning of texts; to tie text to personal experience or to link it to other texts; to explain and argue with passages of text; to make predictions based on the texts; and to compare and evaluate texts or related situations (Heath & Hoffman, 1986), regardless of the texts' connection to print. Oral literate activities were, nevertheless, evident around alternative conceptions of text. Family members, in extended conversations sparked by fragments of symbolic representations of text, used analytical strategies that built upon the meanings embedded in symbolism. They collectively responded to the gestalt of the shared text in such media as a television program, newspaper want-ads, environmental print, and photographs.

Oral knowledge, such as that gleaned from a piece of folklore, a gossiper's tale, or an incident in the family's history, presented learners with opportunities to objectify language, (i.e., to differentiate between what was said and what was meant) an activity previously associated only with written text (Hilyard & Olson, 1982). Children's school experiences, adults' reminiscences of life in the old country, and advice for physical, social, and spiritual well-being, as recommended by community health practitioners, Christian layleaders, and such high-status members of social networks as grandparents, offered many opportunities to give form and context to a variety of encounters with knowledge. These encounters, as well as those that took place in connection with institutional and personal documents, provided individuals with the opportunity to engage in the manipulation and abstraction of texts.

Thus, text and context have become mutually constituted by the varied cultural and linguistic resources available to Mexicanos in the east side. Although traditional culture continues to maintain a very powerful influence on the lives of the four families, other sources of knowledge are beginning to manifest themselves in their conversations. It is a case of a dynamic and creative response to change rather than a culture and language refractive to change. The members of the four families read their world, making analogic comparisons, evaluations, and interpretations of information using resources available in both new and old cultures. The sections below sketch a brief portrait of the complex social reality that supports language use and emergent literacy among the four families of the study.

The East Side: A Mexican Immigrant Community

When considering statistical data on the educational standing, residential patterns, and employment trends of Latinos, it is often difficult to disaggregate Mexican immigrants from the official category of Hispanic, or even from the long-standing category of Mexican American—i.e., people of Mexican origin who have been in the United States one or more generations. In many ethnic enclaves, however, the statistics do represent an identifiable immigrant population. California Tomorrow (1988), an advocate group, reported that 29% of the student population in California was categorized as Hispanic. Of this number, 33% were classified as Limited English Proficient (LEP), indicating that they were probably foreign-born, or, as in the case of the children of the four east side families, came from immigrant homes.

Mexican immigrants continue to travel northward on migratory arteries formed long before either Mexico or the United States achieved nationhood. Typically, it is males who immigrate first; most return home eventually for a bride or family. These family groups then resettle where there is work, raising their children in low-income communities made up of many other ethno-linguistic groups. For example, California Tomorrow (1988) has identified eight elementary school districts in California where more than 50% of the student population is designated as LEP, testifying to a high concentration of immigrants in these areas. The school and community in the east side reflect this kind of aggregation (Shannon, 1987; Vasquez, 1989). According to Shannon, up to 70% of the student population of two elementary schools in the heart of the east side reported Mexico as their parents' birthplace.

The sights and sounds of the east side's residences and business establishments reflect a strong Mexicano presence. Radios and televisions tuned to Spanish-language stations are the norm in the neighborhoods. Moreover, proprietorship and clientele from the rural regions of the Mexican state of Michoacan are evident in the names on commercial signs and on the goods stocked on the store shelves. The yards accompanying some homes and apartment complexes also signal a rural descendency. Arable spaces are planted with corn, fruits, vegetables, or medicinal plants imported from Mexico.

The four families in my study lived in the heart of the east side. However, their community spread through a series of overlapping social networks composed of kin, friends, and acquaintances, beyond the physical boundaries that set the east side off from the rest of the city.[5] The four families did not belong to one another's immediate social networks, but they knew of one another and of one another's personal histories. This is not surprising. Members of different networks tended to flow in and out of one another's groups in a continual stream of interactions of exchange. In intimate interactions and in large social functions, family members exchanged goods and services as well as information about people's lives and adjustment experiences in this country. These encounters supplied the "funds of knowledge" (Vélez-Ibañez, 1988) members of the social network shared to help one another meet the exigencies of daily life.

Language samples for this work were collected from members of the Cristobal, Orozco, Neruda, and Zapata families over a period of 7 months.[6] During this time I lived within walking distance of the families. I paid almost daily visits to the homes and attended many of their social functions, audiotaping conversations in which family members talked about things they had heard, read, or experienced. Analysis was conducted on verbatim transcriptions of selected conversations that centered on information entering the daily lives of the four families.

Although the four families shared many characteristics with immigrant populations in other parts of California and the United States (California Tomorrow, 1988; Muller & Espensade, 1985), they also deviated from these larger groups, and from one another in some respects. Briefly, the families were large, young, and had come to the United States from Mexico during the last 20 years. All adults had initially entered the United States without immigration papers. All of the 38 members of the families spoke Spanish as their first language.[7] The older children were bilingual and the 8 youngest—born in the United States—were monolingual Spanish speakers. With the exception of Mr. Zapata, all adults had fewer than 6 years of schooling in Mexico (none of which they received in the United States); all spoke little or no English; and all were employed in low-skill, service-related jobs. Mr. Zapata, on the other hand, had studied at a community college, was a supervisor at his place of employment, and owned his home. At the time of the study, Mexican-born members of both the Cristobal and Zapata families were applying for amnesty and the Neruda and Orozco families had acquired permanent resident status. Some members of the Neruda family were collecting documents needed to apply for citizenship.

Language Socialization in an Immigrant Community

In the east side, as elsewhere, children are born into an oral world. What makes the east side children's experiences different from their White counterparts' in other U.S. cities is that orality in a language other than English is a major component of daily life. Eastside children grow up using oral language as a tool to understand the world around them and to build upon their existing oral knowledge. Frequent cross-generational interactions at home and at large family gatherings involve the children I observed in numerous extended discussions of family history, national and regional legends, segments of telenovela episodes, and other shared experiences.

Written language received much less emphasis than oral language in the homes I visited. In fact, the few encounters with extended written language were functional and goal-directed collective endeavors. In many cases, family members brought written materials into the home in order to recruit assistance in translating English and in understanding the cultural norms undergirding the particular form of written language. Homework and applications of different sorts are examples of written materials that required help from more knowledgeable bilingual individuals. Sometimes the school and the local churches disseminated written materials in the neighborhood. For example, the school district occasionally communicated district-level decisions or announcements of special functions in Spanish. Religious groups distributed Spanish-language leaflets in attempts to recruit followers from the community. Unless these communications were mediated by personal contact, however, they were likely to be ignored. For example, the Jehovah's Witnesses were more successful than the school in communicating their views. Members of this sect used printed materials to sustain adults' attention in the message they delivered personally during home visits. Written communications from the school held little meaning for adults who did not speak English and less still, for those who were unable to read, regardless of the language. As a result, information about their children's precarious educational standing and/or misconduct often did not reach these parents until a school official made a belated personal call.

The Bible, novels, or other books written in Spanish were infrequently read in these homes. Nor did I find either of the two Spanish-language newspapers sold at the grocery stores nearby in any of the four homes during my visits over a 7-month period. The English-language paper to which Mr. Zapata subscribed was often piled high—and unwrapped—on the hearth. Also absent from these homes was the seemingly ubiquitous set of encyclopedias I have encountered in other Mexicano/Latino communities. The few books written in English that I noted in the homes were school books used primarily by the children. The language and educational background of the parents usually precluded their involvement in the substance of their children's homework. Thus, children labored through their school assignments on their own, drawing assistance from older siblings or, occasionally, from me.[8] On many of my visits, when children requested my help with their homework, their parents sat in the background listening to the interaction and issuing an occasional admonishment to listen carefully to what I was saying.

In spite of the relatively little use of print materials in these homes, I did observe the families talking about written language. These extended, cross-generational discussions centered on deciphering the language of official documents, which often seemed cryptic and jargon-ridden, besides being written in the second language. These problem-solving activities prepared the limited English-speaking member of the family to take part in intercultural transactions outside the home. These interactions served to provide resources for interpreting the language of the document and to decide on subsequent action. In a series of steps, family members made decisions on when to go to a particular institution, whom to see once there, what to say, and what documents to take along. Another common collective endeavor was the reading and rereading of occasional letters to and from relatives in Mexico. These letters usually related important events and/or pending visits.

Members of the four families gained knowledge of the world through many sources. In transitory encounters, community health practitioners, religious layleaders, and the neighborhood gossipers, all archetypical figures in Mexicano neighborhoods, doled out information along with their goods and services. They disseminated local and world news, what-to and how-to advice, and rules of social and religious decorum. This knowledge often resurfaced in family discussions as aspects of amusement or problem solving. One such incident involved the local baker who circulated through the neighborhood selling *pan dulce* [sweet bread]. In the brief moment during which he was in the Orozco home, he sold his bread and related the evening news: A commercial airliner had crashed in South America, killing everyone on board. After the baker left, the Orozco's tuned the television to a news station and talked for hours about related incidents and movies.

Family members also provided one another with a wealth of information, as Luis Moll et al. (1990) have noted in other Latino communities. East side adults frequently shared family and community oral histories both involving experiences from the United States and Mexico. They retold stories they had heard as children or related personal events that had become part of their respective family's history. These stories not only taught children family and community history but also socialized them to family values and tradition. For example, Mr. Orozco's retelling of a story about the apparition of the devil to a wayward son emphasized family and religious decorum. The message was to obey one's parents or risk losing one's life to the devil (Vasquez, 1989).

Carrying out daily chores also provided opportunities to share information. Carlos Vélez-Ibañez (1988, and more recently in collaboration with Moll et al., 1990) has examined the types of knowledge that are communicated in relations of exchange between members of social networks:

> Funds of knowledge include information and formulas containing the mathematics, architecture, chemistry, physics, biology, and engineering [necessary] for the construction and repair of homes, the repair of most mechanical devices including gardening, butchering, cooking, hunting, and of "making things" in general. (p. 38)

Adults and children in the east side, like their Chicano/Latino counterparts in Tucson, New Mexico (Moll et al.'s, 1990, research community) exchanged theoretical and practical knowledge in the context of social relations. I remember an incident in the Orozco's backyard while Mr. Orozco was preparing *chicharrones* [pork skins]. His neighbor, noticing the sizzling lard, told of the explosion that can occur when hot oil and water are mixed, an imminent danger in preparing refried beans.

Knowledge acquired from these home and community sources, in combination with information brought into the home through television, interethnic communication, and symbolic representations from both cultures (i.e., religious symbols, flags, brand names) resulted in patterns of interaction that reflected the influence of mainstream society on these immigrant families. Although the homes and the community were a stronghold of Spanish language and Mexican cultural values and socialization practices, U.S. pop culture was evident in the choice of foods, music, dress styles, and entertainment activities, particularly among the younger generation.

The interfacing between the two languages and cultures generally was smooth and unobtrusive. Family members acquiesced to the influence of both worlds without much reflection, as was evident in a conversation among Mr. Neruda and several of his children. The discussion, held mostly in Spanish and spiced with baseball jargon in English, centered on the current baseball career of a popular U.S. pitcher. In a home where traditional Mexican food still predominated, change was evident. Fourteen-year-old Junior, sporting the latest fashion in tennis shoes and jeans, talked about the game in between bites of his bologna sandwich.

At other times, however, the value systems of the two cultures came into direct conflict, creating family dissension that left both children and parents unable to find adequate solutions. The apparent clash in cultures was particularly evident in disputes over the rights and privileges of children. These situations were particularly difficult to resolve. One example involved a family party where the eldest daughter in one of the families violated gender lines when she and her male guest formed a group apart from the acceptable male and female circles. According to traditional norms, her young friend's rightful place was in the men's group on the periphery of the party. The couple's behavior thus blatantly breached social convention. Their action attributed unsanctioned importance to the friendship and jeopardized the young woman's reputation. The young woman defended her behavior in light of White social rules: "I was trying to be a good hostess," she explained.

Extensions: Reading the World

In a dynamic intersection of language, culture, and knowledge, members of the four families jointly interpreted their world. Extended discussions of four or more speakers averaging 20 turns sprung up spontaneously within the broad context of family activity. These collective deliberations were initiated when family members were called upon to stop short their involvement in other activities and redirect their attention to a specific piece of information. These calls to attention initiated the pattern of Extensions in which family members jointly elaborated on their visual or auditory experience; as such, they read their world in collaboration with fellow family members.

On the surface, this discursive pattern appeared as a break in the conversation. On closer examination, however, I found it was a redirection of attention to an oral or visual form of text—for example, photographs, television programs, or a variety of materials in print. An Extension-starter invited everyone within the small quarters to participate in a collective experience. It called for a thoughtful, joint consideration of aspects of their multicultural reality. Examples of common Extension-starters included summonses to comment on the events of a telenovela; to verbally play with a linguistically intriguing nickname, (e.g., *candingo* [weasel], *chino* [curly haired]); or to interpret the contents of a photograph or a piece of environmental print. Questions, such as *¿Va a pagar la aseguranza o si no que me diga?* [Is the insurance going to pay for this? (a hospital bill) If not, it should let me know (so I can pay it).]; *¿No ves a Oyuki?* [Do you watch (the soap opera) Oyuki?] frequently acted as Extensions-starters. Directives leading to Extensions included such statements as *Mira en lo que se convirtió* [Look what she transformed into (in reference to the television program *Wonder Woman*)]. Declaratives, such as *Mi mamá siempre sale de lado* [My mother is always photographed in profile], also opened Extensions. Extensions tended to end as abruptly as they began.

I found that Extensions took form around three types of texts—two that were literacy-mediated and one connected to print only vaguely and indistinctly but grew out of a shared cultural and linguistic background. Specifically, the two literacy-mediated Extensions involved discrete printed texts that were either present in the immediate social situation or codified elsewhere. The third type involved an expanded notion of text without print. This third type of extended analytic discussions was triggered by shared understandings of linguistically interesting words such as nicknames, double entendres, or anglicisms as well as live media broadcasts.

Conversations about applications, letters, wall hangings, brochures, and environmental print (e.g., traffic signs, billboard ads, directional signs on buildings) are examples of literacy-mediated Extensions centering on a printed text that formed part of the immediate social context. The second type of literacy-mediated Extensions involved discussions about telenovelas, newscasts, and written materials such as institutional documents encountered outside of the home. These discussions constitute second-order, literacy-mediated Extensions because they centered on oral information the printed form of which was once removed from the immediate social context. The third type involves an expanded notion of text based on shared understandings acquired through common socialization or other collective experiences. The deeper meaning, or the gestalt, embedded in such words as *candingo* [weasel], *nuevo* [new, young, again], and a multitude of symbols and environmental print was the actual basis of these Extensions.

Although the Extensions I observed were constructed around different types of texts, they shared similar analytical possibilities. The most salient difference is the degree to which the text was made explicit in the conversations. Only 29% of the conversation turns in the language samples that made up Extensions referred explicitly to the text. In general, these turns were found among the literacy-mediated Extensions in which text was present. This apparent difference, however, can be partially explained by the conversant's inability to read in either Spanish or English. Bilingual individuals, in most cases children, made the text explicit as they translated it for the monolingual Spanish-speakers.

Inability to read and lack of English fluency, did not, however, affect the level of analytical activity surrounding the interpretation of texts. For example, when planning a trip to the grocery store, the Cristobal girls excitedly read the grocery ads to their father, who could not read English or Spanish: "¡Mira papí! La carne a uno setenta y nueve la libra [Look Dad, the meat is $1.79 a pound]; Bolonia a noventa y nueve centavos" [Bologna at 99 cents]. The girls bridged language, literacy, and social context to facilitate further discussion of the items in the advertisement. As they translated the written text, they simultaneously interpreted it for their parents, proposed which items to purchase, and encouraged their mother to take part in the decision making (Mrs. Cristobal could not read Spanish or English and she did not customarily accompany her husband on shopping trips).

With the assistance of a more knowledgeable person, individuals who could not speak or read English could nevertheless share their points of view regarding the printed texts in the world around them. In this respect, the three types of Extensions were similar. Individuals based their analogic comparisons, interpretations, explanations, and argumentation on printed texts present in the social context as frequently and qualitatively as they did on the other two types of texts. It is nevertheless instructive to examine the three types of Extensions separately to demonstrate the differences in the texts that shape each.

Literacy-Mediated Extensions: Print Present

Print initiating the first kind of literacy-mediated Extensions generally was fragmented or symbolic, and was sometimes accompanied by illustrations. These Extensions centered on written language in personal and institutional documents and in environmental signs and symbols. Members of the four families shared contents of letters, requested assistance in filling out applications, and collectively consid-

[handwritten margin note: How might this fact impact young children, not necessarily bilin guids who can interpret the texts before they can read?]

ered illustrated want-ads, travel brochures, report cards, and checks. For example, the presence of written text in the environment prompted one Extension I observed. A sign on the door of the Orozco family's home read, *Este hogar es Católico y Apostólico* [This is a Catholic and Apostolic home]. This text elicited an extended conversation among Mrs. Orozco, her daughter, and a neighbor about the sign's acquisition, its purpose, and the choice of language. The sign was to ward off Spanish-speaking proselytizers who descended daily on the neighborhood. Mrs. Orozco's evaluation of the sign, "Así se los quita uno, tu sabes, de encima. Ya ven, ellos no llegan " [This way you get them out of your hair. You see, they don't come around] prompted her visitor to announce his personal preference, "Para que hubiera en inglés tambien para poner uno en casa ahí—donde vean los testigos de Jovah" [If these were in English I would put one on the door to my house where the Jehovah's Witnesses could see it]. The Mexicano families in the east side, bound by cultural norms of hospitality, as in the case of the Khmer refugees (Welaratna, this volume), have learned to deflect culturally uncomfortable situations through the use of print.

Although these printed forms were usually in English, the message was generally negotiated in Spanish. Bilingual children frequently acted as language brokers, interpreting the language and cultural norms embodied in the texts, making it possible for monolingual Spanish-speakers who cannot read to enter into deliberations about printed materials. Individuals who did not speak or read English equally contributed background information to contextualize the text in terms of time, space, personal attitudes, and previous associations. Everyone involved could provide descriptive details on use, historical context, and other aspects of the text associated with their personal lives. For example, in the conversation about grocery shopping among the Cristobal girls and their father, one daughter challenged the logic posed in an advertisement: "Mire, usted. ¿Cree que uno de esos va a costar cuarenta y nueve centavos? Y dice que agarra dos gratis. Están locos porque eso cuesta por tres." [Look, Dad. Do you think that one of those will cost forty-four cents? And, it says that you get two free. They are crazy—because that's what three cost.] (Cristobal Tape, 1988).

Laura exposed the store's ploy to trick them into thinking that the merchandise was on sale: "They are crazy because that's what three cost." The price of one item plus two free ones was the same as the price for three of the items. Once the text was communicated to the individuals in the conversations, they had an opportunity to abstract and manipulate it.

Literacy-Mediated Extensions: Print Not Present

The second type of literacy-mediated Extensions encompassed texts the printed form of which was found outside of the immediate social context. Media events (e.g., telenovelas, children's television programs, and newscasts; and written forms individuals had experienced elsewhere, e.g., references to report cards, letters, and immigration forms) typically gave rise to these Extensions. The analytic activity in this type of Extension centered on a second-order reference to the text. That is, explanations, evaluations, and elaborations centered on an evolving oral text that individuals were then experiencing or that they had previously experienced.

For example, Luisa Cristobal, who could not read or write in either English or Spanish, initiated an Extension on Canadian coins she had found in a hotel room she had cleaned. She had recognized that the print on the coins indicated that the money was not legal tender in the United States, but she kept the coins anyway, viewing them as useful playthings for her children:

Luisa: El otro día me encontré [—] un ceniserillo llenos así de dinerillo. 'Verdad,' dije, 'Para el bus. No hombre, son puros de Canadá!' Por ahí está el sobre, son muchos. [. . .] Y ya los iba hechar a la basura y dije, 'Ha de menos para que juegen las chiquillas.'

[*Luisa:* The other day I found [—] an ashtray full of coins. 'Great!' I said, 'For the bus. Oh, no! They are all from Canada.' They are around here someplace in an envelope. They are many. [. . .] I was going to throw them out and thought, 'at least the girls can play with them.'] (Cristobal tape, 1988)

Although Luisa would be considered illiterate by most standards, because she could not read the print on the coins, she read the text and made appropriate decisions based on her reading: (a) She could not use the coins for her bus fare; (b) she would not throw them away; and (c) she would take them home for her children.

127

Extended Extensions:
Beyond Print

The third type of text in Extensions is neither physically present nor codified elsewhere; it is beyond print, codified in shared understandings. For example, the linguistic and cultural underpinnings of phonetically interesting words and media events that were not previously scripted sometimes provided a basis for extended collective deliberations. One example was the manipulation of the phonetic characteristics of the word *computadora* [computer] to achieve a social goal. Without a visible or audible stimulus, but rather, prompted by a memory of hearing her niece incorrectly pronounce the word computadora, Laura opened an Extension with the question, "¿Han oído como dice Luz computadora?" [Have you heard how Luz pronounces computer?] She proceeded to take advantage of her niece's naiveté and articulation problem to challenge the social convention of using improper language, *puta* [whore], in the presence of adults. Laura was encouraged in this verbal game by her Uncle Jorge, who frequently visited the home:

Laura: Luz, di computadora.	[*Laura:* Luz, say computer.
Luz: 'Putadora.	*Luz:* 'Putadora.
Jorge: Putadora.	*Jorge:* Putadora.
Laura: Luz, di com.	*Laura:* Luz, say com.
Luz: Com.	*Luz:* Com.
Laura: Pu.	*Laura:* Pu.
Laura: Ta.	*Laura:* Ta.
Luz: Puta.	*Luz:* Puta.
Laura: Do.	*Laura:* Do.
Luz: Ra.	*Luz:* Ra.]
(Cristobal tape, 1988)	

What appeared as an innocent lesson in pronunciation had been a ploy to trick 6-year old Luz into saying *puta* in a formal setting. Everyone present understood that a social convention had been breached, and that Laura's performance had been a success. Laura had orchestrated Luz's language so skillfully that the proper response was laughter rather than discipline. Rules of social decorum constituted the text shared by Laura, her uncle, and the audience. Luz was the only one who operated on a different principle; she had not yet reached the necessary level of socialization to understand either the rule or its breaching.

Another example of an Extension based on shared understandings occurred in an extended conversation among Mr. Neruda and two of his children. Assumptions about the game of baseball and the careers of its players served as the basis for making analytical comments (in bold) about the game the family was watching:

Junior: It was two zero and Canseco made a home run.

Ramón Sr: **Pega duro el büey.**

Rosa: ¿Y cuántos años tiene, twenty-three or twenty-four?

Junior: Twenty-three.

Ramón Sr: **Así empezó Valenzuela con twenty-two o twenty-three y ahorita [—]**

Rosa: ¡Ja! **Pero ahorita ya no sirve pa' nada!**

[*Junior:* It was two to zero and Canseco made a home run.

Ramón Sr: **The son of a bitch hits hard.**

Rosa: And how old is he? Twenty-three or twenty-four?

Junior: Twenty-three.

Ramón Sr: **That's how old Valenzuela was when he started. Twenty-two or twenty-three and now [—]**

Rosa: Ha! **But now he is no good!**]
(Neruda tape, October 1988)

This fragment of the Neruda family's discussion illustrates the analysis of a specific text held in the minds of these individuals. Evaluative statements, in this case the power of Canseco's batting and the deterioration of Valenzuela's pitching, were made on the careers of two baseball stars. Family members not only compared Canseco's great start to Valenzuela's earlier glory, but they also predicted that Canseco would end up like the veteran Dodger: "Ya no sirve pa' nada." [Now, he is no good.]

Although it could be said that Junior's comment, "It was two [to] zero and Canseco made a home run" was specifying the text, the complete text was based on the assumption that "two [to] zero" was the score, and "Canseco made a home run" meant that Canseco had just batted. Descriptive details, background information, and personal association contributed to a tacit understanding of the text. In other words, while the text was fresh in their minds, participants critiqued and justified aspects of the conversation.

Individuals offered brief explanations or justifications for agreeing or disagreeing with some aspect of the text equally across the three types of Extensions. Individuals also pointed out discrepancies in the contents of the texts, as when one of the Zapata girls corrected her grandmother about the rescue of Wonder Woman—"Pero la que se encontró a la mujer maravilla era el hombre" [But the one who found Wonder Woman was the man]. The grandmother had wrongly assumed that Wonder Woman had been rescued by another woman.

Evaluative statements that reached beyond the contexts of the texts were common across the three types of Extensions. For example, one of the Orozco daughters informed me of what I could do with a 3-Star lottery ticket, "You send them to get a chance to spin the wheel." But she also assured me that I would not win, "They don't pick Mexicans." These kinds of far-reaching generalizations also occurred in Extensions with print not present—the rating of telenovelas; and also when the text was coded in shared understandings—the predictions about Canseco's career. Another example is the comment by Mrs. Orozco's youngest son while looking at a photo I had taken of participants at a baptism: "Todo el mundo está enojado." [Everyone (in the picture) is angry.]

Educational Implications

Examining samples of Extensions provided a glimpse into the ways members of the four immigrant families read and collectively considered knowledge in multiple forms. These language activities clearly illustrate a continuum in the oral manipulation of oral and written language rather than a dichotomy. Extensions offer concrete examples of socialization practices that are available to Mexican immigrant children as they deal with the exigencies of every day life. In these extended discussions, they evaluate, compare, explain, and argue with the information being presented to them. They point to an important interconnection between reading, writing, and language and reality. It is in these sorts of settings that Mexicano children learn to perceive relationships, a training for the later skill of critically reading text.

These findings have several educational implications. At one level, conceptions of language competence and literacy preparedness of Mexicano children need to be revisited. As demonstrated, the cultural and linguistic context of the east side of Lincoln City provides ample opportunities to use language in complex and unique ways. Children from this community, and many others like it, come to school using language in ways that are similar to those considered literate in the context of the school. Instructional techniques and curriculum need only to open opportunities for children to access the knowledge and skills they have learned outside of the school setting. Literacy-mediated activities in the classroom, in particular, lend themselves to an opening that accommodates content from the children's life experiences. Children need not base their literacy activities solely on the printed page. They can also enrich their lives and those of others with the many unique experiences they bring to the learning setting.

Another important implication of this work is the use of oral language in the classroom. Orality as a form of practice in the classroom merits more attention. In fact, as has been shown above, orality connects text and context in a blurring of the lines between oral and written language. Given authentic opportunities to engage in a dialectic of one's knowledge and that of others, individuals learn to collaborate and cooperate in the reconstruction of their reality. The workplace in the U.S. corporate world is calling for skills in collaborative problem-solving. Children cannot learn how to solve problems jointly by answering the questions at the end of the chapter. This can only be accomplished in dynamic interactions among participants and not through isolated activities. Teachers and children can learn much about relationships, knowledge sources, and the various cultural backgrounds from discussions of telenovelas, environmental signs, and linguistically interesting words.

... has strong implications for the use of drama ... how drama can bridge the oral w/ the written ...

Summary

This chapter examines a discursive pattern that forms part of the everyday conversations of four Mexican immigrant families living in a northern California community. Referenced texts of conversations in which participants collaboratively discussed information in their social sphere demonstrate a convergence of cultures and languages from both the native and host countries and a connection to literacy. The analytical strategies used by members of these four families to talk about print-based texts, present or not in the immediate social situation, as well as those texts that are beyond print (e.g., photographs, traffic symbols, phonetically interesting words) ignored boundaries between oral and written language. In other words, comparing the analytical strategies used by these individuals to the literate behaviors conventionally associated with print yielded no real distinction between the ways these individuals talked about oral and written language. This finding leads us to reconsider Mexicano children's linguistic repertoire and reading readiness from a recognition perspective of the viable background resources these children bring to the learning setting.

Acknowledgment

This research was supported in part by the National Council of Teachers of English (NCTE) and a University of California, San Diego, Chancellor's postdoctoral fellowship.

Discussion Topics and Projects

1. The work presented in this chapter is based on a distinction between literacy skills and literate behaviors. Using this distinction, discuss the proposition of literate oral activities.

2. Literate behaviors are conventionally associated with written texts. Explain how the notion of text is expanded to encompass oral-based texts as sources of literate activity.

3. Mexicano children in east side experience varied and complex uses of language. Extensions are one such use. Compare Extensions to other possible uses of language in the homes of the four families.

4. Describe the three subtypes of Extensions and explain how text is employed in each.

5. Mexicano children are exposed to knowledge sources from a variety of learning domains. Name possible domains and probable knowledge sources available in each.

6. The notion of knowledge in this chapter varies from conventional notions. Discuss the basis for the different points of view and design an instructional lesson plan that incorporates both views.

7. Select an ethnic enclave in your area and identify salient sources of knowledge. Where do residents get information to conduct their daily lives? Contrast findings to those of other ethnic centers in and around your city. This activity can be conducted in a family setting, a specific locale (restaurant), or in a classroom.

8. Observe a language arts classroom for types of Extensions. Classify sources of knowledge by types of texts.

9. Audiotape several family discussions and section off Extensions in your transcription. Determine knowledge sources used by the family.

Further Reading

Research on language and literacy in minority homes that recognizes the cultural and linguistic resources available to minority children is in its nascent stage. Recent work examining literacy issues in a Mexicano setting include Martha Allexsaht-Snider (1989), Lucinda P. Alvarez (1986), Concha Delgado-Gaitán (1983, 1989), Juan Guerra (1990), *The Quarterly Newsletter of the Laboratory of Comparative Human Cognition* (1991, January), and Henry T. Trueba (1984).

Research on language learning and language socialization in a Latino setting include Diaz, Moll, and Mehan (1986), Flores and Diaz (1991), Shannon (1987), and Vasquez, Pease-Alvarez, and Shannon (forthcoming).

6

A Khmer Perspective

Connections Between Khmer Students' Behavior, History, and Culture

Usha Welaratna
University of California, Berkeley

When Pol Pot's autogenocidal Khmer Rouge regime was over-thrown in 1979, thousands of Khmer (Cambodian) people fled their country in search of refuge in the West. Of the approximately 150,000 Khmer refugees who arrived in the United States, the majority have now lived in the country for more than a decade. Nevertheless, educators, researchers, and refugee service providers frequently de-scribe Cambodians as people who are slower than other refugees, particularly the Vietnamese, to acquire the behaviors and values of the dominant culture.

Although Cambodian refugees comprise only a small fraction of the total population of the United States, their distinctive culture has much to offer people in the United States. The Cambodian world view and life style may prompt Americans to think about their own world

From Beyond the Killing Fields: Voices of Nine Cambodian Survivors in America, *by Usha Welaratna, to be published in 1993 by Stanford University Press, Stanford, CA. Copyright © by Usha Welaratna. Adapted with permission of the author.*

in new ways. To show this, I will provide an overview of the history, culture, and world view of the Khmer people; discuss the common shared traditions of the Cambodians; discuss their areas of diversity to dispel the popular belief that the Cambodians are a homogeneous group; and examine the frequently cited claim that the Khmer are unwilling to adjust to the United States, in particular, to its classrooms. By delineating the differences between U.S. and Cambodian values and ways of life, we can not only increase our understanding of cultural diversity but also come to understand why many Cambodians choose to adjust to the United States in ways that may be overlooked or rejected by other Americans.

The Cambodian perspectives presented here are those expressed to me by the refugees themselves in extensive life history narratives. Their names have been changed to protect their identities. The teaching strategies are those I have employed in teaching English to adult Cambodian refugees in their own homes, during an ongoing ethnographic research project I started in 1987.

Historical Background

Historians believe that many elements connect the present-day Cambodians, or the Khmer, to their ancestors. These include prehistoric human skulls and bones found in caves in the northern region of Cambodia, remains that show resemblance between present day Cambodians and their ancestors; methods of pottery production going back 6,000 years; and other social elements such as pile dwellings, domestication of pigs and buffalo, village games played at lunar new years, slash and burn cultivation, animistic beliefs, ancestor worship, and consumption of large amounts of fish.

With the exception of the 3 years and 8 months when the Khmer Rouge forcibly severed the people's connections to their historic past, this thread of continuity has been maintained through many different eras of Cambodian history up to the present time. Although continuity does not mean that the Khmer are averse to change, it has been an important element in their adjustment to new social and cultural ideas through the centuries.

The first major transformations came at the beginning of the Christian era when Indian culture and thought spread into Cambodia. India never colonized Cambodia, but Indian influences spread through the exchange of ideas via traders and travelers between the two countries.

However, their significance was such that Cambodia's egalitarian social system was replaced by a monarchic system and a strict social hierarchy similar to that in India. The Khmer also acquired from India a vocabulary for the social hierarchy, a system of codified law, a writing system, meters for poetry, a pantheon, Theravada Buddhism, architecture, iconography, and astronomy. Although these changes continued for more than 1,000 years, the Khmer did not embrace every aspect of Indian culture. Instead, they developed their own distinctive culture by choosing selectively from the Indian model.

Around the 9th century, Cambodia ascended to a period of political and cultural brilliance known as the Angkor period, and the Khmer reigned over parts of today's Burma, Laos, Thailand, and Vietnam. By the 15th century, however, the Cambodian empire had begun to lose power. Thailand and Vietnam had gradually usurped much of Cambodia's territory. Although the Khmer rebelled against both these invaders, the Thai, with Theravada Buddhism and Indianization in common with the Khmer, were tolerated. The Vietnamese, whose culture was influenced by China, were deeply resented and mistrusted.

During their control, the Vietnamese removed large portions of territory and thousands of ethnic Cambodians from Cambodian control; stories about their mistreatment of Khmer people became legends passed on through generations. In addition to exercising military control, Vietnam tried to exert cultural control over Cambodia by colonizing the region with Vietnamese and attempting to reform every aspect of the Cambodian life: language, dress, eating habits, patterns of measurement, and agricultural methods. These actions, bound to fail because "the two peoples lived on different sides of a deep cultural divide, perhaps the most sharply defined of those in effect in nineteenth century Southeast Asia" (Chandler, 1983, p. 127), caused deep resentment and anti-Vietnamese feelings that persisted through centuries and are present among Cambodian refugees even today.

When other Asian countries began opening trading posts to Spanish and Portuguese traders, the Vietnamese closed Phnom Penh to foreigners. The few Christian missionaries who gained entry were unsuccessful in their missions because Theravada Buddhism was especially strong. Thus, when Western culture and thought began to spread to Asia, Cambodia was not exposed to either.

Cambodia became a French colony in 1864, with French rule spanning nearly 100 years. But the French administrators did not as a rule speak Cambodian; to govern the Cambodians, they imported

Vietnamese proficient in French and familiar with French ideas. Thus, the Cambodians remained largely untouched by Western influences, particularly because at least 90% of ethnic Cambodians were rural farmers. French influence was limited to the capital city of Phnom Penh, occupied mainly by Vietnamese and Chinese immigrants. Only about 3% of the capital's population was ethnic Khmer and these were mainly the elite.

Even after independence in 1954, Cambodia's rulers, particularly King Sihanouk, considered as a modern day 'god king' by the masses, continued to emphasize traditional values based on Indian culture and Buddhist teachings, values that had evolved over 2,000 years. (See also Edmonds, 1970; MacDonald, 1987; Ross, 1990; Steinberg, 1959.)

Cultural Background and Worldview

Cambodian social values emphasized respecting those higher in social status for their position and those older for their wisdom. These ideals were also reflected in the Khmer language, which had four different registers denoting social differences in speaking to or about royalty, monks, elderly or respected members of society, and equals. For instance, the verb *eat* differed according to whether monks, nobility, ordinary people, children, or animals ate; or whether one spoke formally or casually. These differences, clearly defined and consciously used by the people, were further distinguished by appropriate body language.

Because Buddhism taught reverence for life for all levels of society, Cambodian social values included nonviolence, nonaggression, honesty, generosity, harmony, tolerance, and cooperation. Words were as important as actions in achieving these goals: Im, a 30-year-old refugee from a rural area, explained, "When you speak to a person, it fosters feelings of love, harmony, and goodwill towards others and no one has to regret afterwards."

These values were also shared by Vietnamese and Chinese Cambodians. Even though for historical reasons the Vietnamese were regarded as outsiders by ethnic Cambodians and they lived in clusters among themselves, they attended government schools and had business and other interactions with ethnic Cambodians. Chinese Cambodians had integrated with the majority population so successfully that intermarriage between Chinese and ethnic Cambodians was quite common, especially in the city. Nya Srey, a Chinese Cambodian who grew up as a daughter of middle-class parents and who later married a lawyer from Phnom Penh, told me she liked her husband because he was "very kind to people. He was nice and polite in the way he talked, and in the way he acted." Thus, Cambodians from Chinese as well as Vietnamese origins shared with the larger society a common worldview and cultural values.

Family Life and Education

In prerevolutionary Cambodian society, whether a family belonged to the upper class or the peasantry, and whether they were ethnic Cambodian, or of Chinese or Vietnamese origin, the mother dealt with all household matters, child rearing in particular, and the prosperity, well-being, and reputation of the household depended mostly on her. The father dealt with the outside world and provided major family support. Because social norms based on Buddhist teachings promoted male-female equality, many women engaged in business ventures. When necessary, children helped their mothers to earn extra income, and there was usually a strong empathy between mothers and children. Even after children married and set up their own nuclear households, they continued to interact closely with their parents and siblings for mutual physical, emotional, and financial needs.

The legal and cultural norm of duty to family members based on Buddhist precepts covered such things as parental authority, arrangement of proper marriages for children, provision of support in the event of divorce and in old age, inheritance, adoption, guardianship, and provision of proper funeral arrangements.

Children generally received a great deal of affection in the first few years of life not only from parents, but also from other adults and adolescents. But as they grew, older children were expected to conform to norms of politeness and obedience. Although some competition was present in games, the stress was on playing rather than winning. Bopha, a Vietnamese Cambodian refugee who was a first-year college student when the Khmer Rouge came into power, stated these rules of behavior for her 5-year-old daughter, born in the United States:

> She must behave well. She must be nice and polite to people. She must share her toys with other kids, and not hurt their feelings by saying mean things like "You are not my friend." She has to respect old people.

When we have guests she should greet them, invite them to sit down, and offer them food and drink. Even if she is mad at someone, she must not show her anger, but be nice to that person.

By age 10 or so, both sexes had been taught basic skills necessary to be useful members of society. Boys, particularly in villages, learned agricultural techniques, while girls learned household duties. In adolescent years, the two sexes were segregated in school, which was strictly a place for education, and not for entertainment or romance. Premarital sex was deplored and sexual knowledge not considered suitable for children because it was considered to lead to desire and trouble. Adults also did not display physical love publicly even after marriage. Ideally, marriages were arranged by parents.

Traditionally, students in Cambodia learned by rote, and the emphasis was on learning Khmer history, language and literature, and Buddhist doctrine. French was the main European and second language in Cambodia. English was introduced only around 1967 and only in cities. Sanskrit derivatives were common in the realms of government and literature, while Pali was used in Buddhist canon.

Unlike in the West, in Cambodian villages (where about 85% of ethnic Cambodians lived), education was considered more as a way to grow up to be good men and women who were useful members of society, rather than as a means to secure future social and financial advancement. Due to poor communication methods, the Western ideas of the French colonizers did not spread to these areas.

When it came to education, even the poor families considered the welfare of the individual child before that of the family, even when the child's contribution to the welfare of the family was most necessary. But when the needs of the family became severe, the children had to stop their formal education until times were better. Pu Ma, an ethnic Cambodian who helped her destitute peasant mother earn a living by selling homemade sweetmeats, said: "My mother was very, very, poor, but she insisted we must go to school." Pu Ma obeyed her mother's wishes and attended school until she was 9 years old. Then,

my king, Norodom Sihanouk, visited my school. My teacher said I had to learn Cambodian dancing to perform for the king. I learned to dance, and my teacher said I had to buy some white fabric to make a butterfly costume. I knew my mother had no money to buy the fabric, and I did not want her owing money to people. So I quit going to school.

140

Pu Ma says that though she did not return to school, her mother taught Pu Ma and her siblings the social norms of obedience and respect so that they would grow up to be good members of society.

The Chinese and Vietnamese Cambodians who lived in the cities had a more Westernized view of educational achievement as leading to economic advancement. This was important because as minorities, they could not easily obtain a high social status through any other means. Mum, a Chinese Cambodian recalled:

> Our dad really pushed us to learn. We had to go to two different schools. In the morning we went to the Cambodian school, and in the afternoon we went to the French school. Sometimes we had tutors in the house too.

However, even in the cities where the French style of education and French cultural values spread, government schools continued to guide students in the awareness of their civic duties, and all students in cities and villages were expected to obey and show respect to their teachers. Niseth, an ethnic Cambodian refugee and the daughter of a highly educated veterinarian who attended a government school before the Khmer Rouge eradicated education, recalled how Cambodian parents instructed their children to behave in school:

> When you go to school, you belong to the teachers, so you must not do anything bad or disrespectful to them. You must always listen to the teachers and do whatever they ask you to do.

The Khmer as Refugees

With their ascendance to power in 1975, the Khmer Rouge initiated a social, economic, and cultural revolution by completely desecrating Cambodia's ancient culture and by turning the country into one of the most horrifying death camps ever known. Of an estimated 7 million people, 1 to 2 million, mostly the healthy, the educated, and Westernized, were killed or died due to starvation and sickness in this autogenocidal holocaust. When the Vietnamese defeated the Khmer Rouge, thousands of survivors, most originally from rural areas, fled their homeland in search of refuge in third countries.

When Khmer refugees first arrived in the United States they were part of a large influx of other Southeast Asian refugees from Vietnam and Laos seeking refuge here when their countries fell to the communists after the withdrawal of U.S. forces. Although the United States was partly responsible for the destruction of Cambodia (Shawcross, 1979, pp. 24–26), refugee resettlement workers and the U.S. public in general were largely unaware of Cambodia as a nation. Because refugee service providers knew little about Southeast Asian refugees, at first they treated the Cambodians as part of a homogeneous Southeast Asian refugee group. This misunderstanding resulted in much hardship for Khmer refugees, particularly because the Khmer and the Vietnamese had a long history of enmity and distrust. The problem was compounded because the Khmer themselves had no knowledge of English and so could not communicate their needs. Further, they did not have a group of people who had already emigrated from their country and settled here, a group who could have provided a support service to the newly arrived refugees. These problems were not unique to Khmer refugees. For instance, Vietnamese refugees also faced similar problems when they first arrived here. But the Khmer were less educated and had been less exposed to Western behavior and beliefs than the Vietnamese prior to their arrival here, and because the Western country known to the Khmer was France, even those who came from the city were generally not aware of the technological or economic advances of the United States or its culture. Thus, as refugees in the United States, they had to learn not only a new language, but also a new culture.

Traumas inflicted by the Khmer Rouge also cause various problems for Khmer refugees. They sometimes find it painful to sit in one place for too long due to physical injury resulting from beatings and other abuse. Many suffer from digestive disorders caused by starvation. When they see students sitting together, some refugees are reminded of the Khmer Rouge indoctrination sessions; this upsets them so much they must leave the room. They believe that the abuses they suffered under the regime have impaired their memories and that it affects their learning abilities.

The Khmer in the Classroom

When Niseth arrived in the United States as a refugee, she was 17 years old. She had just finished fifth grade when her country fell to the communist regime, under whom her education consisted of building earthen dams by hand, planting rice, and listening to communist indoctrination. After the Vietnamese liberation, she worked for a year in a tire factory to help her family survive, after which they escaped to a Thai refugee camp where Niseth learned "very basic English like *Hi, How are you?*" before she came to the United States as a refugee. Niseth remembered her first day in a U.S. high school:

> I was admitted to a sophomore class even though I did not know any English and I had a terrible time. I remember on the first day I was given four classes: PE [Physical Education], Science, ESL, and the most basic math class. When I went to class the teacher asked to see my schedule. But I didn't know what 'schedule' was until she took it from my pocket book. There were some Cambodian students in the class, but the teacher did not ask them to help me. She wanted to try to talk to me, to see how much English I knew, but I didn't understand a word. After she checked the schedule and made sure I was in the right class, she said "OK, you can find a seat." But I didn't understand. I just stood there. Again she said, "Find a seat." And then the guy back there told me in Cambodian, "Find a seat." So I finally got the seat, but it was most embarrassing.

Niseth's experience was typical of almost every other Khmer refugee student, but unlike most others who came with minimal exposure to education, Niseth came with a strong educational background, at least up to fifth-grade level. Through sheer hard work and commitment to learning, Niseth has now succeeded in gaining entry to a 4-year college. Talking about her college experiences, she recalled an instance when one of her professors gave her an *F* grade for a term paper because it contained grammatical errors. Although Niseth told her professor that she was an ESL student who had come to the United States with no knowledge of English at all, the professor refused to reconsider her decision. When I asked Niseth how she resolved the matter, her response was:

> I did not tell anybody about it because I thought it may have been my fault. Because of the way I was brought up, I think the teacher is always right. I have gone through high school and college in America, but I have never felt it was right to complain about the teacher. I don't know if my feeling is right or wrong, but I think most Cambodian students are like that.

Clearly, respect for teachers kept Niseth from seeking help from someone else. An outsider who is unaware of her cultural values may easily conclude that she remained quiet because she was passive in her speech and social interactions. In fact, this view of Khmer refugees is often expressed by researchers and educators and is cited as one reason for their lack of successful assimilation to mainstream society in the United States. The Khmer, however, view themselves in a different way. As Mum said, the aggressive style of communication reflects not success, but conflict, and it goes against the social ethics based on harmony and cooperation:

> If you see one of my girl friends, you would think that she was born here; she is so Americanized. The way she talks, the way she acts, what she wouldn't do. . . . She is a year older than me, but she acts like a kid. I can't recall getting into an argument with my friends, but when we get together she always fights with my friends.

Mum's views were echoed by Pu Ma's 15-year-old daughter when she said "I never fight with anybody, I just make friends."

To maintain harmony and goodwill, the Khmer generally avoid face-to-face confrontations and open competition between individuals. Even in troublesome situations, they do not generally assert themselves, complain, or fight for their rights as Americans might do, but look toward a third party to act as mediators. These ideals are especially strong among refugees from villages because in their home settings, they had looked to monks for guidance in secular as well as in spiritual matters.

In addition to conflicting cultural values, the educational and social backgrounds of the Khmer refugees also contribute to their varying degrees of academic and social success in the United States. As Mum and Nya Srey, as well as other refugees who have succeeded in learning English, observe, their early exposure to education and to the French language helped them to learn English quickly and to move away from the crime-ridden neighborhoods in which they were first settled. In contrast, Pu Ma and her daughter, who received minimal education in Cambodia, have experienced enormous difficulties in school. Without regular employment, they cannot hope to move from their depressed neighborhoods. They further believe they will never be able to find suitable jobs because they have not acquired English skills and they think that because they cannot retain what they learn, their inability to learn is due to "problems with their brains."

My research revealed, however, that Khmer refugees who arrived here illiterate or minimally literate continue to be unsuccessful in their

English acquisition not because of inability or lack of interest as claimed by some teachers, or because of impaired memories, but because ESL lessons address the needs of middle-class Americans and not those of refugees living in socially and economically depressed areas. As such, the lessons have no meaning in or application to their daily lives and do not help the refugees retain what they learn. For instance, the immediate needs of the refugees are not to learn how to borrow library books or how to greet friendly neighbors, but to learn how to overcome the problems of exploitation they experience and how to call the police or the ambulance in case of violence or sickness. It is also important to keep in mind that their teachers will obtain best results if they respect their students' cultural values. For instance, I witnessed an encounter between a 40-year-old male refugee and a missionary who stepped into the home as soon as the door was opened. Although the refugee was a Buddhist and had no wish to change his religion, he entertained the missionary for the next half hour, which prevented him from picking up his child from school on time. After the missionary left, I told my friend that he did not have to allow missionaries into his home and that if they forced themselves in, he had the right to ask them to leave. But he said it was wrong to be inhospitable towards visitors who came to his door. I then told him that if he felt uncomfortable about asking missionaries to leave, he should ask for their literature and let them know he would call them later. That was an appropriate suggestion; it provided a solution without violating his cultural values.

Conclusion

Khmer refugees are not less able or less motivated than other refugee groups to learn English or to assimilate. However, given their distinctive cultural and historical experiences, including the Pol Pot experience, they make adjustments somewhat differently from other groups. With lessons developed to meet their present needs, which pay attention to their cultural values, we teachers can help the Khmer refugees to learn English and to adjust to the larger community with ease and thereby become a productive segment of the larger U.S. community.

In addition, by working with Cambodian students and by learning about their ways of life, teachers may come to see aspects of the United States that otherwise might have gone unnoticed. Aggressive or assertive behavior is not the only way to resolve problems. Cambodians succeed on their own terms, not by abandoning humaneness, but by emphasizing it. Success also comes from stressing familial cooperation and consensus. By considering Cambodian values, teachers can not only enhance their understanding of cultural diversity, but also contribute to cultural literacy.

Summary

In the United States today, there are approximately 150,000 Cambodian (Khmer) refugees who were forced to flee their country to escape the excessively traumatic rule of Pol Pot and the Khmer Rouge. The vast majority of Khmer refugees came from a cooperative, rural, and non-Western background. This paper provides an overview of the history, culture, and worldview of the Khmer people, discusses similarities and differences among Cambodian refugees based on their diverse ethnic and socioeconomic backgrounds, and examines the impacts of their early socialization on their adjustments to U.S. society as well as to the classroom. The Cambodian perspectives presented here are those expressed to me by the refugees themselves in extensive life history narratives.

Acknowledgments

Although, by mutual arrangement, refugees quoted in this article will not be identified, their support and friendship is gratefully acknowledged. I also thank James M. Freeman, professor of Anthropology at San José State University, in California, for his guidance with this work.

Discussion Topics and Projects

1. Khmer refugees are worried about their retentive powers, so techniques should be developed to help them discover that they can remember what they learn. This recognition will enhance their self-esteem and accelerate learning. One successful method to achieve this is to have students memorize names and objects on picture cards. Teachers distribute an equal number of cards to each student; then everyone takes turns at collecting as many cards as possible by calling out for them. Clues can be given when asking for the cards instead of actually naming the object; this not only expands refugees' vocabulary, but also demonstrates that they are able to remember more details than just a name. What other methods can you foresee as effective?

2. An example of teaching assertive communication methods to Khmer refugees while respecting their cultural values is given in this chapter. Are there other ways to achieve this?

Further Reading

For Cambodian history and culture, see May Ebihara (1968, 1987), David Chandler (1983), and Sun Him Chhim (1987). Autobiographies by Someth May (1986), Haing Ngor (1987), and Pin Yathay (1987) record the horrors of the Khmer Rouge period. For information on teaching English to Khmer students see Mory Ouk (1988) and Usha Welaratna (1988). On adjustments of Cambodian refugees, see Ebihara (1985) and Welaratna (1989, 1990, in press).

7

Cultural Diversity and Socialization

A Case Study of a Hispanic Woman in a Doctoral Program in Sociology

Christine Pearson Casanave
Keio University, Japan

This chapter concerns the relationship between culture and the process of academic and professional socialization. In it, I portray two "cultures in contact," that of an academic community and that of a young Hispanic woman, Virginia M. (not her real name), a New Yorker of Puerto Rican descent, who spent a year in a PhD program in sociology at a West Coast research university.

These portrayals highlight the conflicts that are perhaps inherent in the socialization of graduate students into a fuzzily defined social science discipline, as sociology is thought to be. But the story told here also raises questions about the nature of the graduate school experience for a culturally diverse graduate student population. (See Johns, this book, for the story of a Lao student learning to cope with academic culture at the undergraduate level.) It leads us to ask (simplistically, to be sure) whether disciplines should socialize all students into a preordained set of values and practices, or whether

148

they should accommodate the cultural diversity of the populations they serve and thus open themselves to change (cf. Walters, this book). The story of the clash between the cultures of an academic community and that of an individual with little experience in that community reveals that the answer to this question is far more complex than it might at first seem. Nevertheless, we will see that the sociology program in which Virginia was enrolled missed valuable opportunities to appeal to and draw on the cultural diversity in one small group of first-year doctoral students.

Understanding Socialization

I would like to contextualize the story told here within a framework of socialization. Understanding the multifaceted nature of the socialization process will help explain why Virginia left her PhD program and why easy solutions to her conflicts will elude us. It will also help us understand the meaning of the term "culture" as I use it here, to refer to the many large and small worlds that we learn to inhabit as part of growing up, finishing our schooling, and entering the workplace.

As part of his early studies in the sociology of medical education, Robert Merton (Merton, Reader, & Kendall, 1957) defined the phenomenon of socialization in a way that highlights the many kinds of knowledge that inductees into professional communities must acquire:

> The technical term socialization designates the processes by which people selectively acquire the values and attitudes, the interests, skills, and knowledge—in short, the culture —current in the groups of which they are, or seek to become, a member. It refers to learning social roles. (p. 287)

Peter Berger and Thomas Luckmann (1967) refer to two kinds of socialization: primary socialization (that of children into their home cultures) and secondary socialization (that of adults into socially sanctioned roles at home and at work). Children learn how to behave appropriately within their culture and to value those things their cultures value. Adult acquire social and occupational roles that have become well established in the social structure. This process takes place for the most part socially as the individual interacts with significant others (Berger & Luckmann, 1967; Merton, 1957) through direct learning (didactic teaching) or indirect learning (association with faculty, peers, colleagues) (Merton, 1957, p. 41). As Berger and Luckmann (1967) point out, "language constitutes the most important content and the most important instrument of socialization" (p. 133). It is through language that social experiences are objectified and reified and eventually incorporated into the self as internal realities (Vygotsky, 1978, 1986).

Central to this chapter is the role that the graduate school plays in the socialization process. However, as Dan C. Lortie (1975) reminds us, formal schooling is only one way that novices are socialized into occupations. They may also become part of specialized groups by means of apprenticeships and by "learning-while-doing." The role that each of these types of socialization plays in the lives of novices probably depends in part on the type of school and occupation that is involved. For example, in a study of the socialization of lawyers, Lortie (1959) found that "laymen become lawmen only partially in law school. . . . [T]he important transformations take place in the hurly-burly of work after graduation" (p. 367). Other researchers have identified the graduate school as "central . . . in developing professional identification" (Becker & Carper, 1956, p. 341). Similarly, Merton et al. (1957) and Howard Becker, Blanche Geer, Everett Hughes, and Anselm Strauss (1961) found in their studies of medical education that the medical school experience was central in socializing students.

However, in the process of acquiring the culture of the profession they are about to enter, students are simultaneously immersed in a school culture into which they must also be socialized. These two cultures may clash. For instance, in the early years of training in medical school, students are forced into a dependent, subservient role as a result of the crushing demands the authoritarian system places on them. Yet these students are being trained to become independent-minded doctors who are responsible for people's lives (Becker et al., 1961; Broadhead, 1983). In graduate schools, too, students are caught in the conflict between this authoritarian educational structure and the goal of developing into independent scholars (Rosen & Bates, 1976).

We can add to this the fact that something different is expected of students in graduate and professional schools from what is expected in lower levels of schooling. In other words, the cultures at the different levels of schooling may themselves clash. Anne Dyson (1984) talked about how young children learned to "do school." Shirley Brice Heath (1983), too, has documented how children learn about the peculiar (to some) language-related practices of schools, such as how to answer the ubiquitous display question, in which the teacher is clearly asking something to which she already knows the answer.

Although we can probably say that the display question is alive and well even in the graduate school context, there is also less of an interest at the graduate school level in coming up with right answers and more discussion of what it means to pose and investigate interesting questions and to develop the skills needed to practice a particular profession. Simply put, the graduate school (and even the highly skill-oriented medical school, as Fox, 1957, discovered conflicts with the school culture at lower levels in that it sends students the message that there is a great deal more uncertainty in the adult professional world than they were led to believe. Part of what it means to be socialized in graduate school, then, is to recognize that some things about the school culture will look very familiar to students, but others will overturn or conflict with previously learned school norms, such as the "training for uncertainty" (Fox, 1957).

The sparse literature on the socialization of graduate students presumes a native-culture student population and addresses not at all in what ways the socialization experiences of minority or second language groups might differ from those of the dominant culture. However, it is a fact that increasingly large numbers of students from abroad, particularly from South and East Asia, have been enrolling in U.S. universities (Barber, 1985; Zikopoulos, 1987). Furthermore, many universities are making concerted efforts to enroll more minority graduate students though various incentive and scholarship programs. Graduate programs are thus likely to encounter student populations that are increasingly heterogeneous both linguistically and culturally. It is as yet unclear just what "socialization" means to such diverse groups or how graduate programs and professors are coping with this diversity. It seems clear, however, that to ignore the diversity is to overlook the reality of our graduate student populations and to pass up the opportunity (particularly important in the social sciences) to enrich a discipline's theoretical and empirical knowledge base as well as its membership.

To sum up my points so far, in general, socialization has tended to refer to a shift in the individual's self-perception from that of an outsider to that of an insider who has acquired the right to the label of the profession (doctor, lawyer, nurse, sociologist), and to the language, behaviors, and beliefs of the group. It has not been described in the literature as an interactive phenomenon in which a culturally diverse student population helps—by its very diversity—shape a disci-

151

pline. Rather, the socialized individual is said to have "internalized the subculture" (Lortie, 1975, p. 61) and acquired the sense of belonging to a cohesive, well-identified group and come to be comfortable over time with language, behaviors, and values that are not talked about, but are rather lived and practiced.

The particular nature of such values may remain unnoticed until such time as they are violated. A breakdown of some sort, in other words, will raise these previously hidden values to a level at which we are able to recognize and talk about them. Such breakdowns seem likely to occur where numerous conflicting cultures and subcultures from within and outside the school setting come together. This is the case in a graduate program that admits a culturally and linguistically diverse student population. Breakdowns may also be more likely to occur in situations where the disciplinary culture is not clearly defined or is made up of a number of subcultures (as it is in some of the social sciences) or where cultural diversity is not openly recognized as a resource for both the graduate program and the discipline. What socialization consists of in such situations remains to be documented by more studies such as the present one, in which cultural diversity remained an untapped resource. We do know, however, that language lies at the heart of the socialization process.

The Role of Language in the Socialization Process

Much of what and how we learn, both as children and adults, is language-related. From the perspectives of Berger and Luckmann (1967), Judith Langer (1987), Lev Vygotsky (1978, 1986), and others, people first experience the world externally, gaining much of their understanding of it through language-mediated experiences that are gradually internalized. Language creates and shapes our world by reifying our experiences and making them memorable and concrete. Language is thus inseparable from the cultures in which it is used. Hence, knowing a language constitutes a great part of what it means to know the culture in which that language is used, as many people such as Clifford Geertz (1983), Thomas S. Kuhn (1970), and second language educators have pointed out.

If we view schools as comprising their own peculiar cultures, we will note that in the culture of schools, language has been used in rather distinct ways that help define what school is. As Heath (1983) and others have noted, this fact makes the transition that children make from home to school a potentially difficult one, especially when the ways language is used at home differ greatly from the ways it is used at school, as it does in the United States for groups outside the mainstream middle class. In short, aspects of school language differ from what some have called "everyday language" in ways that can cause difficulty for those who have little experience with this language and the particular ways it is used in school contexts.

School language in the Western context has been described as more abstract and "logical" (in a formal or scientific sense) than everyday language, which is said to deal with concrete here-and-now experience (Bernstein, 1973; Broudy, 1977; Olson, 1977b). Discussions of school language and everyday language have often been presented like this, as neatly conceptualized dichotomies, even if disclaimers and qualifiers are used. Examples include the distinctions between utterance and text (Olson, 1977a), conversation and composition (Bereiter & Scardamalia, 1982), orality and literacy (Ong, 1982; Tannen, 1982). However, it is widely recognized that no clean distinction exists between school and everyday language, or between written and spoken language (Langer, 1987; Tannen, 1982), and that earlier portrayals of the dichotomy were "exaggerated" (Olson, 1980).

Nevertheless, educators, in particular, have long been aware that the oral and written discourse used in educational settings for instructional purposes differs from that which we learn to speak as children and that which we use as adults to conduct our everyday affairs. Jim Cummins and Merrill Swain (1986) portray this distinction not as a dichotomy but as a vertical and a horizontal continuum of contextual support and cognitive involvement. Much of what makes school language difficult lies in the fact that the activities in which it is used are both cognitively demanding and context-reduced. Some of this difficulty lies in the language itself (as in the case of the specialized terminologies and symbols of different fields); a great part of it, however, lies in the uses to which school language is put, that is, in the nature of tasks that "reduce" the context from which meaning can be made (shift it from a here-and-now context to one more distant or abstract) and that place a heavy cognitive load on the language user (defined by Cummins [Cummins & Swain, 1986]) as "the amount of information that must be processed simultaneously or in close succession" (p. 154).

In the graduate school context, the school language becomes even more specialized and thus distant from everyday language, in accordance with conventions in different fields and disciplines. In its written form, in particular, it is used as a tool of abstract and analytical thought, allowing writers to reflect on and develop their own knowledge and to use the accumulated knowledge of others in the field as a resource. Moreover, in academic disciplines at least, the specialized written form of school language becomes the main way that professionals communicate with one another about their work through journal articles, memos, papers delivered at conferences, and so on. This kind of communication requires writers and speakers to be what I will call "selectively explicit" in their use of language. They must be able to assess what their audiences know well enough to decide when they need to fill in gaps in knowledge and when they may take short cuts. Graduate students thus face the formidable task of developing a sense of what others know in their fields and of learning the conventionalized ways of representing knowledge in fully explicit and in abbreviated forms.

In short, school language can be characterized not only by what it says (its particular content and vocabularies) but also by what it does—by its function to serve as a tool for reflective and analytical thought, as a primary mode of communication among professionals and as an archival source of a field's knowledge. Hence, a major part of what it means to be socialized in graduate schools involves students' coming to grips with the peculiarities of the language that is used there—its nature and its functions—and with the need to shift their relationship with texts, from that of consumers of knowledge to that of producers and communicators of knowledge.

To summarize my sketch of socialization so far, the classic view of socialization is that an individual gains membership in a group by adopting and, some would say, internalizing, its values, practices, and beliefs. Much of what is learned in the process of socialization, whether it is learned through direct instruction or by association, involves language. Language characterizes groups to some extent, as does a group's particular relationship with and use of texts, as we can see in the case of schools, disciplines, and professions. In graduate schools, the process of socialization requires that students gain facility in somewhat different kinds and uses of school language from what they are used to—a requirement that pushes them to tolerate uncertainty and to use language as a tool for abstract and analytical thought as a way for them to develop, not just consume, knowledge.

This view of socialization, though no doubt accurate in many respects, is quite unidirectional. It addresses neither the cultural conflicts nor the resources that a culturally diverse student population might bring to a graduate program. Particularly in the social sciences, cultural diversity needs to be considered not only an object of study but also a resource for helping shape the discipline itself. In Virginia's case, this resource was not utilized.

Introduction to the Study

In the Fall of 1987, Virginia entered a PhD program in sociology at a West Coast research university. From a Puerto Rican family in New York, she was 22, and had just finished a BA degree in sociology at a good East Coast university not too far from her home in the Bronx. She came from a close-knit family in which her father had been a bus driver, then a supervisor, for many years. She and her 11 classmates formed a diverse group. The ages ranged form 22 to 40, and 8 of the 12 students were international students from countries such as Canada, mainland China, Korea, Puerto Rico, and Japan. Two were Hispanic minorities. Quiet, shy, and pretty, Virginia volunteered to work with me over the academic year as 1 of 3 case study participants in a research project that investigated the role of writing in socializing a culturally diverse group of graduate students into a social science discipline.

During this first year of doctoral work, all students had to take a demanding series of required core courses in sociological theory (two courses) and statistical methods (two courses, with a third in the Fall of the second year). For a study of socialization in graduate school contexts, such courses are ideal to track because they presumably are designed to transmit to students the knowledge and skills that are considered fundamental in the field. In fact, one of the core course professors described these courses as bringing a disparate incoming group of first-year students to "more or less the same place." The program in some ways preferred students who did not have previous graduate degrees in sociology, because it did not then have to "un-teach" them so much.

In order to learn what values and practices this program considered essential for novice sociologists to learn, and to learn the role of language and writing in this training, I sat in on all the sessions of the two theory classes, taping and taking notes, and on selected sessions of one of the two first-year methods classes. I also collected handouts, drafts of student papers, final copies of written work, and all written feedback on this work. I interviewed three key participants up to eight times and noncase-study participants, such as professors and other students, up to four times. From the class sessions, documents, and interviews, I not only became familiar with the key issues, goals, and terminology of this particular disciplinary subcommunity, but I also developed a sense of the 12 first-year students as a group. This group became an unusually close group compared to those in previous years. But as is the case with most groups in a classroom situation, roughly a third participated actively and regularly, a third occasionally, and a third was silent.

Virginia was among the silent third. I got to know her slowly over the first few months through regular interviews we had set up for the purpose of discussing her responses to the core courses and to the several writing assignments she had to complete in each one. We talked briefly at first as she completed the first short writing assignments in her first theory class, then at greater length as we got to know each other better and as she struggled with the longer papers that came later.

For Virginia, it was the theory classes more than the rather straightforward, skill-based methods classes that pushed her to decide to leave the PhD program after 1 year. Let me portray these theory classes in some detail because the detail will help convey a clear picture of the culture into which Virginia and the other first-year students were being socialized.

The Core Theory Classes

The first-year core courses in sociological theory had been instituted nearly 30 years before by two of the program's original founders, both of whom were still active and now very influential in the department. The first theory course, which I will call Theory Analysis, was offered in the first quarter in the Fall designed by Dr. Adams (not his real name) who was still teaching it. In spite of some changes made over time, Theory Analysis as taught by Dr. Adams had one main objective—to teach students how to read or analyze theories. A second objective was to acquaint students with "seven of the eight major schools of sociological thought in America today."

To these ends, and to help students use their analytical skills later in the course to write a literature review, Adams had them write three short analytical exercises, following step-by-step instructions provided in handouts. In these papers, students analyzed several old but influential theories, where "analyze" meant discovering the theory's "basic assumptions," its "empirical generalizations," and the definitions of key concepts used in it as well as writing a precis. The third of these exercises asked the students to use their new analytical skills to compare two theories. The three exercises were written in the first month of course and were read and commented on by a third-year teaching assistant, who consulted with Adams in preparing his responses. The major culture shock experienced by nearly all the first-year students occurred in this first month as the students struggled to understand and apply the abstract concepts used in the three exercises to talk and write about theory.

The second theory class, Theory Construction, was a course in how to construct sociological theory. It was offered in the Winter quarter by another of the old guard faculty who had helped establish the department, Dr. Bernstein (not his real name). He had taken over the Theory Construction course 6 years before from its originator and had altered it in 1987, in a team effort with Adams, in order to solve some of the problems he had encountered in previous years in which graduate students had complained about the course's narrow approach. The course remained controversial, but (as was reported to me) less so than before. Part of the problem lay in the fact that Bernstein believed there was a right way to do sociology if one wished to "do science," the presumption being that a scientific sociology was better in some ways than other approaches.

As a way to head off student protests, the 1987 Theory Construction course was team taught by both Adams and Bernstein although most of the teamwork had taken place earlier in the design of the course. Bernstein told me that, among other changes, he was also trying to be less of a "bull in a china shop," that is, to be more accepting of students' work when it deviated from his own prescriptive view of what good sociology consisted of. As for the writing assignments, for the first time since he had taught Theory Construction, Adams and he included four short "working papers" on a research topic of students' own choosing, building up to a final research proposal, rather than a final exam as in the past. As in Theory Analysis, the writing assignments were designed to train students in skills they would need to complete dissertations and to contribute later to scholarly work in the field. The papers had students pose researchable questions, formulate a plan for conducting their research, and test competing hypotheses through formal logical analysis. The approach was empirical and scientific.

Sociology as Science in the Core Course

The intellectual tradition espoused in the core courses (both in theory and statistical methods), I am calling scientific. Issues, values, and practices from the natural sciences and from the philosophy and sociology of science dominated the instruction. As described by continuing graduate students, the program's sociology had a "positivistic, empirical, and formal" flavor, where theory, quantification, and (for professors like Bernstein) experiment played important roles in the work that the faculty did.

The message that science was valued highly was couched in a number of different ways, some overt and some covert. In class lectures and discussions in the theory classes and in interviews with me the professors expressed the following views:

> Sociology isn't a science in the mature sense yet, but it can be if sociologists would just be trained to follow certain standards of language and practice;

> We had a very good, well-liked qualitative researcher here, but she didn't get tenure;

> Sociology is many things, but one of its most prestigious traditions is grounded in practices and values modeled on the natural sciences; if you want to compete as a professional, you should learn this model.

In addition to these views expressed by the professors, a scientific sociology was promoted by the ways in which knowledge was represented in handouts, required readings, and board work, and by the ways in which the students were expected to represent and treat knowledge in their writing assignments. In this scientific tradition, much of the key information was carried in specialized code words, in certain kinds of verbal and symbolic statements, and in images depicting relations and processes. All of these ways of representing knowledge functioned to distance the phenomena under study from the bias of human influence—to present an objectified world view— and to foster a kind of analytical thinking that fit loosely within the scientific tradition of positivism.[1] In this tradition, students were being trained to conceptualize sociological knowledge not just in discursive prose forms, but also in forms that pushed them to think scientifically, that is, objectively, abstractly, symbolically, and analytically.

Although the program did not discourage students from exploring other ways of investigating the sociological world, its own resources were limited because it was such a small department. Moreover, the covert message seemed to be that—if the socialization process worked as it should—the students from this program would adopt the foundational skills and values they were being taught in the core courses as they moved throughout the program and into the professional world.

Three Perspectives of Two Cultures in Conflict

Virginia was one of many in the first-year group who experienced varying degrees of discomfort, resistance, and alienation as they proceeded through their first-year core courses, in particular the courses in theory analysis and construction. This discomfort can be viewed as stemming from a clash of cultures—that of the disciplinary community and that of Virginia's world. To help make her decision to leave the program comprehensible (for many decided to stay in the program despite doubts), I will examine three perspectives from which we can view this clash of cultures. These perspectives emerged as themes over the full academic year. The first concerns language, the second concerns ways of knowing, and the third concerns power and prestige.

The Language of a Scientific Sociology

One aspect of acquiring the culture of a disciplinary community involves learning that community's specialized language: how it represents knowledge in conventional ways to make it accessible to other community members, usually through written documents. Part of what the core course provided for the first-year students was a jargon that united them as a group in at least two ways. In the first place, native and nonnative English speakers alike were joined in the struggle to learn "sociology as a second language." Secondly, the language (especially that of the theory courses) identified the students as a group that was being brought into the fold, so to speak. All graduate students had experienced what it was like to suddenly "begin to understand what they're talking about," as one of the first-year students put it. For most of the students in the 1987 group, this understanding began to emerge after about a month into the Fall quarter. Along with this understanding came the recognition that the specialized language of the theory courses was not necessarily shared by all other faculty in the department. In other words, subcommunities existed within the department itself that may have shared the broad commitment to science but not the language used to talk about theory.

The specialized language of the theory courses consisted of code words (terminology), acronyms, symbols, and certain constrained sentence types. I focus here on the code words because these represented concepts that the students began to struggle with from the first day of class. On that first day in Theory Analysis, Adams used over 50 discipline-specific terms in his 2-hour lecture, most of them nouns. Many of these terms were used throughout the two theory courses as a metalanguage for talking about theory.

Other terms were introduced as central to the writing assignments in both theory courses and were thus quite central to the students' lives: It was difficult to complete the writing assignments without having some sense of what the terms in the directions meant. The following list displays the key code words from the handouts in the two theory courses that described the step-by-step instructions for all the writing assignments. Many of these terms also appeared in Adams first lecture:

Terms from Theory Analysis Assignments
    domain (of a theory)
    basic assumption (underived premise)
    scope (of a theory)
    unsolved problem
    theoretical research program (TRP)
    initial theoretical formulation (ITF)
    current theoretical formulation (CTF)
    elaboration (of a theory)
    degeneration (of a theory)
    proliferants
    competitors
    structure (of a theory)
    metatheoretical presuppositions
    logical implications
    empirical implications
    excess import

Terms from Theory Construction Assignments
    analytical problem
    empirical inquiry
    trivial question or problem
    a "good question"
    empirical studies

160

association between variables
argument
observation statement
knowledge claim
proposition
scope statement/condition
conceptual definition
"system" of concepts
operationalization
indicator
explanatory generality
empirical implication/consequence
heuristic explanation
hypothesis
competing explanation
logical analysis
empirical test
intersubjective understanding

These code words of the writing assignments in the theory classes suggest a scientific sociology, with the values of science embedded in the terms themselves. In the ideal socialization process, the students would learn the words and their concepts and adopt the values embedded in them. However, many of the students were skeptical about the values of theoretical and empirical science reflected in this specialized language. If we look more closely at Virginia's responses to the writing assignments and to the specialized language used to talk and write about theory, we will see how the conflict of disciplinary and personal values materialized for her over the academic year. In particular, we will see that her home languages ("everyday" English and Spanish) came to be less valuable to her over time as tools for communicating her ideas about her work with friends and family in that they were not valued as resources for communication within the department. At a certain point, in other words, she no longer had everyday language for what she was learning.

Virginia's Responses to the Language of a Scientific Sociology

For many students, not just those from non-Western and nonmainstream cultures, the main difficulty in completing the first writing assignments in Theory Analysis stemmed from the code words used to talk about theory and their application to a very discursive piece of theorizing by Merton. The so-called answers, in other words, were not unambiguously obvious in the text. Virginia and others struggled over definitions of terms, then tried to find (as the assignment instructed) sample sentences embodying those concepts. Virginia's first concern was just to get the task done and to fix the definitions of the key code words and their synonyms in her mind.

Having finished the first analytical exercise in Theory Analysis at the end of the second week of school, Virginia talked about the process she went through in writing the assignment. The level at which she was engaged with this first task was that of language and definitions (rather than content) as she struggled to link terms with their concepts, then to identify examples of them in the Merton article:

> I wrote down all the empirical statements and all the lawlike statements. Um . . . from the empirical statements we were supposed to . . . um get—no from the lawlike statements we were supposed to have premises. So I um . . . I selected out the premises from the lawlike statements and—once I got the two lists of lawlike statements and empirical statements, everything else was easy. For me. Assuming I got the right (laugh) empirical and lawlike statements. And if I got that wrong, then you know I'll just learn. For the next time. How to do it.

Here Virginia is trying to use code words that, in week 2 of the program, she had not yet internalized and that had little connection with the world she had just left on the East Coast. But she pushed ahead, and described the value of the writing assignment, again in terms of language, as "reinforcing the definitions":

> I think [the exercises] helped reinforce the definitions in my head. So that now I can tell you what a lawlike statement is supposed to look like. And now I can tell you what an empirical generalization is supposed to be. Whereas before, I was very much confused about the differences.

Virginia also used the dittoed "Glossary of Terms," made available in the first week of class, to help her remember definitions. But the written feedback that she received from the teaching assistant on her first exercise indicated that she (along with many others) had not linked terms and their concepts to examples in the text in appropriate ways. Note the specialized language of the course in the following example of written feedback: "Your list of basic assumptions are not lawlike statements: A and B are categoricals. C is an empirical generalization."

Given this kind of feedback on the first exercise, we can understand the frustration that some students felt. But the specialized language of the writing assignments was not Virginia's only concern. She also felt intimidated in this first theory class by the discussion carried on between the professor and the vocal third of the class. She judged her own competence and that of others, in other words, according to the way they were able to use language in a spontaneous situation. In the comment that follows, she groups herself with the other foreign students, most of whom spoke rarely in class:

> I feel like the others have a—aside from the foreign students, um the Americans in the group have an upper hand in terms of um the way they speak and um the kinds of questions they ask in class. I feel they have a better grasp of the material than I do.

By the end of her first month in the program, having completed three of these short writing assignments, Virginia began to express her misgivings about the way language was used in the Theory Analysis course. She claimed, for example, that the directions for Exercise 3 could have been stated much more simply. "The language sort of covers up the main idea," she said, expressing frustration that the professor had not "gotten to the point" in a way that made the directions clearer. Virginia also began to articulate her discomfort with the abstractness of the specialized language and concepts and to long for discussion that was more down to earth:

> I wish somehow that there wasn't such a big mystery. . . . You know a mysterious air surrounding theory, and what theory is, you know? I wish it could be more concrete.

By the time she returned from Christmas vacation, Virginia was more openly articulating her dissatisfaction with the first theory course. The abstract language, she suggested, held little meaning for her in everyday life:

> I felt the whole course was um . . . was based on these—abstract language, you know, and I wish they could have been more simpler, and more um applicable to everyday things. But I guess theory—you know, that's antithetical to theory. Theory isn't particular.

Her gauge of whether she was using language in the clear, straightforward way she'd been taught in a college writing class was whether she could explain her ideas to her mother. By the end of her first quarter, she was no longer able to do this. She was "learning the concepts in Adams' language," she said, and could therefore find no everyday terms for what she was doing. In other words, new concepts had been created for her out of the specialized language, making it impossible to "translate" into language that her family could understand. "You know," she said, "there's no way that I could explain to [my mother] what I was spending my last 2 weeks before Christmas doing. Just sitting at the computer, Mom."

In the second theory class, given during the Winter term, Virginia's concern for language continued. In this class, the students wrote four working papers that led to a final paper in which they were to systematically identify and propose a solution for a research problem. As part of the class requirements, the students shared their four working papers with each other and critiqued them publicly in class, according to guidelines established by Bernstein. This system of public critiquing allowed the students to see everyone's writing, which Virginia found in some cases to be "awful." She lamented the fact that the students were getting no feedback on their writing and claimed, "If you can't understand the writing, how can you understand the concepts?"

But she said a month later, after having completed three of the four working papers, that the working papers could not have been done orally, "off the top of your heads," without being written first. The reason for this, Virginia explained, was that "they expect us to use that strict language—which isn't normal everyday language." Using this language meant "writing for Dr. Bernstein" rather than for the wider audience she wished to communicate with. It meant, as Virginia phrased it, "using Bernstein's language and the stuff from his lectures."

By the end of Theory Construction, though not happy with the specialized language, Virginia expressed more confidence than before at comprehending it. But after a Spring break, she began her third quarter facing an incomplete on her final paper in this class because of a flaw in the logical analysis of her hypotheses. Over the break, some of the meanings of the key code words had already begun to slip away. In the following quote, Virginia is rereading Bernstein's guidelines for completing the paper:

It says demonstrate by logical analysis that the two observation statements or two hypotheses are the consequences of the two *explanans*.
(small pause, small chuckle) I just feel like I'm gonna have to go over
some of these words, definitions. (laugh)

Well into the third quarter, Virginia was still convinced that good
writing in sociology was written in terms accessible to nonsociologists:

Although I use "proper" terms, I still use simple sentences, and um
simple phrases, um. . . . I try to be as clear and to the point as possible,
. . . uh . . . so in some respects I use words which I feel nonsociologists
have an idea about. Even though they don't define the term as a sociologist. Something like the word theory.

By Spring, Virginia was also ready to label many of the terms used
in Theory Construction as "useless—all of the Latin ones, instantia-
tion. . . ." Yet she now saw the value of learning something about
these words, not just in terms of surviving a class assignment, but in
more political terms:

I think it's valuable to me (. . .) to know more or less what theoretical
sociologists are talking about. Trying to sort of you know learning how
to speak their language. In case they try and pull one over on me. (small
laugh)

In sum, by the end of the academic year, Virginia recognized the
extent to which the theoretical sociologists in the program used language that was different from what she used in everyday life, including their use of so-called common terms in technical or quasitechnical
ways. Nevertheless, in her own writing, she continued searching for
a way to express her new knowledge in language that was accessible
to her friends and family, though she found this increasingly difficult
to do. Her desire to maintain ties with nonsociologists by means of
language reflects her growing sense of alienation from the sociologists
from whom she was receiving her training. Language in some ways
lay at the heart of her self-identity by helping define who she was and
with which reference group she would align herself. By "using Dr.
Bernstein's language" she was aligning herself with scientists, not
with the populations with whom she wished to communicate at home
and in future work: women, ethnic minorities, educators in racially
and culturally mixed neighborhoods. She rejected this alignment, but

had no convenient linguistic substitute because so many of the new concepts seemed to be created out of the specialized language itself. As a resource for communicating her new knowledge to her home community, Virginia's everyday language had become ineffective.

Hence, although Virginia began developing a "shorthand" for communicating with other sociologists, the sociology program missed an opportunity to help Virginia become a pipeline for communicating its knowledge to the community and to add her perspective to that knowledge. The knowledge produced by this particular academy would probably remain relevant only to a fairly small circle of specialists.

Hand in hand with Virginia's growing awareness of the role of language in defining the people who use it came a greater sense of the different world views, or ways of knowing, that are reflected in language and a realization that she was learning only one of the many ways a sociologist might understand the world.

Ways of Knowing

Kuhn (1970) described the scientific community as a group of practitioners of a scientific speciality who share language, beliefs, and practices. Language lies at the core of the community in that a group's "knowledge of nature [is] embedded in the language" (p. 272). When novices learn a group's way of knowing nature by learning how to solve a field's classic problems ("exemplars"), they are acquiring a "language-correlated way of seeing the world," says Kuhn, without which "we do not see a world at all" (p. 274).

The notion that a field's specialized language shapes how group members see worlds has been explored by Charles B. Bazerman (1981, 1988). Bazerman focuses on the ways in which field-specific written texts embody a group's knowledge and its conception of what knowledge is and does in that field. Kristine Hansen (1988) used this idea as the core of a study in which she demonstrated how the different theoretical conventions in two social science texts on the same theme reflect very different epistemological assumptions. One text was a qualitative study in social anthropology that Hansen refers to as a "particularized representation" of a small number of kinship networks among several African American families. These families appear, along with the author, as real people in the document. The other was a quantitative empirical study within the sociological tradition of

survey and experimental research. In this study, the author represented several hundred African American families abstractly as numbers and objects. The author himself did not appear as a persona
in this "objective" portrayal, hence the frequent use of passive and
agentless nominalizatons. Nature, in this portrayal, revealed itself to
the author, who played the role of nature's messenger (Gilbert, 1976).
Each type of text, in other words, reflected different assumptions of
what can be known, what is worth knowing, and how we can come
to know it. As I have suggested above, the texts written and read in
Virginia's sociology program fit the latter tradition.

Virginia and others came to recognize that they were being indoctri-
nated (their term) into one way of knowing the sociological world. As
she put it, she felt she was "learning not to view certain types of works
as sociological." Her first theory class, she said after just one month
in the program, made her realize that

> there are going to be certain types of works that [we] are not going to
> be reading about in this course, descriptive sort of works you know.
> Um . . . comparisons, just you know comparisons between maybe two
> ethnic groups.

Rightly or wrongly, by the end of the first month, Virginia had
gotten the idea that descriptive works were atheoretical and nonscien-
tific, and that, whereas such works might be considered "sociology"
in one sense by practitioners working in other "paradigms," they
would not be valued highly in this program.

It is at this point, early in her first year, that Virginia began to
express a sense of discomfort in the program. Her first real clue about
the exclusive nature of the department's instruction in theory came
early in the first quarter, during a guest lecture that Bernstein was
giving in Adams' Theory Analysis class. In this lecture, Bernstein had
highlighted one of Adams' messages to students—that there were
many ways to approach the study of sociology, even though other
ways were not discussed in depth or practiced in the core courses.
Virginia expressed the frustration that resulted from this discovery:

> I think the Bernstein lecture also made me realize a couple of comments
> that Adams had said throughout his lecture about the way other sociolo-
> gists view sociology. You know um the question just kept coming up
> more frequently, well what do they—how do they view, you know, and

167

what kind of arguments do *they* use to support their own view of sociology.

In response to her frustration, her Hispanic classmate, Laura, reminded her that any department will enculturate its students into its preferred way of viewing the world. As retold by Virginia, Laura said, "*Well*, Virginia, if you go to a department that's very heavily into Marxism, you're just gonna hear about Marxism!" Understanding this helped Virginia realize that there was a very pragmatic side to her socialization into this department. This involved simply learning to do the work in the ways that were expected in order to get through the program, and somehow separating this pragmatic aspect from the personal, epistemological one. In fact, by the time she returned from the Christmas break, she saw that the highly structured writing tasks in Theory Analysis had helped her know what Adams expected in class and what the department expected on a dissertation literature review. But she also noted that the way she expressed herself in these writing tasks was constrained, as was her thinking: "I'm really not knowledgeable," she said in January, "about the way other sociologists think. So I'm just learning one type of sociology. I'm just learning how to think a certain way."

Later in the Winter quarter when she had finished three of the four working papers for Theory Construction, Virginia could express more clearly than before some of the values she saw being promulgated through writing assignments and class lectures: Good sociology is theoretically based—it deals in abstractions as well as in particulars; it is not enough to critique a theory—one must also improve it; empirical research is highly valued when it is exact and precise (numbers are needed); a good question is one that is nontrivial and one for which there are logical and scientific explanations as well as empirical evidence. Moreover, as she was taught in Theory Construction, formal logic is valued by some social scientists as a way to test the consistency and logicality of sets of hypotheses. Of all the valued ways of knowing in the core courses, this one met with the most resistance from Virginia and numerous other students, who found the requirements of formal logic to be a waste of time and effort. As Virginia phrased it, "converting knowledge to ps and qs" was not her idea of a fruitful way to understand the world.

In short, in Virginia's eyes (and those of other first-year students), the way of knowing that was promoted in the department's core theory courses pushed students to distance themselves (their biases, personal values) from their objects of study, in essence to remove themselves to the extent possible as sentient human beings from the research process. Knowledge could then be represented abstractly and quantitatively so that it could be compared, tested, publicly critiqued, and perhaps added to the discipline's body of knowledge.

Perhaps because of their sparse backgrounds in sociology, some students like Virginia felt constrained, even trapped, by the core-course emphasis on what they felt was a dehumanized way of knowing a very human sociological world. They missed the engagement with issues involving real people: women, minorities, immigrant cultures, families. They witnessed their thinking being shaped by the language and practices they were exposed to, yet felt somewhat helpless to explore other ways of knowing for reasons of time (of which there was none), pragmatics (the need to get through the coursework), and resources (the absence of other kinds of researchers in the department). The department, for its part, was small, and admitted having limited resources. It had opted to specialize in some types of sociological research and not in others in order to graduate PhDs who were competitive in a job market that held scientific ways of knowing in high regard. Given these restrictions, it might still have been possible for the department to demonstrate from early in the core-course sequence how issues of gender and ethnicity could be encompassed in a more "human" way within some kind of scientific framework. A move away from the strict hard science model of knowledge, on the other hand, would have allowed the department to draw more easily on the cultural resources within its own graduate student population. As it was, these resources were overlooked.

Students' decisions to stay in or leave the program thus hinged on a complex array of personal and pragmatic factors. In Virginia's case, many layers of conflicts having to do with language and ways of knowing contributed to her decision to leave. A third factor that fed into her decision was her recognition of who the powerful and prestigious people in this broad community of "scientists" seemed to be and her increasing sense of discomfort at imagining herself a part of this group.

Recognizing Where the Power Lies

When phrases like "knowledge produced by the academy" (e.g., Bazerman, 1987) are used, we are led to ask what the composition might

169

be of this prestigious group that presumably has the privilege of shaping a discipline in quite fundamental ways. As implied by Bazerman (1981), David Olson (1980), and Karl Popper (1979) among others, this group consists of a discipline's writers and researchers—those who are published and whose publications are incorporated into a field's "archives." If we view writing as a "social and collaborative act" (Bruffee, 1983), then a field's publications can be thought of as joint productions of writers and the colleagues who exchange ideas with them. The academy of knowledge producers, then, would consist of the community of people whose publications influence the field or subfield and the colleagues who contribute to the knowledge that finds its way into print.

Geertz (1983) describes "most effective academic communities" as "not that much larger than most peasant villages and just about as ingrown" (p. 157). He claims that the relations among the individuals in these "intellectual villages" are not only intellectual, but also political, moral, and personal. Students in doctoral programs will eventually be obligated as part of the dissertation process to align themselves with one of these groups, both for the short-term pragmatic purpose of completing the program and for the longer-term purpose of forging professional alliances. However, the nature of this developing relationship with the profession is not fully understood.

Some scholars, inspired by Paulo Freire, have described the relation between an academic community and the students it serves as that of the oppressor and the oppressed (Bizzell, 1982). In this view, politically oppressed students need to master the discourse of the academy in order to be able to understand critically, and thus resist, its oppression in the academy's own terms (p. 196). Although this view may be too strong for some, it is still the case that part of the socialization process involves learning to recognize who's who in the field, learning to "speak" with them in their language (as Virginia put it), and eventually making decisions about the "intellectual village" one wishes to pay taxes in. In the social sciences, novices making such decisions need to achieve enough political awareness to have a sense of which subcommunities are the most influential or interesting or intellectually and ethically compatible with their own developing beliefs and values. This is not an easy task when numerous intellectual traditions exist and when the novice has little background or experience in the field, as was the case with most of the minority and foreign students in the sociology program in this study. However, students in such a situation may not realize that their own backgrounds constitute a resource for an academic program in the social sciences. From this perspective, Patricia Bizzell's (1982) portrayal of students as oppressed by the academy is misguided, because it does not consider the active role that a culturally diverse population might play within the academy.

But most new graduate students will probably not recognize their own potential as a resource for the academic community. They will attempt, as did many of the foreign and minority students in Virginia's program, to develop a relationship with the profession on the community's terms. In some cases, this may mean shifting the goals they had on entering the program. Like a number of other students, Virginia had decided to pursue a PhD in sociology so that she could gain the knowledge, skills, and prestige to be able to return to neighborhoods and schools she was familiar with and make a difference in people's lives. She felt particularly committed to the plights of women and ethnic minorities and wished to find ways to better understand and alleviate their difficult lots in life. It was thus understandably difficult for her to see the relevance of learning how to identify basic assumptions in a theory, to "convert knowledge to ps and qs," to trace the development of a theory over time, and to run regression analyses on massive data sets she was not particularly interested in.

But added to this difficulty was Virginia's gradual recognition that the people she was most interested in were grossly underrepresented in all aspects of the sociology she was learning: in the faculty in the department, in the theories they read, in the field's best journals, and in the issues that were discussed. In the third week of the program she said only, "I have some reservations, but I don't know where it's coming from." By the middle of the academic year, she had gotten the sense that theoreticians constituted a powerful group within the field and that there was something unbalanced about the gender, ethnicity, and focus of this group:

> I'm more skeptical [than last quarter] about the place of theory in sociology, um . . . who determines what a theory is, who writes theory and what is the theory about, um . . . . I think I'm looking at it in terms of a race issue. Most—I guess almost all of the theorists we heard about were White males.

One particular example struck Virginia as quite odd. She had chosen a topic for her Theory Analysis literature review (a paper and an oral presentation) on collective violence—a topic she assumed would deal to some extent with populations in the third world, particularly

171

Latin America. But to her surprise, there was nothing in the bibliography that she had been assigned to read that was either written by a Latin American scholar or that was on the topic of Latin America:

> One thing that struck me as I was reading all the literature that was assigned to me for this presentation was that there was no mention of Latin America at all. And this was a theoretical program on collective violence. And there was no mention of Latin America.

She thus took this to be a good starting place for her next writing assignments (a paper in Theory Analysis and her project in Theory Construction) because this seemed to be a fruitful arena for research. Indeed, she received positive feedback from both professors on her choice of topic and was pleased to be investigating a topic that interested her in spite of the paucity of studies.

Nevertheless, Virginia found herself questioning the way she was required to treat her topic in both theory courses—analytically, abstractly, and logically, according to guidelines prepared by two White male professors who had been trained more than 30 years before in the Talcott Parsons school of thought. Both professors, for example, commented to Virginia in written feedback about her needing to "press harder in the future for more analytical power in conceptualizing the problem," but did not appear to take an interest in her personally. Bernstein, moreover, gave her an incomplete on her final paper because she had not completed the formal logical analysis of her hypotheses correctly. She eventually did complete the assignment, but concluded that grades were based less on hard work and creativity than on students' ability to complete the assignments according to what she called the recipes of the professors. These recipes, Virginia came to believe, were the products of a sociological world run by White middle-class European and American males, theorists, as she called them.

When Virginia began the program, she had been somewhat skeptical about the people she labeled "the theorists"—who they were and what they were doing, but was "willing to give them a chance." By this she meant she was willing to "be open to their message," and to learn how theory was constructed. But by the middle of her first year, she was fairly certain that this group did not speak to her concerns:

> Well, um . . . I found that throughout the long process of how theories develop that it's very elitist, it focuses on just a few theorists who get

published, who come from certain schools of sociology, so ah . . . My views have changed. I've become a little bit more closed minded.

This view of who controls what work gets done, how it gets done, and what gets published, and her perception of who was left out of the process, contributed greatly to Virginia's decision to leave the program, and persisted after she left the program. After having had 8 months to reflect on her experiences, she said in a taped response to a questionnaire that I had sent her in New York:

> This university's sociology is scientific and formal. My opinion about doing sociology in this way is that I think that it's an elitist way of doing sociology. It's um, especially when you don't combine the scientific and the formal with the informal, the normal, everyday language that is needed to communicate with people outside of sociology. So I find it elitist, um, very exclusive way of doing sociology.

Some months after returning home to New York, Virginia took a job as a research assistant in a small nonprofit Puerto Rican educational organization. Her experiences there put her in touch with the people she wished to work with and help. Yet she felt a great deal of frustration at not being able to use some of the skills she had acquired the year before. From the inside, this time, rather than from the outside, she felt the need for something more—for further training that would give her a more influential voice in what was being done. Having stepped into a world where being elitist gave one a voice, she agonized over where she might fit in. In a letter written a year after she left the program, she commented, "I understand why I felt alienated (. . .) but I have not figured out whether the experience means I should not do [study] sociology, or I should not do sociology at that university."

In correspondence with me up to the time this chapter was written, Virginia continued to struggle with how to identify herself professionally; with what further education she might pursue that would be more relevant to her interests in culturally diverse and underprivileged populations, yet that would still give her an influential voice; and with what discipline-specific language, practices, and values she felt comfortable with. Of one thing she was certain: "Having a Masters in sociology is not enough to get people to listen to the ideas of a young Puerto Rican woman."

Hence, wishing to add her voice at a more practical level within the power structure in the world of social science, she decided 2 years

173

after leaving her PhD program with a Masters degree to accept the offer of a scholarship for a second Masters in social work at an East Coast university. Just 25, with many years ahead of her in which to educate herself even further if she one day chose to, Virginia had opted to leave the theorists to their work and to move ahead with her own more concrete, here-and-now agenda. Those in charge of her sociology program missed the chance to let Virginia help them see the sociological world with a new set of lenses.

The Dilemma of Socialization and Cultural Diversity

Virginia's story is one of several like it in her first-year group. It could no doubt be retold endlessly in graduate social science programs across the United States where minority and foreign student populations are growing. In such programs, these students, and mainstream U.S. students as well, face the tasks of learning the language, values, and practices of the disciplinary (sub)communities in which they are immersed and of deciding which "intellectual village" they will designate as their primary professional residence. This is a normal part of the socialization process and is no easy task for anyone. But minority and foreign students face the possibility of being confronted with a disciplinary language and culture so distant from their own that to join such a culture would mean alienating themselves form other highly valued personal and occupational communities at home. Likewise, academic communities with inflexible disciplinary boundaries stand to lose the rich cultural resources in their midst.

We can confront this dilemma from the perspective of socialization into the disciplinary community, which works to maintain continuity of beliefs and practices, or from that of the culturally diverse population, who may find the standardized language, practices, and values irrelevant or alien. These two perspectives are incompatible and therefore not easily amenable to compromise.

From the Perspective of Socialization

From the first perspective, inherent in the concept of socialization is the notion that certain fundamental aspects of a community's life and ways of understanding the world need to be shared by all members. This sharing ensures that individual community members will be able to communicate, that work can be done that adds to community knowledge as well as to individual knowledge, and that standards exist for evaluating that knowledge. Moreover, core values and practices accumulate over many years and many generations; it is their continuity that gives shape to a discipline and that allows us to recognize that a group even exists. Additionally, without a common grounding in what the fundamental values and practices are, novices will not be able to contribute to the community in a productive way, where being productive can be defined not only as continuing a disciplinary tradition, but adding to and modifying it.

From the perspective of disciplinary socialization, novices are expected to shift and accommodate their interests and purposes (or, as those within the community might say, to expand and develop them) if they do not match those of the community. Nevertheless, with the sets of standard skills and values they acquire, they should be able to explore existing interests even if this requires refocusing them. Students from cultures outside that in which the disciplinary culture originated can thus be seen as acquiring skills for exploring their own worlds in ways they can then communicate to the discipline. In this way (the advocate of this view of disciplinary socialization would say), minorities and foreign students may do work within their own cultures that can then be shared with and evaluated by the larger community, with the result that the body of knowledge in the discipline may come to include culturally diverse perspectives.

Finally, from the perspective of disciplinary socialization, it can be argued that in most fields, particularly in the social sciences, numerous subtraditions exist. The individual who is not comfortable with one tradition should be encouraged to try another. Nevertheless, when the individual does find the appropriate group, the socialization process works as it should to shape language, thinking, understanding, perception, and values.

From the Perspective of Cultural Diversity

From the perspective of a culturally diverse graduate student population, other arguments can be put forth that counter those given above. In the first place, we can try to identify the source of a tradition or subtradition and question its fundamental relevance to culturally

175

diverse populations or issues. Just as many have criticized E. D. Hirsch (1988) for his narrowly conceived view of what Americans know and should know, in that the Americans he surveyed were primarily White male academics, so may we question a discipline like sociology that was born and shaped within the confines of the white European and American male academic community. In sociology (or whatever the discipline may be), the very problems that are used as exemplars, the values that are promulgated, and the methods that are employed emerge from a population that historically has had little interest in multicultural ways of understanding the world. What interest there has been takes the form of studies of non-White populations by White academics who impose their own agendas and arrive at their own interpretations. Given the tight hold that the White male academic has on many disciplines, it has been difficult for minorities (including women) and foreigners to make headway in influencing disciplines in any substantial way. This seems to be the case even when individuals from nonmainstream cultures attempt to play by the "White man's" rules.

It can also be argued that the standards of science, now a model for many of the social sciences, also represent a Western male tradition— one that values theory over practice, research over teaching, numbers over people, standardization over flexibility, objectivity over understanding, and abstractions over the concrete hustle and bustle of people's lives. This tradition, the proponent of cultural diversity may argue, cannot and should not be used as the model for investigating all aspects of our world, particularly of our social world. Its values and standards may simply be inappropriate when applied to situations that are not inherently quantifiable or amenable to categorization and precise definition or to situations that are perhaps more political and economic than they are scientific.[2] From this view, then, any sociology based on the model of the hard sciences embraces a world view that is fundamentally incompatible with its own subject matter—the lives, attitudes, and organizations of people. Other models (preferably more than one) should be followed that allow investigators to deal with the messiness of research into people' lives without feeling obligated to tidy and categorize and count, models where values such as creativity and nonstandardization are viewed more favorably. It may even be the case that there are no mature disciplines in the social sciences, in which case the whole notion of socialization into a defined group is a myth. Hence, to the extent that social sciences try to deny or constrain their inherent compatibility with diversity by applying models from the hard sciences, they constrain their own development.

Lastly, the argument can be made that the two notions of socialization and cultural diversity are at base antithetical. Because we cannot have it both ways, the whole enterprise of disciplines, with their exclusivity and their standardization, must be dismantled and replaced with a more pluralistic approach to understanding our world. In this view, the very separation of ways of knowing the world into disciplines feeds into an elitist power structure in which one way of knowing the world will always be perceived as more prestigious than others. Those who adopt the prestige model have the strongest voice; others will be left behind.

Toward a Resolution

The problem is, of course, that neither of these perspectives affords a happy solution to the dilemma of socialization and cultural diversity. Each excludes the positive attributes of the other. What we need to ask is whether it is possible for the phenomenon of socialization, grounded as it is in the notion of core language, values, and practices, to embrace cultural diversity in more meaningful ways than it did for Virginia in her PhD program and in fact to view it as a resource. Likewise, we need to ask whether the notion of cultural diversity can accommodate the need for some core language, values, and practices as a way to make knowledge and research manageable, teachable, and communicable. Our purpose in asking these questions should be to examine ways in which, in the long run, people from diverse linguistic and ethnic backgrounds might gain stronger voices than they presently have in helping to shape their disciplines.

I would like to argue first that field-specific groups, if not full-fledged disciplines, with their own specialized language, values, and practices, are here to stay in the social sciences, but that the scientific model inappropriately occupies the prestige position. Had Virginia and some of the other first-year students felt they were doing *social* science rather than science, they might have become more willing believers of the need to standardize some of the language and practices in the field. Shared language, values, and practices facilitate communication among group members and make it possible for bodies of work to build upon one another. But this is meaningful only when there is equal access by many different groups to a voice in the field, such as to its best journals and jobs, and when the field's knowledge base is allowed to be enriched by the addition of such new voices.

Secondly, individual students need to be given the opportunity to explore and nourish their interests from the very beginning of a doctoral program. In a sociology program, this will often mean that students are deeply committed to issues involving real people. In Virginia's case, as in that of many of her classmates, learning about theory would have been more relevant had the ideas and issues of women, minorities, and multicultural populations been addressed. This could have been done, I believe, within a quasiscientific framework if examples, discussions, and occasional readings had included them, and if frequent suggestions had been made as to how to apply abstract theoretical notions to concrete, real-life situations. It was not a problem that theory itself was conceptualized as general and ahistorical (not committed to particular times and places), but that examples of particulars within the framework of the theories were not regularly drawn from students' own backgrounds. With meaningful examples taken from different cultures, students like Virginia would have found the hook to draw them into the world of the theorists. Similarly, if the professors had avoided very esoteric home-grown jargon and had attempted to translate concepts into everyday terms, many more students would have been drawn into the subject matter and the discussion of sociological theory from the beginning of the core course sequence. Eventually, moreover, the theories themselves might have been enriched as students like Virginia enter the professional world.

Thirdly, students like Virginia need to work with established faculty who share both the training of the community and the interests of minority and multicultural populations. In Virginia's case, an African American professor, trained in the same program, turned out to be one of the few people she felt took a personal interest in her: He helped her in great detail with the revision of her Theory Construction paper and, later in the methods classes, provided her with a meaningful database from which to write her methods papers and learn statistical procedures. Virginia's most valuable learning experiences took place as a result of her contact with this professor and with the methods professor who allowed her to use this database rather than the one other students were using. The African American professor, however, learned he would probably not receive tenure, and made the difficult decision to leave the university for a position elsewhere. Had he stayed, Virginia said she might have returned to this program.

For their part, the other professors could have learned more about the cultures and culture-specific goals of their students. The two theory professors, for instance, believed Virginia to be a Chicana until well into the academic year, when in interviews with them I reminded them that her background was Puerto Rican. In a small, culturally diverse program, such ignorance is hardly excusable. Core-course professors, then, as well as advisors, need to ask the following questions: Who are their students? Where are they from and what are some of the basic values and goals they hold? For what do they wish to use their sociology? Will they be working in the Bronx, Korea, China, or the Hispanic Southwest? How might key concepts and skills be presented in ways that students from such diverse backgrounds would find relevant?

Finally, well-established programs in the social sciences need to re-evaluate themselves and their goals in light of the populations they serve. A program that admits half or more of its doctoral students from outside the mainstream White middle-class culture needs to consider seriously the question of how relevant its socialization practices are to a culturally diverse group. If certain skills and values are deemed fundamental, how can they be transmitted more meaningfully to people who may have no inherent interest in the intellectual inventions of White males? Similarly, if such programs are committed to educating culturally diverse populations, they should also be committed to breaking down barriers that exist for such populations in hiring and publishing practices. This will mean, in no uncertain terms, taking the risk of breaking with tradition. Socialization must come to be seen as an interactive process in which tradition and standardization do not prevent change from multicultural sources, but provide the foundation for it.

Summary

In this chapter, the relationship between academic socialization and cultural diversity is discussed. A case study of a Hispanic woman, Virginia, in a doctoral program in sociology is used to highlight several fundamental issues in the socialization of a culturally diverse graduate student population. One of these is language. A second issue concerns ways of knowing and understanding the world, both of which are revealed in a community's language and practices. A third issue concerns the perceptions of community members as to who shapes the

179

field. In all three of these aspects, Virginia's sociology program can be characterized by its scientific, "White male" flavor. Over the academic year, Virginia came to feel increasingly out of place in this sociology subcommunity because its language and values seemed to alienate her from the community in which she had grown up and wished to work. She perceived that the language was too abstract to deal with concrete real-life issues, that the scientific way of knowing was lacking in human elements, and that the people who controlled the (sub)field were uninterested in issues of race and gender. The chapter concludes with several perspectives on the dilemma of socialization and cultural diversity, which seem to be fundamentally incompatible. With some adjustments in the educational setting, however, students like Virginia might find socialization experiences less alienating and better suited for nourishing their interests in things human.

Acknowledgment

I would like to thank the National Council of Teachers of English (NCTE) for a research grant that partially funded this project.

Discussion Topic and Projects

1. What characteristics of the specialized language and associated values and ways of knowing can you identify in the program in which you are studying (or have studied) or the field in which you are working? To what extent and in what ways are the specialized language and ways of knowing brought to the conscious attention of community members?

2. Consider the three perspectives of socialization discussed in this chapter: language, ways of knowing, and power and prestige. What socialization experiences have you had that can be highlighted from these perspectives? What other aspects of your socialization stand out as significant?

3. In some ways, learning the specialized language of a discipline or profession is like learning a second language. In an English-speaking university setting, native and nonnative English speakers alike need to learn this language. Assuming advanced competence on the part of the nonnative English speakers, do native English speakers necessarily hold an advantage in this situation? What examples can you find from your own education?

4. Given your understanding of socialization at the graduate level, what do you believe to be the responsibilities of a graduate program to a culturally diverse population?

5. With one or more classmates, make a list of the specialized language used in your program to talk and write about key issues in your field (theory, methods, and so forth). Include specialized symbols and specialized ways of displaying knowledge in writing. Characterize this language as best you can and try to interpret the values and the world view, or way of knowing, that is embodied in it.

6. If you and others in your program form a culturally diverse group, devise a questionnaire or a short structured interview that is designed to elicit a multicultural view of what it is like to be socialized into your disciplinary subfield. If possible, compare the views of students who are relatively new to the program or field with those who have been in it for a while. Draw on categories from this chapter if you wish or devise your own categories. Pay particular attention to socialization

phenomena in the academic culture that seem to clash with other aspects and levels of culture in students' lives.

7. Interview a native and nonnative English-speaking student in your program and one professor. Compare the three opinions on what the role of the graduate program should be in socializing students from different cultures into a disciplinary community.

Further Reading

For a sociolinguistic view of the many ways in which language reflects social norms, see John Gumperz (1972). Two classic qualitative studies of the socialization of medical students are Robert Merton, George Reader, and Patricia Kendall's (1957) *The Student-Physician: Introductory Studies in the Sociology of Medical Education*, and Becker, Geer, Hughes, and Strauss's (1961) *Boys in White: Student Culture in Medical School*. Geertz (1983, Chapter 7), in his usual rich literary style, discusses perspectives from which to understand the academic community. Fascinating analyses of texts in different academic communities have been undertaken by Bazerman (1981) and Hansen (1988), and the experiences of undergraduates learning to write in different academic communities have been documented by Anne Herrington (1985), Stephen North (1986), and Lucille McCarthy (1987). Few studies exist of the socialization of graduate students, but several that focus on the role of writing in this process are John Ackerman (1991), Carol Berkenkotter, Thomas Huckin, and John Ackerman (1988), Christine Pearson Casanave (1990), Elaine Chin (1991), and Paul Prior (1991). With the exception of Casanave (1990), studies of the graduate socialization of multicultural student populations have not yet been systematically undertaken. Ruth Spack (1988) takes a strong stand against what she calls "initiating ESL students into the academic discourse community" (p. 30), a position that we should continue to examine as we learn more about how students of all kinds interact with such communities.

8

Toward Developing a Cultural Repertoire

A Case Study of a Lao College Freshman

Ann M. Johns
San Diego State University, California

I'm a Lao. I'm proud I'm a Lao. I live in the United States, but that
doesn't mean I can't be a Lao . . . go to my temple and speak my
language. I don't reject my people for anything else.

A university freshman spoke these words. Grounded in her first
culture, she was determined to succeed in U.S. academic culture
as well. Like many culturally and linguistically diverse students in
English-speaking countries, she derived her core values, language,
family, and friends from her own culture, and her first loyalties and
emotional ties will always be to her Lao heritage. Because she lives in
the United States, however, she wants to acquire other cultures so
that she can survive and succeed. This is the story of her initial contacts
with a U.S. university and her efforts to add an academic culture
without compromising herself or her core values.

Studies of Freshmen

The subject of this case study was a freshman college student in my English class at San Diego State University (SDSU). She was part of a group of 20 "at risk," culturally diverse freshmen assigned to a bridging program of reading, writing, and study skills classes, all satellites to Cultural Anthropology 102. The subject was one of several students interviewed in an on-going project to study the challenges, successes, and frustrations of culturally diverse students entering a large university. Similar projects exist on a number of university campuses (See, e.g., Brinton, 1990).

We decided to interview students at this point in their academic careers because the freshman year at a university represents one of the major literacy transitions in a student's academic life. In any literacy transition, language users "must . . . master the ways of speaking, reading and writing that are appropriate to the new community" (Berkenkotter, Huckin, & Ackerman, 1988, p. 12). The transition into tertiary education can be particularly difficult (Johns, 1990). As a result, the overall dropout rate after freshman year at large comprehensive universities is generally more than 30%; it tends to be even higher among culturally diverse students (Sprotte, 1990).

There are a number of reasons for this sizable dropout rate. One reason, certainly, is the new literacy challenges at the university level (Carson, Chose, & Gibson, 1990). In many cases, for example, this is the students' first exposure to formal lectures requiring note-taking. Students often don't understand why they are taking notes, and they lack the skills to take them effectively and efficiently enough for use in papers and on examinations. New reading challenges are also presented. High school reading experiences are generally from a limited number of genres, for example, novels and textbooks. In their first college year, students may be assigned law cases, monographs, historiography, and disciplinary essays, among other genres. They also may be required to write papers in a variety of new formats, for example, case studies and critiques (Horowitz, 1986a). Writing assignments tend to differ in each class, thus causing confusion for students most familiar with the five-paragraph essay (Kroll, 1979). Lucille McCarthy (1987), speaking of the writing assignments in these early university years, notes that her case study of a native-speaking White student

> adds to existing research which suggests that school writing is not a monolithic activity or global skill. Rather, the contexts for writing may

184

be so different from one classroom to another, . . . that the courses may be for the student writer like so many foreign countries. (pp. 260–261)

Studying for examinations is often challenging as well because students must integrate information from the lectures, the readings, and class discussions; and, from it all, they must decide what is important and control the information well enough to reformulate it in a timed examination response.

In addition to literacy demands, there are factors relating to classroom organization and power relationships that can make this transition to university work challenging. In many high schools, students are able to negotiate classroom activities and change assignments. There are situations in which students openly circumvent a teacher's plans and modify the classroom agenda:

> Students may make mistakes, which may alternately be classed as moves in a different game. Instead of being an incompetent move in the teacher's game, the behavior in question may be a very sophisticated move in a students' game, a move calculated to manipulate the teacher's normative arrangements to accomplish items on the students' agenda. (Mehan, 1980, p. 147)

In addition, most high school teachers educated in language pedagogy and child development provide guidance for students in completing classroom tasks. Barbara Rogoff and William Gardner (1984) examined the educational interactions between mothers and children in which a mother guides a child-novice in performing a task, allowing for trial attempts and responding appropriately to requests for help. Arthur Applebee (1981), who investigated the interactions between teachers and secondary school students, also noted this guiding-responding relationship, which he, and others, call *scaffolding*, that is, "providing support which allows a child to engage in a task which would otherwise be too difficult while also learning general procedures which eventually make the support unnecessary" (p. 8). Frederick Erickson (1988) refers to scaffolding in the public schools as

> a matter of social relations as well as of subject matter content. In everyday teaching scenes . . . the scaffolding relationship is jointly

constructed. The child has [the] right to ask for a range of kinds of help. (p. 215)

In university classes, however, new students may be in for a rude shock because many faculty provide little of the guidance or scaffolding to which Applebee and Erickson allude. There are a number of reasons for this difference in attitude, when it exists. One is previous education: High school instructors may be taught to guide and scaffold in education classes. University faculty are, for the most part, taught nothing about pedagogical approaches in their PhD programs; their major concern is covering the content. University instructors do not scaffold for other reasons, as well. In my several years as a university writing-across-the-curriculum director, I discovered that most faculty believe that providing models for writing and examination tasks and offering guidance in completing assignments is tantamount to teaching remedial courses and giving away high grades. ("I'm not lowering my standards!" they assert.) Many university faculty argue that those students who cannot catch on without guidance should not be enrolled in the university in the first place.

To compound these difficulties, freshman students find that many so-called introductory classes in which they are enrolled are not introductory at all. Much prior knowledge of the discipline, of Western culture and values, and of sophisticated "rules of use" (Hymes, 1980, p. 11) are assumed by the faculty and by the readings that they assign (Benson, 1991).

These differences between high school and college and between faculty and students can result in frustration and disappointment for all of those involved. Students generally blame themselves for their difficulties, claiming that they are "dumb" or that they have poor high school preparation. Most faculty tend to blame students for their poor academic performance. They complain of student "illiteracy": of their inability to read, of their lack of planning in writing, and of their poor vocabulary (Johns, 1991a).

Because my colleagues and I are concerned about student failure and self-esteem, and because we would like to raise faculty awareness, we have undertaken a series of case studies of culturally diverse freshmen in order to determine factors contributing to their frustrations and to their successes. Because we can learn most from successes, I am presenting here a case study of one student who seems to be beating the odds.

One Case Study: A Lao Freshman

Tic, the subject of the study discussed here, is a friendly, outspoken, and hard-working Lao student. Because of her willingness to talk, her mature manner, and, most importantly, her determination to succeed at the university, I selected her as a subject for one of our case studies. During her first semester, I interviewed her for 20 minutes each week, observed her in Cultural Anthropology, and collected all of her papers: her essays for the adjunct English classes, her examinations and projects for her anthropology class, and her various reflective essays written for her portfolio throughout the semester.

Like many recent refugees, Tic's education has been scanty and interrupted; in fact, she had had few school experiences before coming to the United States. Her family was very poor after their escape from Laos. Stranded in Thailand, she had sold fruits and vegetables on the street for 6 years to support her mother and sister, as her father had died immediately after the family arrived in Thailand. On her arrival in the United States at 13, when she began junior high, she had experienced fewer than 4 years of formal schooling, all of which were in Thai medium (ages 6–12) schools.

Tic's first responsibilities in the United States were to what remained of her family. Her mother had arranged for her sister to marry a Lao man living here to make it possible for the family to immigrate. Tic and her mother lived in a small house with this sister and brother-in-law. During the semester in which she was my student, Tic was under considerable pressure from her mother to marry an established, older Lao, "because they are calling me (at 18 years) a loose woman" and because the mother was disappointed with the low salary that her current son-in-law was making at his airport job. This in-law also had expectations: Because Tic had learned to be a good salesperson in Thailand, he had bought a number of toys in Mexico for her to sell at swap meets during the evenings and on Saturdays.

None of the members of her immediate family saw a value in prolonging the education of this young woman or realized that if she achieved her goal, to receive a BA in accounting, she might be able to raise their standard of living. Yet there were people in her community and at her temple who encouraged her to continue; and her own feeling of self-worth and pride in her culture and accomplishments, inspired by years of adversity, kept her going.

When she entered my class, Tic had already experienced considerable academic success. In high school, she quickly learned enough English to be able to use it for her purposes and was often encouraged by her favorite English as a second language (ESL) teacher to express herself: "I could write about what I wanted to. The teacher liked to hear my stories." Tic had already passed the university entrance writing competency examination, though her written language still evidenced a number of sentence-level errors. She was beginning to exhibit strategies for success in her university classes, strategies that eventually earned her *A* grades.

The purpose of our interviews was to determine what made Tic successful in school, what enabled her to succeed and enjoy her success despite numerous outside pressures, limited knowledge of Western culture, and a limited formal education. Many of the diverse students at SDSU, particularly women, experience the ambivalence within families that Tic experienced; yet their survival in a new culture is often enhanced by the core values of their first cultures, values that may not be held by their immediate families but are passed down through the elders, the religious leaders, and the oral and written traditions of the community.

Why did Tic do well during her first semester, when many of her U.S. classmates were experiencing difficulty? First of all, she took her education very seriously because "in my culture, we think being educated is very important." Along with other new immigrants in the class, principally Hispanics, she felt that native speakers took their education too much for granted: "These American kids, they don't know how lucky they are and they don't take a lot of this seriously." She never cut a class; she listened carefully throughout the lectures for the subtleties that other students missed ("In anthropology, the most important stuff he says at the very end [of the lecture]."), and took copious notes, which she reorganized immediately after each lecture. She set aside time in her busy schedule to study, and she was always prepared with her reading before the lecture. She didn't want to miss anything, often asking me or a classmate to define words or phrases from the lectures.

There is a copious contrastive-rhetoric literature, beginning with Robert Kaplan's famous (1966) "doodles" article and continuing with John Hinds' (1987) work, indicating that some cultures require readers and listeners to be more responsible than others; that is, it is the responsibility of the reader or listener to puzzle out a discourse because the writer/speaker may present important information in a subtle or round-about manner. Coming from a more reader/listener-responsible culture than her U.S.-born classmates, Tic demonstrated that she was a very proficient receptor. She was able to digest and restructure much more from the lectures than most other students, and, because of her study habits, she could remember and interpret lectures that she had heard several weeks before.

In addition to paying careful attention to the new discourses to which she was exposed, Tic enjoyed her academic experiences, particularly if she could interpret and exploit them to meet her needs and interests. She explained that from the first time she began reading and writing in English, she looked for information and assignments that interested her and that related to her life and culture. In high school, she was assigned a term paper in her favorite ESL class, the class in which the teacher encouraged her to "tell her stories." After seeing a film on the Holocaust, she decided to write this paper on that topic, "Because these people had a very hard time, like me, and they had to come to America and start again so I thought it would be interesting to write about." In the anthropology class, each student was to complete a data-based project. There were a number of possibilities: participant-observation of a religious service, bathroom graffiti analysis, a proxemics project, or a life history. Tic chose to do a life history, that is, to report on an interview detailing the adaptation strategies of an individual (outside of her own culture) who had immigrated to the United States in adulthood. Searching for something that would appeal to her, she first chose to interview a Lao, "because it's important to remember our history and our culture and all . . . and that's what I know best." However, for good reason, the professor would not negotiate the task parameters, maintaining that if Tic were to understand research in anthropology, she had to take a relativist attitude toward the "other" and interview someone outside of her primary culture.

Tic was determined to make the project meaningful to her, despite the failure of her attempt to negotiate the task with the instructor. She found a middle-aged Vietnamese man in adult school; although working at a menial hospital job, he was a doctor and aspired to professional employment. He wasn't a Lao, but she sympathized with his plight because "I could understand his problems. I felt sorry for him because he is never going to make it but he hopes."

She also found interest and relevance in most of her reading and lectures, even about people as distant as the hunter-gatherers of the Kalahari or the horticulturalists of the Amazon. During our interviews, she would remark "Now isn't that interesting!" or make a comparison with what she knew, "That sounds like X," when we would discuss a topic. Whereas some other students in Cultural Anthropology 102 showed little interest in the topics they studied, viewing them as irrelevant to finishing college and making money, Tic seemed to derive pleasure from it all: studying, testing herself through the exams, writing the project, and, of course, receiving high grades for her efforts.

Deborah Brandt (1990), in *Literacy as Involvement: The Acts of Writers, Readers and Texts,* claims that literacy is not found in texts themselves but in reader/writer interaction and involvement: "Literacy requires learning how to become purely and attentively entangled" (p. 67). Tic is a good example of such a growing literacy. Her pleasure in learning guaranteed a personal investment in the subjects she studied, beyond the basic memorizing of material for examinations that was common among her classmates.

Tic persevered and listened; she related her academic experiences to her own life and found pleasure in making those connections. In addition, she attempted to make analogies between current and past academic tasks, even if they were only tangentially related. She remembered that her favorite high school English teacher "emphasized on analyzing, looking for something that it's supposed to mean. I did lots of analysis for English class. . . ." When her anthropology project required analysis, she was able to transfer that skill to a new kind of task, something that many novice university students have difficulty doing (Johns, 1990). Thus, after writing about the interview for her life histories project, Tic said she thought that some analysis in the conclusion would help: "You know, something about what happened in their life that determines who they are."

When preparing for essay examinations in anthropology, her focus was also upon making analogies. She could deconstruct the prompt in a sophisticated manner, remembering how the professor had presented an issue in class: "In this question, he was asking us to list three reasons . . . , in this essay he was asking for us to compare." After the first examination, she could predict both topics and essay prompt types from her previous experiences. She also realized that she must plan her essay-taking time, especially because she wasn't a native speaker of English. After one test, she said, "I had a lot to say about the Yanomamo and I could integrate and all that but I had to end writing and go on to the short answer and multiple choice that I don't like because I had to get lots of points."

In his chapter entitled "Whose Culture? Whose Literacy?", Keith Walters (this book) argues that E. D. Hirsch and his colleagues define literacy principally as the mastery of a body of facts and values re-flecting "monoculturalism." Walters contends that Hirsch's view discriminates against the diverse students in our schools and is inappropriate for the future of the United States and other English-speaking countries (see also Ballard & Clanchy, n.d.). Tic's approach to adding a new literacy is much more sophisticated than that implied by Hirsch. She knows that she does not share the background knowledge of the American-born students in her classroom; she also knows that her written and spoken English are far from perfect on the sentence level. Thus, she has developed other, more efficient ways to acquire the new culture: She looks for underlying structures and concepts rather than concentrating upon the facts alone. The information in any course is useless, she has discovered, if it is not related to the core values, concepts, and structures of the discipline. In this endeavor, she was aided by her anthropology instructor, who provided more scaffolding and guidance in understanding the discipline than any general education instructor I've encountered during my 6 years in the program. He selected a textbook that focused on concepts, and he repeated core concepts and values in his lectures. Despite his efforts, many of the students failed to understand that he was building a "history of the discipline" (Nelson, 1990, p. 365), and they continued to attempt to struggle with unrelated facts. Tic, on the other hand, listened carefully to her instructor's emphases and followed his lead.

Throughout the course, Tic continued to develop her abilities to search for concepts central to the discipline and for ways of thinking that would enable her to organize her study and her reading and writing. Her notes were organized around the course concepts, and her study was based upon the relationship between concepts and examples, one of the most critical aspects of academic literacy, as identified by university faculty (Johns, 1991a). Therefore, when the anthropology professor asked during the final examination review for an identification of core concepts, it was Tic who knew them all, and who, with some embarrassment, reiterated them to him in front of his large class.

Her focus on concepts led her to concentrate upon other organizing principles as well, such as macrostructures of texts, a skill that would enable her to produce writing in genres with which she had been unfamiliar (See Benson, 1991). She realized that "deciding how to write is hard for me because I haven't written as much as the American kids, so I always decide carefully what I'm going to do. I choose the project or essay that has structure." Because, like many university faculty, her anthropology instructor was reluctant to give too much assistance in producing papers, she listened carefully for any guidance that was offered. With some trepidation, the anthropology instructor distributed a student paper from a previous life histories project "as a good example, but not to be copied from" and provided some hints for conducting the interview, "with really broad questions, like 'Tell me about your coming to the United States'." Therefore, Tic had two good reasons to choose the life histories project: "I liked it because it would make me think about my life, and I kind of knew where to start because you don't start chronologically or anything."

In the first draft of her paper, her project introduction was similar to the professor's example; but her goals, organization of the data, and analysis were very much her own: "I just needed some help to get started and then I went OK." She was sensitive to the fact that the professor "didn't want me to copy [from his student example]," but that he also had a text structure in his mind, based upon anthropological research, that would determine the criteria for grading, though he did not reveal these criteria to the students.[1] After writing her rough draft, Tic asked me to help her with tightening up the final version, evidencing faith in my ability to understand "what the teacher wants." I finally conceded, although at first I had refused to help, attempting to use the standard "writing process approach" by requiring her to share the draft with her fellow students for peer editing. However, she didn't have much faith in peer review of a paper for an academic class, "because they [the students] don't get the structure. Sometimes they don't know as much as me."

Tic also kept the structure and concepts of the class in mind when completing essay examinations. As she studied, she looked over previous examinations for the organization required by the prompts, then related the required organization to the class concepts. When she felt that she had developed a good sample question, she practiced writing out a response. This practice led to a kind of automaticity that is the bane of process-oriented writing teachers (Raimes, 1985) but is of great importance to the success of some ESL students when they must write quickly at a high conceptual level (Johns, 1991b).

Related to Tic's ability to benefit from past experiences and her interest in relating the concepts and structures of the courses in which she was enrolled was her uncanny grasp of audience. Though she could not articulate why her ability to "psych out" her faculty audience was so keen, it is my hypotheses that she draws from her cultural values for this competence. In her culture, where there is great respect for traditional education, the teacher is the sole source of information and insights (Scollon & Scollon, 1981); therefore, Tic's sensitivity to "what the teacher wants" is probably keener than that of some of the students whose only education has been in U.S. schools.

One aspect of this audience awareness was her sensitivity to disciplinary vocabulary. Tic was aware that her anthropology instructor expected her to use "just the right words," to sound like an anthropologist and to "understand what anthropology was about." She attempted throughout the class to understand how the specialized terms could be integrated with the concepts and examples and with the questions that anthropologists raise. This developing "understanding of the history of the class itself" (Nelson, 1990, p. 365) was of great assistance to her throughout the semester. It was she, for example, who immediately caught onto the juxtaposition of relativism and ethnocentrism in anthropology and who understood from the class films that anthropologists in the 1990s must have new responsibilities to their subjects. She integrated her understanding of the discipline and its vocabulary and concepts on the final examination, and she was rewarded for her efforts.

Her sense of audience also enabled her to realize that her anthropology professor would not penalize her for her sentence-level errors on examination responses.[2] She knew that for him, content, organization, and understanding of the discipline were much more important than grammar and mechanics. Therefore, she took no time to correct her work as she sped through the examinations. In other classes, and in her anthropology papers, she monitored her writing more carefully. In my adjunct English class, she was particularly aware of syntax and morphology because English teachers "care about all of your verbs and stuff." There were still a number of errors in her writing, however, perhaps because she felt that certain grammatical features of language, for example, the third person singular *s* morpheme, were not important to meaning. I often found an *ed* missing from a past participle ("My attitude towards life and future also have change") or from a past tense verb ("I learn to and experienced the pressures that have been put upon me by my peers and family"); and I discovered a number of other sentence-level errors as well. Nonetheless, I could be assured that she would carefully edit for metadiscourse features such as connectors, validity markers (*perhaps*) and narrators (*according to*).[3] For example, she concluded with an essential conjunct in her reflective essay for her portfolio: "*Therefore* this paper shows that I was wrong in thinking that my future would be so easy" (emphasis mine). No doubt even her English teachers have been so impressed by her sense of organization, metadiscourse features, and essay development that the sentence-level errors, often unnecessary for deriving meaning, have been ignored.

In her (1990) essay entitled "This Was an Easy Assignment," Jennie Nelson notes that "successful student writers are, above all, sensitive decision-makers. They are able to size up a writing situation and adapt their goals and approaches to meet the demands of different classroom contexts" (p. 388). Tic's approaches to writing (and thinking) in anthropology and in English provide evidence for the mature and effective decision-making of which Nelson speaks.

Conclusion

Tic may fail in her attempts to keep her first culture and add an academic one. She has experienced great pressures from her family to leave the university, pressures that are somewhat different from those of some other culturally diverse students, especially males, whose parents make great sacrifices to ensure their schooling. Thus, even though her first semester was successful, it was also a sobering experience, as her responsibilities and the realities of her life closed in upon her.

In her reflection for her personal essay, assigned as part of the class portfolio assessment, she wrote:

> The paper "Where I Am Now" is a reflection of my experiences and what I have learned at San Diego State because I have grown academically and maturely in taking my education more seriously than ever. My attitude towards life and future also change. I no longer think life would be so easy and freedom that I have to think and make my own decisions will not always be mine. I learn to and experience the pressures that have been put on me by my peers and family. After I have written "Where I Am Now," I began to loose my confidence of what I thought my life in the future will be like because in one month, I have experience more frustration and pressures than any student would have experience in their whole life.

Though she was frustrated, there were other factors that gave her confidence and the will to continue. For example, the strategies and skills discussed here were very satisfying to her. She was aware of these strategies and mentioned a few, with some pride, in the second reflective essay from her portfolio:

> The second paper that I choose to write my reflective essay is that project I did for Anthropology 102. This project's main objective is to explore the ways an individual adapts to the change in culture socially, economically and spiritual. This project demonstrates my abilities to organize and analyze which I have learned in this semester to be very important and are necessary to succeed at any university. The project also reflects that I have learned to follow the criterias that the profesor expects me to have a knowledge of.

> In summary, the both papers that I choose in writing this essay show my changes in attitude about life through the experiences that have faced this semester. They also demonstrate my ability to analyze and organize my written works.

Tic's initial successes in the university can be attributed to a number of personal and cultural characteristics. She was quite emotional and unanalytic about her family and her first culture, and she was concerned that the recent demands by her family would mold a future not of her own choosing. However, the second culture, that of U.S. academic life, is one upon which she could look intellectually and with pleasure. She could manipulate some of her academic experiences for her own purposes, following her own intellectual instincts rather than attempting to memorize the required vocabulary mindlessly (cf. Hirsch, Kett, & Trefil, 1988). Her rational approach to cultural acquisition enabled her to stand back and examine the rules—rules that enabled her to make analogies about tasks, to understand the nature of higher order thinking skills (e.g., analyzing), to exploit models and to structure new discourse. She found pleasure in coming to terms with this foreign culture and its distant faculty. Going to school was a treat after years of adversity, and she was determined to be gratified by each school experience. Her intellectual stance and her determination to derive pleasure released Tic from a slavish adaptation to a new culture, which leaders from her first culture may fear.

Tic demonstrated that she could maintain her voice as a person and as a Lao, yet she could vary that voice to meet the needs of the new sociocultural situation. She looked for tasks that meant something to her and to which she could bring her past experiences. She empathized with people outside of her culture, like the Jews of the Holocaust, and she was able to use that empathy to construct academic papers. When she realized that she couldn't write a life history about one of her own people for anthropology, she found someone with whose life she could identify, and she brought to her final anthropology project her empathy for someone "who is middle-aged and can't get ahead in America."

Many refugees in the United States are involved in a balancing act, attempting to satisfy the requirements of their primary cultures and of their families and to succeed in new lives within a demanding new environment. Time will tell whether Tic can balance the demands upon her life. She may marry the middle-aged Lao man her mother has chosen and become a housewife, selling toys at the swap meets.[4] However, Tic is also aware that the general values of her culture, if not of her family, favor education. Thus she may, in fact, be successful in becoming a "good" Lao woman, while adding the U.S. academic language and rules to her repertoire.

Tic is the kind of student who would please both literacy camps, those who believe that students can and should have primary power over their academic lives and literacy (see Bizzell, 1987; Spack, 1988) and those who believe that in order to succeed in a university, students must, first of all, understand the academic rules and be given a chance to play by them (Horowitz, 1986b; Swales & Horowitz, 1988). She is an excellent example of a student who can build cultural and linguistic repertoires, adding an academic culture without diminishing herself or her cultural values.

Implications for Instruction

Some of what Tic knows and values cannot be taught. However, there are other features of Tic's success that could become an integral part of any English for academic purposes (EAP) curriculum, a curriculum that can, in my view, be best realized through an adjunct program such as the one in which Tic was enrolled during her freshman year at SDSU.[5] Important to the success of any EAP program is the realization by all instructors that the students' cultural and linguistic diversity can be a positive force in their success. Like many of our diverse students, Tic brought to the classroom useful values, for example, a respect for education, a keen sense of audience, and a strong ego. Unlike some of the other students I have interviewed, she understood her own learning strategies (e.g., the need to practice writing essay examinations) and her strengths as an individual. Our principal responsibility as teachers is to assist our students in recognizing and enhancing their abilities, rather than insisting that they adopt strategies that have been discovered as successful in native speaker populations (e.g., as discussed by Carey, Flower, Hayes, Shriver, & Haas, 1980).

One of my objections to most codified approaches to "the writing process" is that ESL teachers attempt to make students into clones of successful native speakers. Teachers force students into peer review, when, in fact, it may be useless for some academic tasks because, as Tic points out, peers "don't understand what the teacher wants." The idea of practicing (and, in some cases, memorizing) essay examination responses (Johns, 1991b), a strategy that Tic and others have found successful, would be forbidden by many process advocates. It is my contention that rather than impose native speaker "rules," we should encourage diverse students to do what works for them, whether it is theoretically correct at this point in time or not.

A second teaching implication relates to the nature of cultural literacy and how it can be enhanced. If academic literacy requires gaining complete control of the standard grapholect and a specified body of facts (Hirsch et al., 1988), then Tic and many of her multicultural friends will never be literate. However, she and others are demonstrating that success in academic classes, which should require the "accepted" literacy, can still be achieved. For Tic, literacy is not acquired through a kind of digital learning, that is, memorizing of facts, but through creating a private view of disciplinary scaffolding, by identifying concepts, looking for structure, comparing assigned tasks with previous tasks, and developing a keen sense of audience. Beyond this, successful students involve themselves in the literacy experience, personalizing the tasks as much as possible and finding pleasure in the experience.

In EAP classes, adjunct classes in particular, instructors can assist student in recognizing concepts of an academic discipline, tying them to examples, and building a network of learning that assists them in reading, recalling, and producing texts (See Carrell, Pharis, & Liberto, 1989). Using models of new genres for reference, asking students to relate present tasks to previous ones, and requiring them to visually portray and integrate the topics and concepts of a discipline are all useful in building academic repertoires.

Thus, it seems that our most important tasks in assisting diverse students to survive in university are to encourage their own successful strategies and values, enhance their involvement in the disciplines, and provide the scaffolding and guidance that many university professors seem unwilling to give. Most of all, we need to listen carefully to our students because it is from them that we can gain insights into how individuals from diverse cultures successfully add new cultures to their repertoires.

Summary

This chapter describes a case study of a Lao university freshman who was successfully adding the rules of use of an academic discipline to her cultural repertoire without compromising herself or the values of her first culture. It discusses the various attitudes and strategies that led to her success: her ability to listen and interpret new discourse; her attempts to make each assignment meaningful and relevant to her life; her talent for making analogies between current assignments and those made in previous classes; her search for concepts and terms central to the discipline in order to create a mental map, her sense of text moves and macrostructures; and her audience analysis skills.

The study provides evidence for what instructors have always known: Academic literacy does not require the mere memorization of a body of information or a set of values. Instead, it requires an assurance of self and first culture that can be juxtaposed to the second, and an ability to see through apparently isolated facts to the basic concepts and mental structures that drive a discipline.

Discussion Topics and Projects

1. This case study examines attitudes and strategies of one successful student. What other successful tactics do students use? Think about your own student experience. What reading, listening, speaking, and writing activities assisted you to understand a discipline and to demonstrate that understanding in assignments and examinations?

2. Johns argues that teachers "should encourage diverse students to do what works for them, whether it is theoretically correct at this point in time or not." Do you agree? Or are there certain strategies employed by students that should be discouraged?

3. What assignments can an ESL or content teacher give to students to encourage successful strategies? How should they take notes? How should they approach their reading? How should they approach writing assignments?

4. What attitudes and beliefs are detrimental to the successful addition of a culture such as the one described in this anthropology class? What instructor attitudes obstruct students? What attitudes do students bring that may inhibit their motivations?

5. Can most students develop diverse cultural repertoires without damaging their relationship with their first cultures? Must we shed many of our first culture values before successfully taking on others?

6. Conduct a study of an academic classroom, using questionnaires, interviews, student writing (especially journals), faculty reports and any other methods that seem to be viable. You might pose research questions such as the following:

   a. What do students perceive as the rules of the discipline in general and this class in particular?

   b. How do they interpret the cultural data they collect in the classroom and from their readings?

   c. What do they perceive as the instructor's objectives for them as students?

   d. How do they deconstruct the assignments written by the academic instructors?

e. What types of problems did they face when they attempt to understand the lectures or readings?

f. What cognitive or affective goals do they have? How do they operationalize these?

g. What linguistic, conceptual, or cultural problems do they face?

h. How do they make the concepts, terms, or assignments their own?

i. How do they perceive their instructor (as an audience)?

7. Conduct your own case study of a student whose culture is not well represented among the teachers in your academic institution. Either use a scripted interview or use a nondirective approach, that is, merely asking the student on a regular basis how the class is going.

If you choose to use a script, you might want to try the following questions (after you have determined a considerable amount about the student's background and previous educational experiences):

a. What's most important in the class? Listening, reading, speaking or writing? How do you know? How do you successfully perform the important skills?

b. What is the purpose of this reading? Who is it written for? How do you know? How do you go about understanding this reading? How do you relate it to the lecture?

c. What problems or questions are important to the discipline you are studying? How do you know? What do you do to relate these problems or questions to your studying and writing?

d. How do you go about preparing to write an assignment or examination? How do you write? When you have time to revise, what do you do?

e. Can you relate what is said and done in the class to your life or first culture? If so, how?

8. Perform a careful, complete description (see, e.g., Doheny-Farina, 1986; Goetz & LeCompte, 1984) of one or several academic classrooms. What's going on there? What is the importance, in your view, of the lecture? How is the lecture organized? What kinds of questions are asked? Are questions encouraged? How do students respond to the

lecture or the class atmosphere? What and how much does the instructor tell you about the discipline?

9. With a partner, devise some classroom activities that will enhance the learning of students about academic disciplines. Why do you think these exercises will be successful?

Try out the activities, then ask students to assess them. Did they understand your instructions? Did they understand what motivated the activities? Did they believe that the exercises were useful?

Further Reading

For discussions of academic literacy and university freshmen, see Sarah Benesch (1988) *Ending Remediation: Linking ESL and Content in Higher Education.* A presentation of literacy acquisition from a process orientation is provided by Deborah Brandt (1990) in her *Literacy as Involvement: The Acts of Writers, Readers and Texts.* There is an excellent "Educational Perspectives" section in the more general volume *Perspectives on Literacy,* edited by E. R. Kintgen, B. M. Kroll, & M. Rose (1988).

Academic discourse communities and their characteristic genres are well presented in John M. Swales' (1990) *Genre Analysis: English in Academic and Research Settings* and in a number of articles in *Written Communication* and *College Composition and Communication.* Discussion of models for academic instruction, for example, the adjunct, can be found in Brinton et al. (1989) *Content-based Second Language Instruction.*

Second Language Writing (Kroll, 1990) and *Writing in Academic Disciplines* (Jolliffe, 1988) provide insights into the attempts by novice authors to produce academic texts. They also suggest a number of approaches to research into academic literacy.

Most of the volumes on teaching academic English focus on writing. Two of the most recent are *Richness in Writing: Empowering ESL Students* (Johnson & Roen, 1989) and Ulla Connor and Ann M. Johns'(1990) *Coherence in Writing: Research and Pedagogical Perspectives.*

9

Diversity Among Individuals

Eight Students Making Sense of Classroom Journal Writing

Tamara Lucas
ARC Associates, Inc., California

It has become a cliché (at least in some parts of the United States) to say that our schools are increasingly characterized by diversity. Discussions of this diversity elicit varied reactions from educators. Some of us express fear of facing classrooms of students with widely differing backgrounds, some feel inadequately prepared to teach such groups of students, some want to eradicate differences as quickly as possible, some deny the importance of differences, and others celebrate the richness of diverse classrooms. Whatever our responses to classroom diversity, we tend to think of it as being manifested in racial, cultural, and socioeconomic characteristics. In this chapter, I will address another kind of diversity that is found in any classroom anywhere in the world: the diversity that arises because no two individuals share the same life histories, personalities, values, or expectations.

More specifically, I will report on the diverse ways in which 8 students from six different countries responded to classroom journal writing. The individual diversity among these students' responses is consonant with current views that portray individual writers and readers as actively making meaning when they write their own texts and when they read texts written by others:

> When we read, we comprehend by putting together impressions of the text with our personal, cultural, and contextual models of reality. When we write, we compose by making meaning from available information, our personal knowledge, and the cultural and contextual frames we happen to find ourselves in.

> (Petrosky, 1982, p. 26)

This conception of readers and writers has grown out of three major bodies of thought: first, that learners play an active role in learning rather than the passive role hypothesized by earlier behaviorists (see, e.g., Britton, 1970; R. Brown, 1973; Brown & Bellugi, 1964; Halliday, 1975); second, that learning in general and language learning in particular are social, interactional phenomena (see, e.g., Bruner, 1978; Halliday, 1975, 1978; Vygotsky, 1962, 1978; Wells, 1981); and third, that our prior knowledge—organized as schemata or frames[1]—determines how we perceive and interpret the world, including texts (see, e.g., Adams & Collins, 1979; Carrell, 1983, 1984, 1987; Carrell & Eisterhold, 1983; Johnson, 1981, 1982; Langer, 1984; Rosenblatt, 1978; Rumelhart, 1980). The last two of these perspectives can be seen as in conflict, as yet another version of the nature versus nurture dichotomy (see Lemke, 1988). But they need not be. These two models of learning are complementary, both contributing to a more complete picture of how we learn—the cognitivist (nature) model, focused on the role of individual mental processes, and the social/contextual (nurture) model, focused on the role of social interaction and context. Lev Vygotsky (1962, 1978) argued that learning begins in social interaction and continues on an individual level, "first *between* people . . . and then *inside* the child . . ." (1978, p. 57, emphasis his).

On the one hand, all meaning is social. That is, it is learned through social interaction, it has social functions, and it is socially meaningful (see Lemke, 1988) within particular cultural and socioeconomic contexts: "through *culture* humans share learned systems for defining meaning" (Erickson, 1986, pp. 32–33, emphasis his). On the other hand, as people make and use meanings, they do so through the filters of their own individual frames, each of which—though constructed through social interactions—is unique. This "underlying diversity" (Erickson, 1986, p. 33) may not be obvious at first glance. In many situations (including classrooms overflowing with students), it may be necessary to concentrate on similarities in people's attitudes and behaviors rather than trying to sort out individual differences if we want to get anything accomplished (e.g., teaching a lesson, making a business decision, maneuvering through a busy intersection). At the same time, we should not lose sight of the fact that—despite similarities in important aspects of their lives such as social, cultural, and economic backgrounds, gender, and age—different people make sense of their environments in different ways, ways that influence their interactions with and within those environments.

In this chapter, I will concentrate on the responses of individual students to a written classroom genre, individual responses that, to be sure, are shaped by cultural and social contexts and that occur simultaneously with cultural, social, economic, and other types of diversity. By focusing on diversity across individual students—rather than on behaviors, values, and expectations shared by members of social, cultural, racial, and socioeconomic groups—I have chosen to take a perspective that is often ignored, perhaps, because it seems obvious and, at the same time, is too complex to capture adequately. In examining the ways in which 8 students responded to a particular writing task, I have captured some of the influences on their individual approaches to and completion of the task. I have uncovered some of the actions, thoughts, and feelings of these students, some of the available information and personal knowledge that they drew upon in response to being asked to "make meaning" within a particular genre.

The Study

The students whose writing I examined were enrolled in one of two sessions of an English as a second language (ESL) writing class called Writing for Fluency, which was offered through Extended Education at a U.S. West Coast urban university and was team-taught one evening a week for 10 weeks each semester (for more detailed descriptions of the course, see Vanett & Jurich, 1990a, 1990b). I collected data in two Writing for Fluency classes, in consecutive Fall and Spring semesters. The purpose of the study was to examine the teaching and learning of a written genre within the context of the class. Classroom personal journal writing was the primary ongoing writing activity of these classes. Most of the journal writing, on topics assigned or

suggested by the teachers, required the students to describe and examine their past experiences from various perspectives. Each week the
teachers also wrote a journal entry on the same topics and distributed
them to the students. The data for the study consisted of (a) a student
questionnaire distributed at the beginning of each semester; (b) field-
notes, audiotapes, and course materials collected during observations
of all twenty class meetings; (c) interviews with teachers and students;
and (d) the journals written by both teachers and students. Here, I
will focus only on the students.

In this chapter, I will present one part of this larger study: the
individual variation that occurred in 8 students' approaches to the
journal writing. These students, who served as subjects for case studies, were from six different countries. All females, they were selected
for the study primarily on the basis of their interest in participating.
I examined all of their writing and interviewed each of them three
times during the 10-week course in which they were enrolled. Six of
the students were Asian (Keiko and Kaoru from Japan, Sita and Sunee
from Thailand, Irene from Vietnam, and Elizabeth from the Philippines) and 2 were Latina (Raquel from Puerto Rico and Alicia from El
Salvador).[2] Keiko, Kaoru, and Sunee were foreign students in the
United States; the other five students were immigrants. Their ages,
lengths of time in the United States, educational levels, and experiences with different types of writing varied somewhat, as you will see
below. Of particular interest for the study was their experience with
self-motivated personal and imaginative writing (see Applebee, 1984,
pp. 14–16)—journals, poems, and stories. Four of them (Kaoru, Sita,
Irene, and Raquel) had had extensive experience with this type of
writing and spoke of the joy and fulfillment of writing. The other 4
students had written primarily out of obligation at school, at work, or
to family and were more likely to describe writing as a chore than as
a pleasure.

Conventions of Classroom Personal
Journal Writing

Before discussing the diverse ways in which the students approached
the journal writing, I must first describe the conventions of the writing
to which the students were responding. The teachers of the Writing
for Fluency classes were not consciously teaching a genre. They did

not have specific expectations about how the students' journals should be organized or to what extent they should include reflection in their journals, nor did they explicitly teach the conventions of the writing that I will describe below. They wanted the students to become more confident and competent writers in English, and they believed that allowing them to write about content that they both knew and cared about (i.e., their own lives) would provide a context in which the students could do so. Students received a credit for the class if they fulfilled the assignments and attended classes; no grades were given. Thus, students were not criticized or punished for failing to follow the conventions that were implicitly presented. Nevertheless, as I observed and participated in the classes, I realized that the students were "learning" a type of writing that was unfamiliar to them—classroom personal journal writing—from a number of sources: the teachers' oral instructions for in-class and at-home writing, written assignment sheets, the teachers' written responses to the journal entries, classroom materials, such as an excerpt from a piece by Lillian Hellman (1974)[3], and the journals written by the teachers and distributed to the students. I examined these data to determine the characteristics of the journal writing that were presented to the students.

I focused on three elements in my analysis of the journal entries and other prose texts presented as models—organizational features, linguistic features, and content—in an attempt to determine genre conventions, following Charles Ferguson's (1985) definition of genre as a

> unit of discourse conventionalized in a given community at a certain time, having an internal sequential structure and a set of features of form, content, and use that distinguish it from others in the repertoire of the community. (p. 207)

In analyzing organizational features, I drew upon William Labov and Joshua Waletsky's (1967) approach to describing the "overall structure" of oral narratives. In analyzing linguistic features, I drew upon their analysis of the "basic framework" of narratives (p. 20), using the clause as the unit of analysis, as they did, focusing on the extent to which actions occur and affect people and things and who the participants are and what their roles are within the actions (see Halliday, 1981). I approached the analysis of content, the third feature of the writing I examined, with "the general pretheoretical notion of [content] as 'what is being talked [i.e., written] about'" (Brown & Yule, 1983, p. 71), following my intuitions as an experienced reader and writing teacher as well as considering specific features of the writing such as vocabulary, verb tenses, and verb types. I also examined the data (teachers' journals and other prose texts as well as instructions, assignment sheets, and teachers' responses to student journals) to describe functions (Ferguson's "uses") and audience. In analyzing functions, I focused primarily on vocabulary; in analyzing audience, I considered who read the journals and how they responded as well as what students said in interviews about responders and responses.

Using these analytic approaches, I was able to describe particular functions, content, audience, and organizational and linguistic forms of the writing as it was presented to the students. The most salient features—the personal, reflective characteristics of the writing—are highlighted on the following page (see Figure 1).

The combination of representational and reflective functions is one of the salient features. Writers describe and then reflect on the roles and importance of events, people, objects, and issues in their lives. In this way, the genre is similar to personal journals written outside the classroom. The content, another feature distinguishing this genre from most other classroom genres, is focused on the personal experiences and feelings of the writers. The fact that there is an audience (the teacher and occasionally other students) for this personal genre makes it different, not from other classroom writing, but from personal journal writing done outside the classroom. That the audience responds to the content rather than to the form of the writing and does not "correct" the entries, reacting as an interested reader rather than a teacher or evaluator, constitutes a radical departure from the predominant audience for school writing, which continues to be the teacher-as-evaluator (see Applebee, 1981, 1984; Britton, Burgess, Martin, McLeod, & Rosen, 1975).

The element of organizational form that most distinguishes the genre is the reflection that typically occurs at the ends of entries on the meaning or significance to the writer of the event, person, object, or issue described earlier. Finally, several linguistic features characterize the genre: in particular, the predominance of the first-person singular participant (as subject and object) and the expression of the writer's thoughts, feelings, and attributes (i.e., reflection) through certain syntactic structures. Examples of journals discussed on the following pages show how these features were manifested in student writing.

Figure 1
Features of Classroom Personal Journal Writing

Functions

    Representational—description of events, people, issues, objects in writer's life.

    Reflective—discussion of the influence and importance of events, people, issues, and objects in writer's life.

Content

    Personal—experiences, ideas, and feelings of writer.

Audience

    Responsive to the content of the writing only, not to form or correctness, as interested reader rather than as evaluator or teacher.

Organizational form

    Beginning—identification of time, place, person, and theme.

    Middle—thematically unified description of event, person, issue, or object accompanied by some reflection on significance for writer.

    End—concluding reflection on significance of event, person, issue, or object described previously.

Linguistic form

    First-person singular (predominantly)—writer expresses thoughts, feelings, and attributes through three primary syntactic structures:

    1. First person subject + stative verb + adjective (noun)

       Examples: I was scared; I was a shy child.

    2. First person subject + mental verb + clause/phrase

       Example: I assume that I missed my mother's attention to me.

    3. Questions

       Example: How could I do what was expected of me?

Student Diversity in Responding to Classroom Personal Journal Writing

These 8 students responded in diverse ways to the writing assigned in the class. Though they can be grouped according to their general approaches to the writing, the groupings cross ethnic and cultural lines and therefore appear to reflect individual propensities and experiences rather than general social or cultural values or customs. Their responses to the writing required by the class illustrate individual differ-

ences and remind us that we must be cautious in making generalizations about how students may perform in our classes based on the
social, cultural, and economic groups with which they are associated.
Below, I attempt to portray the richness of the diversity in their perceptions of and approaches to the writing. Providing examples in the
students' own words to illustrate, I will describe four different ways
that the 8 students approached the writing: embracing the genre,
struggling successfully with having an audience for personal writing,
developing their own agendas for the writing, and escaping the genre.

Embracing Classroom Personal Journal Writing

Sita. Sita, at 38 the oldest of the 8 students, had immigrated to the
United States from Thailand 9 years before the study with a BA in
Mass Communications from a Thai university. She planned to enter
a graduate program in counseling. She had written stories in Thai and
had kept journals in both Thai and English. She was the only student
who embraced the classroom personal journal writing without reservations or conscious efforts to adapt to its conventions. In her second
interview, she referred to the writing she was doing in the class as
"writing therapy," saying that it "helps you keep in touch with your
feelings." She saw that she was different from many of the other
students in her attitude toward the writing:

> I realize that not everyone in the class has the same ideas and purpose.
> From listening to their writing, I've found that many come with business
> reasons [i.e., to improve their writing skill for business purposes], but
> I come with my heart. If I were the one to read first [when students
> share their pieces in class], I might embarrass myself from reading
> something so personal.

In trying to explain why she was learning so much about herself
through the writing, she said that it was not just because of the writing
but also because of her stage in life and her experience:

> I think it's a combination, not just the writing [that's causing me to learn
> so much about myself]. In 1983, I had been through heavy tragedies
> and I think that really shook me. And maybe my age also; I'm thirty-
> eight years old now. So it's like everything is just ripe.

Throughout the course, she continued to feel positive about the personal writing she was doing, even writing a journal describing her experience, from which the following is taken:

> I [have] found that the more I opened myself up and wrote, the more I learned about my feelings and life. I wrote about the past that either I tried to forget because it was too painful or I fail to remember because the distant of time, brought all the memories back to life again. This time, though, I relived them with new perspective, it helped me to understand myself better than ever. As I wrote the journal for the class, I felt as if I were a weaver who woved the past and present of my life, line after line, in to one tapestry.

Sita described significant personal experiences and reflected upon them in her journals, even from the beginning of the class. In her first piece, written in class on the subject, "Where are you in your life right now?" she described her recent difficult decision to quit work and go back to school, revealing her feelings of "depression, irritability, and unhappiness" during the previous year and changes that made her "feel alive again." In her second piece, also written in class, she revealed that she lived with her boyfriend and described her feelings of happiness and contentment after returning from a trip away from him. She continued to write such reflective pieces throughout the course, including a long and moving letter to her deceased mother expressing guilt and sadness about some of her actions.

Struggling with Audience

Five of the students (from Puerto Rico, Japan, and Vietnam) struggled with the fact that they had an audience for the personal writing assigned in the class and came to satisfactory resolutions with the struggle.

Raquel. Raquel, 27, had a BA in Elementary Education from Puerto Rico and was preparing to take an examination to qualify her to teach in the United States. She struggled with two issues involved in writing within the genre: communicating her feelings in English rather than in Spanish, and settling on just how personal she needed and wanted to be in the writing. She had kept a personal journal in Spanish for 13 years, her "closest companion," in which she had "explored, understood and brought out some of [her] deepest feelings." Thus, though she was accustomed to exploring and expressing her personal concerns, feelings, and experiences in writing, she had never done so to any great extent in English or for an audience beyond herself. Doing the writing in the class made her realize that, as she wrote in one of her journals, it "is very hard to express your most intense feelings, ideas or thoughts in another language which is not your native language." Yet she wanted to develop her ability to do so: "In spite of this, I would like to do my best in this class because I want to translate or share the bea[u]ty that could be in my heart with the people who are now around me."

Having kept a personal journal for so long, she was aware of the difference in the degree of the personal disclosure she engaged in in her writing for the class and in her own journal. She reported that she felt comfortable writing about herself in the class, but acknowledged that "some personal things you don't want to communicate. You have to use vocabulary, not to hide, but to give only some information, not all." She used the teachers' journals as models to help her resolve this issue: "The teachers' journals show you that you can write about yourself and not be threatened. You can tell significant things without being very personal."

This issue—just how personal to be in writing for her audience—continued to be of concern to her throughout the course. Still, she consistently wrote about and reflected upon personal experiences. That is, she followed the conventions of the genre to a greater degree than most of the other students. In fact, all of her entries were about personal experiences, most of them quite significant in her past and present life; she was the only student who did not choose to write at least one or two of her entries about insignificant or incidental events, people, or issues. Raquel was well aware that she was avoiding personal disclosure, not telling her "most inner, deepest feelings," yet her standards for what constituted disclosure had been shaped by her own personal journal writing and allowed her to describe significant personal experiences more easily in this more public genre than other writers who had done little personal writing in any context, such as Sunee, Alicia, and Elizabeth. Raquel's journal entry below, about her mother's death, describes a significant personal event and presents her reflections on the effects of that event on her life. These elements of Raquel's piece contrast sharply with the approach taken by Sunee in her piece about her father (see p. 222):

When I was 21 years of age the most important person in my life, died.

My mother, my sister and I lived in a nice town in my country. Our life was like the life of many working families: my mother worked to support the family and my sister and I studied to be proffesional and to support my mother in her old age. My parents were divorced since I was ten years old. My father never took out the responsabilities I think that as father he should take. Thus, all the family burden leaned over my mother's shoulders. She spent almost all her life working and working hard to give a good education to her two daughters.

When my mother was going to see the fruit of her efforts in terms of our education, she got a cerebral stroke that put her in 5 days of comma. We were not expecting this hit in our lives. Those days were the worse days in my life. My mother was the most important person in my life. She was the meaning of my existence and I was losing that in those days of agony. The feelings I experimented with in those days were unknown for me. I was rebeled with every thing, especially with God. I didn't understand why that was happening to us. She was too young to die. I was totally unable to stop the death and that made me feel angry when I saw my own weakness in front of the death. Even the doctors couldn't do anything.

After five days, my mother died. The following days and months were months of completely loneliness, sadness, and emptiness. Her absence was evident in every moment of my life.

As the time went by, I got envolved in different activities. The death of my mother left another taste in my life. I started to see the life from another perspective, from the perspective of somebody who had suffered the lose of the beloved one. After that I could understand the suffering of different people because I was sensitive to this. I was alert of when [?] was happening around me and started to rebel against all kind of injustice, oppresion and suffering.

Keiko. Like Raquel, Keiko found the personal nature of the writing difficult, though for different reasons. Thirty-six years old, Keiko was a senior in International Communications and was hoping to become a journalist when she returned to Japan. Keiko had never done much personal writing, in fact had never written outside of school and work. She described herself as "not an enthusiastic writer." Most of her writing had been done because of "obligation," and she reported that she did not like to write about herself: "I'm shy; I prefer to write about not private things."

In fact, "openness" and "disclosure" emerged in interviews as important personal issues for her, issues that she had become especially aware of after having experienced the contrast between the Japanese and American cultures by living in the United States for several years. In Japan, she had been considered "strongly opinionated," an eccentric trait in Japan, where, she reported, "you can't have [a] strong opinion." However, in the United States, she had found herself to be "very, very Japanese," that is, much less open and assertive about her ideas than most Americans. She had come to feel that in her own life she had "had very little self-disclosure" and that she had therefore not been aware of the effects of various events on her personality and her relationships with other people.

Her attitudes toward her openness in the journals changed as the class progressed. After a few class sessions, she reported that the writing for the class was "easy." She found it easier to "disclose" herself in English than in Japanese because in Japanese "you have to restrict yourself. There are too many ways to be polite." She also found that she enjoyed the journal writing more than academic writing. This was a revelation to her: "I didn't think I felt that way; I thought I didn't like writing about myself." Her perception of the degree to which she could and would "disclose" herself also changed as the semester progressed. By midsemester, she had realized that the writing was easier for her than she had imagined and acknowledged that she enjoyed it: "Since we are forced to think back and draw something from our memory, it is a very good experience. I really like it." Still, she saw limits to what she could comfortably disclose at that time: "It's difficult to disclose myself. I've tried to choose topics with less disclosure." She discussed her difficulty writing about one important incident in her life in particular:

> I had a very good childhood, I think. . . . [But], of course, I have a bad memory, too. I mean like [being] kidnap[ped]. I included that one in my Steppingstones,[4] but so far I haven't had the courage to write it down. But maybe in the future I can write about that one too. . . . Usually I avoid it. But if I have a chance. . . . , I might include that.

A few days later, she did write a Steppingstone piece about her kidnap and molestation at the age of 5, one of the two "big events" of her childhood:

213

When I was five years old, I experienced being kidnapped or rather molested. I was a very quiet girl. I wanted to ask for help and I wanted to run away from his hands but I couldn't. I was so timid.

I left alone when we finished a kindergarten. I took time to put on my coat, hat and gloves, so my cousin and her friend whom I went home with everyday left the kindergarten, in spite of my asking them "Wait for me!" When I climbed up the stairs and reached to near the entrance of an elementary school, an old man talked to me whether or not more children were coming from the kindergarten. I don't remember how I answered to him but I remember he graved my hand and started walking. When he turned left where I was supposed to keep going, I remember I wanted to say "no," but I didn't have a courage to shake off his hand. He took me to downtown, holding my hand. Nobody was doubtful about us. We looked like a grandfather and his granddaughter. I remember I saw two police men standing 30 meters away on the cross street when we were walking on main street. I wanted to call them but I couldn't. He took me to the top of a department store. There were only a few people on the roof since it was winter. He put me on the bench and touched inside my pants briefly. I thought he was doing a strange thing. I was quiet. A few people, away from us didn't recognize us or even if they did they might have thought that old man helping to fix his grand daughter's clothing. After he finished he taught me the way to go back. I remember he had a peculair accent in pronouncing "a mail box," a post, in Japanese. I walked home. That was a long walk for a five year old child. Even after I became 12, our family never walked to downtown. It was simply too far to walk even for adults. As I came near to the home, I started crying. I guess I became to be able to feel fear. I remember two young women stopped in front of me and one of them asked me what had happened. I just kept walking, crying more loudly. When I came home my crying became even more harshly, crouching in front of the house, relieved as well as terrified with horrible experience I had had.

Those days, in my area, kidnapping or child molesting was not a big problem. It was still peaceful compared with now. My mother told me never followed a stranger. I think the reason why I've been so careful and unreceptable toward men is due to this experience in my early childhood.

In her last interview, Keiko acknowledged that she had extended her willingness and ability to disclose by writing that piece:

Last time, I said I still couldn't disclose myself. But I tried to do it. I didn't totally disclose; I covered some of my feelings, but I tried and I could do it. . . . It was a good opportunity to reveal myself up to a point because I don't do it usually. . . . I was still hesitant, but at least I tried.

Keiko's writing bears out many of her perceptions about herself and her writing. In many of her pieces for the class, she did avoid disclosing, writing about events, people, objects, and issues that were less significant in her life than her childhood molestation. For example, in her second journal, she wrote a largely descriptive piece about a picnic in the park with a friend. In fact, only one quarter of her entries focused on significant personal experiences and included reflection. However, in those pieces, two of them written near the beginning of the class, she conformed closely to the genre conventions, writing classic pieces within the genre (i.e., following most of the features of the genre described in Figure 1). Though Keiko did write disclosing pieces early in the semester, she felt more comfortable writing about personally significant content for an audience as the semester progressed.

Kaoru. A 25-year-old graduate student in Teaching English as a foreign language, Kaoru had been in the United States for only one year. Like Raquel, she had kept a personal journal in her native language, Japanese, for 15 years and she thus had had experience writing about significant personal experiences and exploring her feelings in writing in her native language. Also like Raquel, she was aware of the differences between her personal journal and her writing for the class and she found it more difficult to express her feelings in English than in her native language. Unlike Raquel, Kaoru focused on more formal differences arising from the existence of an audience other than herself when comparing her personal journal writing to the classroom journal writing. She did not report having difficulty with the degree of self-disclosure expected of her, but rather with writing clearly enough for another reader to understand. In comparing her personal journal to the classroom writing, she wrote:

> Writing a jo[u]rnal is different from writing a diary. The latter is written for a writer himself. In the same personal writing, diary is more private writing. In other words, it's enough that only writer can understand what he wrote, and doesn't have to care about topic, organization, grammar, too. On the other hand, a jo[u]rnal should let everybody who read it understand a content. . . .

In the same journal and in an interview a few days earlier, she said that she liked to have others read about her feelings: "It's exciting to express my feelings to others."

Thus, Kaoru's struggle with the genre conventions arose not from the fact that the content was personal but rather from the fact that she had to write for an audience besides herself and that she had to write in English. She described pieces she wrote about Mt. Fuji and her grandmother as "really private" but considered the private nature of the writing a problem only in that she had to express her ideas clearly to an audience, not in that it involved a high degree of disclosure. She was very much concerned with developing her English writing skill and style so that she could express herself "naturally" and effectively, as she was able to do in Japanese:

> In the diary [in Japanese], I use sensitive words. In Japanese, we have a lot of adjectives, really sensitive differences. So I use that difference. But I don't know in English how to express these differences. When I read my English, it seems too simple, too plain, not like my diary in Japanese. I'd like to write in English like in Japanese, like Lillian Hellman, really sensitive, simple sentences with enough feeling to express myself.

She felt that her style of writing in English was inappropriate for "private" writing because it contained too many complicated sentences and obvious transition words such as "first of all, because, and but" but that her style of writing in her Japanese diary was too "emotional" for others to understand. Her goal was to integrate the two styles and to write "logically but also emotionally."

From a reader's and analyst's perspective, Kaoru succeeded in communicating her experiences and her feelings about them in her writing for the class. Even in her first three pieces—about her "mental and physical confusion" about her grandfather's imminent death and her absence from Japan, her decision to go to university after taking a year off after high school, and her feelings about and relationship with Mt. Fuji, respectively—she described significant personal experiences and reflected upon them following the conventions of the genre. She consistently followed the genre conventions throughout the class.

Irene. Irene, a 25-year-old junior in Computer Science, had lived in the United States for 5 1/2 years, having escaped from Vietnam by boat as a teenager. Like Keiko, she had never done much personal writing in her native Chinese and Vietnamese or in English. She had never written about her "feelings" in English before the class. Yet she did not find the writing for the class difficult, explaining, "We have a lot to say about our own things." Like Kaoru, Irene's difficulty with the writing stemmed from her perceived lack of skill in English writing rather than the personal nature of the journals:

> It's a special feeling [to have people read my journals]. I like telling my experiences to people. . . . The way you express your experience to people is very important. I did my best, but I don't think my writing is very emotional. A lot of what I wanted to say, I couldn't; I had to say something else.

She did acknowledge that in other contexts such as "regular classes" she had been "afraid" to write about "very personal" things, but in Writing for Fluency she felt that she did write about personal things, which she described as "mostly about my past experience, sometimes my own feeling, my confusion, things more related to myself than the outside." Despite her reporting no discomfort or other difficulty with the writing, Irene did not fully engage in the personal, self-reflective conventions of the genre in her first five pieces. Her two responses to the Steppingstone assignment elicited her first entries which conformed to the personal, reflective conventions. These pieces were about her arriving in the United States after being in a refugee camp and about her decision to escape Vietnam by boat when she was 18 years old. After those pieces, she wrote 11 more, 6 of which involved relatively high degrees of reflection on significant personal experiences.

Thus, Irene did not report feeling any reluctance to disclose and reflect, to write about "personal things." Yet it took six entries before she did so in her writing. Perhaps, as Irene came to know and trust the teachers more, she came to be comfortable with presenting more personal content. Perhaps also just as Sita's life experience contributed to her readiness to engage in the journal writing to the extent that she did, Irene's life experience, called forth by the assignment asking her to think of significant and meaningful events in her life, stimulated her willingness and desire to engage in the disclosing and reflective conventions of the writing. Having left home and family "to face the edgeless ocean" all alone at 18, having barely survived days on a boat not knowing whether she would ever see her family again, Irene had had "significant" experiences which this type of writing allowed her

217

to explore in a way she had never done before. In fact, she said that when she left home she did not cry because she had to pretend to be strong but that "when [she] wrote about it, [she] got some tears." Reading a Steppingstone entry in her journal below, we can see why she might have felt like crying:

In a raining night in 1978, I packed up my cloths, and left my house without saying good bye to anybody. I knew I will never be back again.

I was a stuff decision to make. I didn't want to leave my parents, my brothers, and my grandma, but I didn't have any other alternation either. I was 15 when the Communist took over South Viet Nam in 1975. Since then, my whole life was changed. I changed from a pure and happy young girl, who didn't have anything else to worry bende [?] her homework assignments, to a girl who had to live in a scary and worried situation every day and night. I didn't know what the local government really wanted from me. They called me to meetings at least three times a week. They wanted me to become a member of the Communistic Party. They wanted me to went to their school. They suggested me to do this, or to do that. I felt totally confuse about my own life and my furture. Finally, in one day in the year of 1978, they suggested me to leave my parents and stayed in the dormitory which located far away from the city. They gave me two choices. Either I jointed them volunter-rily or they would use force to bring me over there. My family was shocked with this new, and I knew it was the time that I had to make a decision. After some careful considerations, I chose to leave my family and escape from the country by boat.

I left my house in the rainning night during the end of October, with the tear drops on the faces of my family. I wanted to cry, really, but I didn't. I had to pretend that I was strong enough to face the furture on my own. Yet, at the bottom of my heart, I was so afraid and confuse to face the edgeless ocean, the uncertain future of myself. I would miss all of my family, my friends, and my little puppy who was grasping my foot and started to cry. Embracing him in my arms, I told my puppy that it was the last time I held him and then we would be separated forever. At 11 o'clock that night, I left my house without a promise to come back. "Mama", I said to my parents as I stepped out the door, "If I unfortully die on the ocean, please forgive me. Please just pretend that you didn't born me, raise me, and I didn't exist in your life at all."

Now, six years had past by. I am still alive, and my family has been reunion. Yet, I never forget that sadness moment in my life. I will never forget my friends, my relatives, and my little puppy who had shared my happiness, my laughter, and my tears.

Developing a Personal Agenda

Two of the students developed their own agendas for the writing, following certain conventions but ignoring others.

Alicia. Alicia, a permanent resident with no plans to return to her native El Salvador, had lived in the United States for 7 of her 26 years. She had written very little in English, primarily business letters and memos at work. She had never "thought of doing this kind of writing before . . . , of writing things that [she] had in [her] mind." In fact, when the class began she had never heard the term "journal" and had never taken a writing class before. Thus, she had little writing experience inside or outside of school with which to compare the journal writing. Yet she quickly developed her own agenda for the writing and was very consistent in following it throughout the course.

Like Irene and Sita, Alicia's life experiences influenced her response to the writing she did in the class. However, rather than being inspired to describe and reflect upon her experiences and feelings, she responded by developing an agenda that completely excluded some genre conventions while embracing others. She described her attitude toward personal writing in her first interview, providing some insight into her reluctance to probe her feelings and to reflect on events:

> Some people get into the habit to do [personal writing], and I never like to do that because I don't want to go back and read something that I'm trying to not remember. Because reading that is like living that again. . . . I wouldn't like to go back and read sad things. Maybe good things, beautiful things, but not sad things. . . . My parents used to have a lot of problems—fightings and things like that. . . . One of my brothers said we should write a book [about] all the things that we've seen. One of us started writing the things that happened every day, but then we destroyed everything. We said, "No. Forget it. We don't want to read those later."

Alicia's writing for the class conformed to this stated desire to avoid writing about sad things. She did not write about the many "sad things" that she told me about in interviews—for example, her father's alcoholism, the fact that her father had been kidnapped on his farm outside San Salvador several years earlier and had not been heard from since, the fact that the guerrilla fighters had taken over the family farm that she loved so much, or her decision to leave family and

219

friends in El Salvador and become a refugee in the United States. She wrote about her childhood on the farm and in town with her aunt, about swimming in the river, eating fruit off the trees, being in school plays, losing her first boyfriend, moving away from the farm to her aunt's house during the school year. In effect, she was true to her word: she did not, for the most part, write about sad things. She also did not reflect on the events that she described in her journals. Her pieces tended to consist of strings of loosely connected events, none of them developed. On the other hand, she did consistently write about significant personal experiences. In effect, she engaged in the personal and representational elements of the writing, but did not engage in the reflective elements. The piece below illustrates her approach:

> When I was 8 years old, I liked to be in shows that the school use to give for Mother's Day and Independence Day, I used to recite and dance I enjoyed doing that very much, all the kits in the school and their parents liked the way that I acted. At the time I was living in one of San Salvador's Town, a beutiful town, My parents liked too. The only thing that my Father did not like was all the make up that I did have to wear to look pretty. I remember one time a friend from school polished my nails when I got home my father saw them, he got so angry that he made me to take the polish off. I never did that again. At the time my preorities were my books earn the best grades, tried to be one of the best students on class, goal that I always achieved, my religious commitment was attended to church every Sunday with my parents at that time I belonged to Girl Scouts, my favorite clothes was to wear mini skirts, my favorite music oh I loved to listen rock and roll, my hobbies swim and read stories and my favorite food it always been seafood.

As this journal shows, Alicia's English skills were among the least developed of the 8 case study writers. However, they were strong enough to have allowed her to reflect upon the events and experiences she describes if she had wanted to. Alicia was very aware of her audience, herself as well as other potential audiences for her writing. She asserted that, just as she would not want to go back and read sad things herself, she would not want anyone else to read what she had written: "I like everything [about the writing]. It's a new experience; it's interesting. [But] I still haven't changed my mind to keep a diary because if I die somebody else would read it."

Sunee. A foreign student from Thailand, Sunee, 27 years old, had been in the United States for 6 years and was a senior in Economics.

Like Alicia, she developed an approach to the journal writing that allowed her to participate and to feel that she had benefited from the course, yet she followed fewer of the genre conventions than any other student. She was also the least forthcoming in her interviews with me, rarely elaborating on her answers and telling me very little of her personal history or family background. She seemed reluctant to simply answer a question without first trying to get a clearer idea of what kind of answer I wanted.

She did tell me that her family did not write much and that she wrote most of the letters that other family members needed to send. She had used English writing only in school. Nevertheless, she reported feeling good

> about the writing I'm doing in Writing for Fluency. If I hadn't taken this class, I would not have written about these things, I'm sure. I think some of the moments [from the Steppingstone list?] are important. Five or ten years later we can look at it and recall the past.

She described the writing she was doing for the class as "a way to express our feelings, what we feel inside" but said that "the benefit of writing about yourself is to improve your English." Her description of the writing, like some of her other interview responses, was a very close approximation of the teachers' instructions to the students to "express their feelings" in their journals. This was one instance of many in which Sunee seemed to want to find the "right" answer for my questions.

In fact, she did not express her feelings in 71% of her entries; she also did not write predominantly in first person-singular in 74% of her entries, but wrote 43% of her entries with first person-plural of equal or greater predominance than first person-singular; she did not include more than three reflective constructions in 43% of them. To a large extent, she did not write within the genre described in Figure 1. Perhaps Sunee's conception of herself as a member of a group made this genre, with its focus on the individual's experiences and feelings, incomprehensible or inconceivable to her. Perhaps the genre lacked saliency for her because she had never reflected on her feelings and experiences. For whatever reason, she did not follow the genre conventions overall, yet she completed the course and felt she benefited from it. The journal entry below is typical of those she wrote throughout the course. Although the piece describes a significant person in

221

her life, it is not presented from a first-person singular perspective and includes no personal reflection:

> My father used to play an important role in my life. My family has five children. Everyone in the family loves him eventhough he had pass away a couple of years ago.
>
> He was a handsome man and had a loud voice. He had brown skin and a bit bald. He was about 5 feet 10 inches. Because of his character, everyone in the family afraid of him. He supported us to have good education and to save our lifes. He worked hard and took full responsibility of his family. When he was alive, he always taught us to respect to other people, honest to other people, be worked hard, and be a responsible person.
>
> We were not close to him when we were little because he left home for work early in the morning and came home late at night. We were closer to him when we grown up because at that time he had a business at home. He always in a good mood when the business was well, otherwise, he was a serious person. He smoked and drank heavily when he was young. He stopped smoking and drinking when he was fifty-five years old because of his health. No one could stop him before that time. He suffered a lot when he was sick in the hospital for four months until he died. Everyone in my family still respect him because he was our father and he was the one we always love.

Escaping Classroom Personal Journal Writing

Elizabeth. Elizabeth, at 29, was a permanent resident in the United States, having lived here for 6 years. She had received a BS in Chemical Engineering in the Philippines and worked as an engineer. She described herself as an "emotional" person, who wrote in her diary, which she had kept off and on for approximately 15 years, about important events and "beautiful" things, about things that "excited" her. She also recognized that personal writing for an audience was difficult for her, yet at the beginning she was enjoying the class:

> Any writing is easier to do when it's formal. It's easier for me to do that, like at work. The kind that we're doing right now [in the class], it's more personal and it's harder to do because it's more expressing yourself. Sometimes people don't want to do that, especially when somebody looks at it. . . . It's hard to express myself in English, to translate my ideas into English, especially these personal things. It's fun though. It

makes me very nostalgic. I remember fun days, write about happy things from the past.

This conflict between her feeling that the writing was very personal and therefore difficult especially because it was to be read by someone besides herself and that it was, at the same time, fun and beneficial, continued to be a part of Elizabeth's experience throughout the course. In the second interview, she again mentioned that the writing was "very personal," that she had written one piece about her wedding that was "too personal" to have the teachers read (or to give to me for my research). She had also written a piece about some of Bishop Fulton Sheen's inspirational writings that she had read in the newspaper, and this piece, too, was "very personal" and "revealing." Yet she said that the writing helped her "get a lot of ideas deep inside" and that it was "nice" to write about Sheen's writings because "it's like telling people what your experiences are, hobbies are." She again mentioned her personality as a factor in her reaction to the writing:

> I think I've learned to be more open because I've always been hiding things within me, but this helps me to open, helps my well-being. It makes you grow and relate to people what you feel.

By the time of this second interview, Elizabeth had written six of the seven pieces that she would write for the class. Of those pieces, five were about her own experiences; five had reflection at the end, though somewhat clichéd (e.g., "She has influenced me in a lot of ways and I'm very greatful"); two addressed content highly significant in her life; and four were predominantly in first-person singular. On the other hand, the amount of reflection in five of the pieces was minimal.

The picture here is of a student trying to conform to the conventions of the genre, to the teachers' expectations of her, someone who found this personal writing difficult but beneficial, someone who was trying to adapt her own needs and values to the expectations of the course but was losing steam. In the second interview, Elizabeth reported that she had been writing fewer entries each week, explaining this by saying, "I'm probably running out of ideas, and my job interferes." In fact, she did not attend three of the last four classes and did not hand in a final revised journal to be distributed to the entire class at the last meeting. In phone interviews conducted after she had stopped attending class, she admitted that her job was an "excuse" and that

223

in fact the writing was simply "too personal" for her to continue with it:

> The writing was too personal. It was hard to write. I can't do it anymore; it was too hard and too personal. . . . It's helped in that I saw I can do something like this. I had never done it before, this kind of writing. I'm glad I was able to do it. But I can't give anymore; it's very personal. I can't write the Fulton Sheen piece to be read in front of the class. [Three days later:] I've tried to write it [i.e., the Sheen revision] and I just can't do it anymore. I'll end up lying. I feel I'm not supposed to write this down; it's too personal, and I decided, "This is it. . . ." The writing is very personal, very revealing. I didn't have a problem with that at first, but when I was asked to develop it, it was hard.

Elizabeth reached a point in her writing past which it was not worth it to her to try to disclose more in this context, as it seems to have been for Keiko and Irene, and she did not adapt to what was being asked of her in a way that would allow her to feel that she was not revealing too much, as it seems Alicia and Sunee did. Though she tried to follow the conventions despite some discomfort, she ultimately found herself so uncomfortable with the personal nature of the writing that she simply had to stop trying.

Implications for Instruction

I hope the above description has left you with a strong sense of these 8 people making meaning of their environment, adapting their own expectations and values in their own ways in order to perform acceptably in a classroom. I have tried to capture their thoughts and feelings in this process of adaptation, their struggles in coming to terms with the writing required in the class. Several implications for instruction arise from the individual diversity reflected in the case studies, some related to teaching in general and some related to the teaching of writing in particular.

Although people are products of their social and cultural contexts, they are also individuals with unique experiences, preferences, and personalities. As teachers, we must balance our understanding of students as members of social and cultural groups with our knowledge of them as individuals. Whereas a knowledge of different cultural values and experiences can make us aware of the influence of culture on individuals, cultural stereotyping can blind us to individual experiences and perceptions that influence learning. Assuming that the Asian students in the class would have been more reluctant to engage in the personal, reflective writing than the Latin Americans because Asians, as a group, tend to be more reserved would not have been a useful generalization, for example. We "need to be able to use knowledge of culture judiciously in order not to stereotype students but to serve them better" (McGroarty, 1986, p. 305).

Just as generalizations based on ethnic and cultural stereotypes can lead us astray in our attempts to teach, so can assumptions based on our own experiences or those of other students we have encountered. We need to find out about the schooling and literacy experiences of the individual students in our classes. In this case, it appears that the students who had engaged in personal, reflective writing before taking the class more readily followed those conventions in the classroom writing. Knowing more about the students' previous writing experiences would have allowed the teachers to adjust their expectations and their responses to student writing accordingly. Other types of questions we might want to ask our students include: Have they had uninterrupted schooling? What educational experiences have they had that are relevant to what we would like to teach them? We also cannot assume that all students have had access to written materials or that such materials are used in the same ways in all families—even within one ethnic or socioeconomic group. And even within the same family, children have different roles and experiences that make them respond differently to different educational approaches. In many immigrant families, for example, one child is given the responsibility of being the literate person in the family, the person who acts as a translator and mediator for other family members when written materials must be dealt with (see, e.g., Trueba, 1984). Such a student will likely have different motivation to learn as well as different previous experience with literacy than a student who does not play this role in his or her family.

Just as students' schooling and literacy experiences influence their learning, so do their personal experiences. When we know something of the lives they have led, we can better understand their motivations, perceptions, and values as they are manifested in our classrooms. Sita, for example, attributed her enthusiasm for and success with the personal, reflective writing she was asked to do to her stage in life and the experiences she had had. It appears that Irene's experiences also played a part in her engagement with the genre. To help us interpret students' responses to classroom tasks, we might want to ask such questions as: Where are our students from exactly (not just the general part of the world or of the United States)? How long have they been in this country or in this part of the country? Why did they come? Who came with them? With whom do they live? What are some of the important events in their lives? Taking the time to find out about students' experiences, interests, and areas of knowledge can help us appreciate the unique contributions of each and more effectively facilitate their learning.

Other implications for instruction relate more specifically to the teaching of writing. All students perform better and become more engaged in learning when what they are learning makes sense to them and is relevant to their lives[5]. With regard to writing in particular, Judith Langer's (1984) findings "suggest a strong and consistent relationship between topic-specific background knowledge and the quality of student writing" and indicate that "different kinds of knowledge predict success in different writing tasks" (p. 41). In the context of Writing for Fluency, this relevance was built in—as student comments above indicate—in that the topics for the writing came from the students' lives. Most classes, however, do not focus on information students already possess. In all situations, we cannot make assumptions about what will make sense or be relevant to our students. We need to ask: What knowledge do students have of the subjects we are asking them to address? What opportunities have they had to acquire formal and informal knowledge that is relevant to what we are hoping to teach them? How do they spend their time? Do they work? Do they have special interests? What concerns do they have about their schooling, their futures, their families? A student who did not watch the coverage of the 1988 Summer Olympics and has never heard of anabolic steroids, for example, would have a great deal of difficulty writing a coherent and convincing essay expressing his or her opinion about the use of such substances in sports and about the justice of Canadian athlete Ben Johnson's loss of his gold medal because of steroid use—though I observed a class in which just such students were asked to write an essay on these issues.

These portraits show different students responding differently to being asked to engage in a particular written genre. Some of them had more difficulty than others participating fully in the assignments and producing the kind of writing that the teachers expected them to produce. We need to recognize that we are presenting discourse conventions whenever we teach writing or require written work. Students

226

may have difficulty in our classes because of the conventions of the genres we are asking them to engage in, not because of the linguistic features of the language or the thought processes required of the assignment. Once we recognize this fact, we can then examine the genres that we assign in our classes and make conscious decisions about which conventions to present and how best to present them, taking into account individual students' experiences with, knowledge of, and attitudes toward the genres. The ability to acquire literacy and to display knowledge in the genres valued by the school are crucial to the success of all students in the United States (Heath, 1986). When teachers assume that students already know the conventions of these genres, all students suffer, but especially those students who do not speak and use language as it is spoken and used at school. "The mastery of something as essential as formal genres needs to be insured for all students regardless of the degree to which their language [and I would add: cultural, social, and individual] backgrounds are consistent with what schools [and teachers] expect" (Lemke, 1988, p. 88).

On the other hand, the influence of what the student brings to the acquisition of genre is one of the things that make such acquisition a complex process (see Fowler, 1982). We cannot expect our students to learn a genre simply because we give them guidelines for their writing, because we give them practice doing it, or even because we give them implicit and explicit models, as these teachers did. The acquisition of genre, like all learning, involves students' previous experiences with writing and with the genre as well as their life experiences and knowledge, their personal and cultural frames, and the classroom context, including the audience for the genre. Some of the students discussed above, for example, seemed to understand the genre conventions well enough but were not always willing to fully engage in them. Their life experiences, writing experiences, perceptions of audience, values with regard to the sharing of personal information mediated between their competence in the genre and their performance at times (for a more in-depth discussion of influences on their responses, see Lucas, 1990).

Finally, these stories of individual diversity suggest that teachers need to take into account the importance of audience as an influence on students' participation in writing (and perhaps other learning) tasks. In interviews, audience emerged as one of the most salient features of the writing for many of the students. Because they had an outside audience for personal, reflective writing, many of them were forced to consciously consider the extent to which they would engage in the conventions of the genre. By writing journals themselves and by responding to the students' writing primarily as interested readers rather than as evaluators, the teachers played roles that allowed students to resolve their difficulties with the audience in their own individual ways. All teachers would do well to consider carefully the audience stance that they are taking with respect to students' performances. When teachers respond as "collaborators" in learning (Applebee, 1984) rather than as evaluators, as these teachers did, they are more apt to understand the processes that different students go through in writing and to respond to students as individuals, that is, to recognize and address individual diversity among their students.

Conclusion

Frederick Erickson (1986) has asserted: "The billiard ball does not make sense of its environment. But the human actor in society does; and different humans make sense differently" (p. 33). The stories I have told here illustrate this sense-making proclivity of humans, illuminating some of the complexities beneath the surface of a teaching and learning situation. From the teachers' points of view, all of the writers were presented with the "same" writing tasks, but by the time the tasks were in the hands of the writers, they were not the same anymore. Each made sense of the tasks differently, responding in her own way, because each brought different knowledge and experiences to the tasks. We need to recognize and celebrate differences among individuals just as we do diversity among different cultural, ethnic, and socioeconomic groups. If we do not, we are ignoring part of what makes us human.

Summary

This chapter examines the diverse ways in which 8 adult students approached a particular type of writing assigned in two university writing classes. The data come from a study that examined the teaching and learning of the conventions of classroom personal journal writing. Eight case study students from six different countries responded in different ways to writing assignments and to the personal, reflective nature of the writing. This chapter, therefore, is not about diversity that is manifested in racial, cultural, and socioeconomic characteristics, but about diversity that arises because no two individuals share the same life histories, personalities, values, and expectations.

The chapter begins with a brief overview of the interconnectedness of cognitive and social/contextual views of learning. That is, individuals learn through interaction within particular cultural contexts, not by mental activities of an isolated mind. At the same time, people learn and make meaning of their environments through the filters of their own individual frames, constructed from their unique experiences. This overview is followed by a discussion of the setting, subjects, and methods of the study and a description of the conventions of the classroom genre. The core of the article provides brief accounts of 8 case study students adapting their individual experiences and expectations to the classroom writing in ways that allow 7 of them to participate in the writing successfully, although differently from one another. One student embraced the genre in her attitude toward the writing and in her writing itself; 5 students struggled with having an outside audience for personal, reflective writing, ultimately resolving their struggles in ways satisfactory to themselves and to the teachers; 2 students developed their own agendas, following some of the genre conventions but ignoring others; and 1 student dropped out of the course, unable to resolve her conflict about the personal nature of the writing. The chapter concludes with suggestions for ways in which teachers can address individual diversity in their classrooms.

Discussion Topics and Projects

1. Most students, especially after elementary school, are not assigned such personal writing as were the students in the Writing for Fluency class described in the chapter. From your own experience, can you think of ways in which the findings of this study might relate to students' engagement with other types of writing, such as academic essays, summaries, and reports? What are some possible difficulties that individual students might have with these other kinds of writing? What are aspects of them that students might want to avoid? What are aspects of them that students might change or adapt in order to succeed in a class where they are assigned such writing?

2. As a follow-up to Question 1, interview two or three people taking classes in which they have to write academic essays, summaries, or reports and write up your findings. Ask them about their previous experiences with writing in general and with the particular type of writing they have to do for their classes. Depending upon the scale of the project, you might focus on one specific aspect of their involvement with the writing, such as their perception of the audience for the writing or what they see as the purpose(s) of writing essays, summaries, or reports. If you have more time, you might try to get a broader view, including their perceptions of audience and purpose(s) as well what they find easy and difficult about the type of writing, what they see as the features of the writing, and how they have adjusted their writing to conform to those features.

3. For many of the students discussed in the chapter, the personal, reflective nature of the classroom personal journal writing caused some difficulty. They wanted to perform acceptably for the teachers, but they found it unusual and therefore difficult to write about and reflect upon personal experiences, knowing that someone besides themselves would read what they wrote. At the same time, the teachers responded as interested readers rather than evaluators; they did not grade the journals but wrote down their reactions to the content of the journals (not the form of the writing), and most of the students were able to adjust their writing so that they felt comfortable. Given what you know about how these students adapted to the classroom journal writing, do you think teachers should assign personal, reflective writing in their classes? What potential benefits might this type

of writing offer to students in general and to nonnative speakers of English in particular?

4. One student discussed in the chapter found the personal aspects of the writing so difficult that she dropped out of the class. The teachers evidently did not know that she was having so much difficulty until she was no longer attending classes. Can you think of ways that the teachers might have prevented this, without assigning a different kind of writing? What advice would you have given the teachers and the student if you could have talked to them before she dropped out?

5. Usually we think of educational diversity in terms of ethnic, linguistic, and cultural groups. This chapter points out that there is another layer of diversity that is relevant to teaching—the diversity that exists among individuals regardless of their group affiliations. As a way to sensitize yourself to the distinction between group and individual diversity, write down all the comments you hear or read within a week in which generalizations are made about minority and majority ethnic, linguistic, and cultural groups. Then, for each generalization, think about how individuals who do not conform might be affected by assumptions that they will conform. When appropriate, think of how students would be affected if their teachers assumed they would conform to the generalizations.

Further Reading

For more information on classroom journal writing, see Toby Fulwiler (1987), Joy K. Peyton (1990), Joy K. Peyton and Leslee Reed (1990), Gene Stanford (1979), and Jana Staton, Roger Shuy, Joy K. Peyton, and Leslee Reed (1988). For good overviews of current thinking on individual differences in second language acquisition, see Rod Ellis (1986) and Peter Skehan (1989). Specific factors affecting second language acquisition are discussed by different authors, for example, age (Hatch, 1983; McLaughlin, 1987; Snow & Hoefnagel-Höhle, 1978); personality (Dulay, Burt, & Krashen, 1982; Schumann, 1978; Strong, 1983); aptitude (Gardner, 1980); motivation for learning the language and attitudes toward the language (Gardner & Lambert, 1972); learning styles (Hansen & Stansfield, 1981; Naiman, Frohlich, Stern, & Todesco, 1978). To pursue issues related to the notions of prior knowl-

edge, schemata and frames from different perspectives, see Frederic
C. Bartlett (1932), the person who first used the term "schema"; John
D. Bransford & N. S. McCarrell (1974), Charles Frake (1977), Kenneth
Goodman (1967, 1973), Stephen Kucer (1987), Roger C. Schank and
Robert P. Abelson (1977), and Deborah Tannen (1979).

Part III

Teaching Diverse Learners

10

Power and the Politics of Knowledge

Transformative Schooling for Minority Language Learners

Daniel McLaughlin
University of Utah

The challenges confronting educators of minority students in the United States are increasing. By the year 2000, African, Hispanic, Asian, and Native American youths will constitute one third of the nation's student body. Within 40 years, the Hispanic population is expected to multiply two-and-one-half-fold to nearly the size of the African American population, from 14.5 million in the late 1980s to 37 million in 2030. The Asian population is expected to quadruple during the same period, from 3.5 to 17 million. Meanwhile, Native Americans, with the highest birth rate in the United States, are experiencing equally precipitous population growth. Already in major cities across the country, even in large states such as Texas and California, more than one half of the overall student body is of minority background.

From Power and Politics of Knowledge: Transformative Leadership and Curriculum Development for Minority Language Learners, by Daniel McLaughlin, 1989, Peabody Journal of Education, *66(3), 41–60.* Copyright © 1989 by Peabody Journal of Education. *Adapted by permission.*

To deal with this pressing diversity, under a general rubric of multi-cultural schooling, educators have developed myriad models, instructional approaches, materials, and teaching techniques. At the risk of oversimplification, most of these can be situated along a continuum from cultural inclusion to cultural exclusion: from strategies that incorporate students' home language, history, and customs, to strategies that aim to promote and reproduce a single common culture. At the cultural inclusion end of the spectrum exist a wide variety of dual language programs that attempt to build standard forms of knowledge upon a foundation of vernacular forms. At the cultural exclusion end exist school programs that operationalize E. D. Hirsch's (1987) notion of cultural literacy, namely, that academic progress and getting ahead in life require the successful acquisition of mainstream concepts, thinking, reading, writing, and speaking abilities.

In this chapter, I speak in support of, and aim to go beyond, the notion of cultural inclusion. For minority students in general, and for colonized minorities in particular, such as African Americans and Native Americans, I will argue for the need to build a bridge from where students are as they come to school, to where teachers want them to go; from the linguistic and cultural resources children bring with them to the classroom, to the skills and concepts that facilitate access to mainstream power and influence. I will argue for the need to build a bridge so that minority students can go back and forth between standard and vernacular forms of knowledge; not, as proponents of cultural literacy would argue, for the necessity of building such a span, having the students cross it, then burning the bridge.

At the same time, I want to take the cultural inclusion argument a critical step beyond calls for the mere incorporation of minority students' language and culture into the content of schooling. What is needed is the creation of conditions in schools whereby students and teachers alike participate in the creation and re-creation of knowledge. The need is for *transformative leadership*—administrative procedures that create "a community of critical, reflective citizens," as William Tierney and William Foster (1989) advocate; and for *transformative intellectuals*—teachers and school administrators who strive to make the "pedagogical more political and the political more pedagogical," as Stanley Aronowitz and Henry Giroux (1985) advise.

Ultimately, I seek to highlight a relationship between school knowledge and power, and to illuminate the role of leadership in shaping, distorting, and mediating not only what goes on inside school but also learners' understandings of the social world. To do so is to recognize that education is not an apolitical, ahistorical entity. Rather, it must be seen as a process of selection and appropriation of particular kinds of knowledge from all available social knowledge for particular purposes within a given political and historical context. Accordingly, the question for educators of minority and mainstream students alike, as Michael Apple (1990) advises, is not *what* knowledge is most worth in terms of school curriculum, but *whose* (p. vii). The question is significant for all students. For students of dominated minority background, however, it is especially important in that minority languages, values, cultures, and voices are those most at risk. To question whose knowledge counts is to raise difficult corollary questions: In what language should instruction be taught? Which aspects of a vernacular culture should be taught? Which versions of truth should be portrayed, debated, and possibly denied?

The purpose of this chapter is to examine the meanings of power in relation to questions about leadership, language, school knowledge, and program development in a community-controlled school on the Navajo Reservation. I will suggest that an understanding of power can play a central role in the way educators conceive of their work, both in terms of analyzing curricular challenges and developing program solutions. After a discussion of power from a critical perspective, I will point out the utility of power as a descriptive device, as a way of diagnosing curricular challenges that confront Navajo teachers and program developers. In attempting to make concrete what are often overly abstract formulations, I will then describe in detail how power can be used as a prescriptive notion, in order to create English and Navajo literacy programs that specify conditions for student and teacher empowerment.

Power in Theory and Practice

Admittedly, the extent to which power infuses all aspects of school knowledge is not readily transparent. In the dominant view, knowledge tends to be obscured from all considerations of power and to be treated in a technical, utilitarian, and objective manner. Underpinning most school activity is an input-output, behaviorist understanding of learning, an understanding of teaching as the imparting of demonstrable skills, and an understanding of curriculum as carefully ordered sequences of skills and skill-related tasks that, for the most part, tend to "teach themselves" and to exist far removed from the multiple discourses with which students generate the meanings of their everyday lives. So thorough is the hegemonic saturation of the technical, utilitarian, objective view not only in schools but also throughout mainstream culture, that it is difficult to see the otherwise common-sense idea that curriculum represents a selection and organization of certain, and only certain, aspects of social knowledge in the broadest sense of the term.

That the curriculum in most schools is less concerned with the distribution of skills than with the distribution of norms and values that shape, and are shaped by, the hierarchical stratification of individuals in society is a central point developed amply in critical analyses of U.S. schooling (e.g., Apple, 1982, 1987, 1990; Bowles & Gintes, 1976; Giroux, 1981; Giroux & McLaren, 1986; Gitlin & Smyth, 1989; Tierney, 1989). I do not intend to belabor the point here. Suffice it to say, however, that where minority languages and cultures are concerned, whole versions of truth are at stake. Where oppressed peoples have been led by dominant processes in schools primarily to assimilate mainstream ways of thinking, speaking, doing, and knowing, nothing less than cultural genocide has been at issue (Simonson & Walker, 1988).

Given that the relationship between school knowledge and power is at the very least problematic, the need is two-fold: first, to recognize how power relations mediate social and school reality and thus reflect people's lived experiences; second, to develop alternate pedagogical and curricular structures that provide students an opportunity to use lived experiences as a basis for acquiring language, literacy, and critical thinking skills. The goal is one of student and teacher empowerment, a process of critical understanding of the self and of the world. Individuals need to be able to develop theories of themselves and their individual strengths; and to develop theories of the world, so that they understand for themselves what problems there are to be solved, and where they fit in. Beginning with the knowledge and language they bring with them to the learning situation, students need to be able to analyze and selectively appropriate knowledge, values, and skills from the dominant culture as a basis for scrutinizing and changing their existing circumstances.

In the following section, before describing alternate pedagogical and curricular structures that take critical notions of power, transformative leadership, and transformative intellectualism as prescriptive starting points, I want to demonstrate the utility of power as a descriptive lens, as a way of seeing how power relations constrain and

238

enable what people think, believe, say, and do. The focus will be on native literacy and language instruction in a Navajo setting. I will analyze the range of opinions Navajos hold about the utility of oral and written Navajo as an instructional device, and show how this range makes sense in light of procedures and ideologies that have developed at local institutions in a community setting for nearly three decades. The analysis is specific to one small, isolated context in the heart of an area far removed from mainstream concerns. Still, the points are pertinent to minority and native language issues elsewhere. In light of the macrostructural processes in U.S. schooling I have briefly highlighted thus far, they generalize readily to communities that hunger in a simple sense, as Dell Hymes (1980) puts it, for mere breathing space within the larger hive.

Power as a Descriptive Lens

Mesa Valley (a pseudonym), where I lived for 9 years, taught, conducted ethnographic research, and was school principal, comprises an area of 200 square miles that is home to 1,800 Navajos, most of whom survive on subsistence farming, livestock raising, weaving, seasonal forest fire fighting, and welfare. Situated among the red rock cliffs of the Four Corner's high desert plateau in the U.S. southwest, the land is sparsely settled, arid, and marginally productive. No local industry exists, and unemployment is high, with estimates ranging between 35–80%. One local resident summed up the low ceiling of opportunity into which children of the community are born: "Other than employment at the school, there's little here for young people. If they want to work, they must leave for town." The nearest centers of commerce, mainstream media, and employment are off the reservation more than 110 miles away.

From outward appearances, Mesa Valley is similar to many other reservation communities. Camp settlements of extended families lie distant from the community's single paved highway and from one another. Entering the center of the community, Mesa Valley splits into four parts. In the resulting quadrants exist a trading post, chapterhouse, mission church, and community-controlled school, that is, institutions of commerce, local government, religion, and K–12 education, respectively.

The area looks no different from other reservation settings, but, in important ways, Mesa Valley stands apart. For the past 25 years, the local community-controlled school has gained an international reputation for its bilingual program. Children who enter school with few or no English skills learn initially to read, write, and count in Navajo. English literacy is introduced in the second grade and maintained along with Navajo throughout the elementary and secondary levels. Gauging from criterion-referenced and standardized tests, the program has been effective. Mesa Valley students have consistently scored higher than other comparable reservation children on tests, written in English, of reading, language, and math.

In addition to effective bilingual instruction at the school, for more than 30 years the local mission church has developed Navajo reading materials to spread the word of Christianity. Community members have led Sunday church services, organized Navajo literacy classes for nonliterates, translated portions of the New Testament, and conducted weekly prayer meetings that focus on individuals' personal problems and solutions that derive from interpretations of biblical texts.

Although different ideologies surround and support church and school practices—an ideology of Christian salvation on the one hand, an ideology of community control of the content and process of schooling on the other—identical political processes have underpinned church and school activities. Cumulatively, they have not only delimited a narrow range of opinions about the efficacy of Navajo language and culture as heuristic devices but also allowed for the partial acceptance of indigenous uses for vernacular print (McLaughlin, 1989, 1992). In light of the nearly universal rejection of Navajo literacy elsewhere, this partial acceptance is and has been news (cf. Holm, 1971; Spolsky & Irvine, 1982; Young, 1977). The political processes are three-fold.

First, for more than two decades, Navajo language and literacy has been painstakingly incorporated into the process and content of church and school activity. Culture brokers who toiled more than 25 years at both settings diligently sought to engineer the acceptance of vernacular language and literacy. The director of the school understood community-control to be one and the same with native language instruction. The pastor of the church, upon assuming leadership of the congregation, soon realized that "if any message was to get through to the people, it would have to come in Navajo from one of them," and that Navajo reading was a powerful way to promote Christian conversion.

Second, the participation of community members in the governance and performance of school and church activities has been highly collaborative. At the school, local individuals teach, create curriculum in Navajo, teach Navajo history and culture, supervise teachers, manage programs, and, as School Board members, oversee all aspects of program development and implementation. All of the employees in the elementary school are Navajo, as are more than two thirds of the teachers in the secondary school and nearly four fifths of the school administrators. At the church, local Navajos perform all aspects of church services in Navajo from Navajo texts.

Third, the overall posture of what goes on at the church and the school has been advocacy-oriented. The aim has been to "build people up," as the church pastor once explained, and "to help students learn about, accept, and affirm their people and themselves," as the school director exhorted at a commencement exercise.

The use of community members' first language, collaborative community participation, and advocacy-oriented activities have underpinned the partial acceptance of Navajo literacy for purposes unconnected to church and school domains and shaped the opinions which individuals hold about Navajo print. In addition to valuative texts at the church and pedagogical literacy at the school, significant numbers of Mesa Valley people at home settings write letters, notes, journals, lists, and songbooks for interpersonal, intrapersonal, representational, and memory-supportive reasons, all in the vernacular— again, a novel development insofar as the macrosociolinguistics of Navajo language and literacy use is concerned.

Surrounding and supporting instructional practices in oral and written Navajo have been a narrow range of opinions, both pro and con, about the utility of Navajo script.

Navajo language and literacy are useful for they help individuals understand who they are. A parent explained, "It's good that students learn Navajo language, literacy, and culture. The Navajo people are made strong by our language and cultural practices. In other areas of the country where other tribes live, different Indian groups have forgotten their languages. They have forgotten their cultures. Because of that, they are not stable, and some Anglos take advantage of them." This person's third-grade daughter added, "I think kids should learn Navajo the most and English the next because we are Navajos. You have to speak your own language and act like Indians. English is good for talking to Anglos, and that's why we should keep teaching both languages. But Navajo is first. Navajo is for the Navajos."

Navajo language and literacy are useful for the promotion and maintenance of Navajo language and culture. A medicineman, administrator at Mesa Valley School, and user of vernacular script to record ceremonial knowledge elaborated, "From the Anglo point of view, teaching Navajo literacy is a useful transition to English, but from a Navajo point of view, the most important thing Navajo reading and writing does is help keep the culture. . . . Navajo language is the basis of Navajoness. . . . I know English is important, but if we forget about our language and only speak English and live in dominant society, then we [will] have melted and disappeared into a melting pot."

Navajo language and literacy are only useful for teaching initial academic concepts to young children. "It's cool for a little kid," said one high school student, "because when he gets older, he'll understand a lot." Yet as the child gets older, English becomes more important, as a recent graduate of the Mesa Valley program explained, "I don't think people should be in a program learning Navajo till their senior year. Learning the English language is much more valuable if you want to survive in the real world."

Navajo language and literacy are not useful; individuals will be judged on English speaking, reading, and writing abilities in later life in order to find jobs. In an article in Mesa Valley School's bilingual newspaper, a student editorialized, "Students need to spend time developing good English skills for their careers. Students are more likely to get jobs off the reservation than on because there are more jobs off the reservation. . . . People need good English skills to be in positions such as these." A translator of biblical texts and prominent writer of Navajo in the community added, "Somewhere along the line, Navajo becomes a hindrance. When [students] go to Farmington, Flagstaff, and other places off the reservation, all talk is in English. . . . Most of the people here, they'd say, 'We already speak Navajo. We already think Navajo. Now we want our children to learn English so they can find jobs.'"

The different beliefs about Navajo language and literacy that comprise the ideological field makes eminent sense in light of the political processes that have undergirded church and school activities. For young students, Navajo language and literacy are useful for promoting initial concepts in reading, writing, and mathematics. As students get older, the medium promotes understandings of traditional culture and of the self. Language and literacy in the vernacular also help them comprehend Christian truths. At the same time, the language of commerce and scarce job opportunities is English. People need to speak, read, and write English in order to get ahead. Moreover, few nonreligious reading materials exist in the vernacular, which makes inevitable the highly personal nature of culturally indigenous uses for Navajo print, such as letters, notes, lists, ceremonial songbooks, and ceremonial journals.

Beliefs about Navajo instruction and the political processes underpinning them speak to the utility of power as a descriptive notion in making clear the fact that the analysis of language, literacy, and knowledge at Mesa Valley cannot proceed inside a political vacuum. Forms and functions for what people think, say, read, write, and do are shaped on the one hand by processes of self-determination and self-empowerment at the church and school, and on the other by powerful economic structures embedded in the larger social order. Thus, the need is to see language, literacy, and knowledge in terms of social context, fundamentally constitutive of, and constrained by, political processes and ideologies that frame what goes on. This descriptive axiom then becomes an important starting point for the design of effective language and literacy instruction, as I elaborate in the next section.

Power as a Prescriptive Notion: Transformative Leadership, Transformative Intellectuals

I aim to describe alternate pedagogical and curricular structures that take critical notions of power as a prescriptive starting point. I will detail the development of two model language and literacy programs for Navajo youngsters—one at the secondary level, the other at the elementary level—that make concrete the often abstract notions of transformative leadership and transformative intellectualism.

Background

Although I ultimately conducted an ethnography of Navajo literacy and became coprincipal of the community school's elementary program, upon first arriving at Mesa Valley, I was hired as a teacher of secondary-level talented-and-gifted students. The approach I inherited in this capacity was an important precursor to one that became central to the development of a model language and literacy program for all Mesa Valley secondary students, not just talented-and-gifted ones, and with considerable modification, to the development of a model language and literacy program for Mesa Valley elementary-level children. Both programs operationalize critical notions of transformative leadership and have created roles for teachers and students as transformative intellectuals.

The definition of talented-and-giftedness in the secondary-level program I inherited was similar to ones commonly employed elsewhere. Students who read at or above grade level qualified for special pull-out instruction. In other words, students who measured at the bell curve's middle or beyond on standardized reading tests gained access to talented-and-gifted classes. For my first year, from a secondary student population of 160, I had 35 students. All but two of this number were children of staff persons at the school or lived within a 2-mile radius of the school compound, which allowed for participation in after-school clubs, field trips, and special events. Access to English language and literacy, and values in support of their use, were clearly integral to stratifying the students academically into mainstream or talented-and-gifted tracks and ultimately placing them into separate and unequal career pathways.

I taught in small groups. The average class had five students with whom I employed a project approach. For each 6-week grading period, students read from a choice of novels organized according to an overarching theme, such as "journey," "commitment," or "adventure." Then they worked in groups to create a tangible product that interpreted the theme: for instance, to write an additional chapter to the novel, dramatize an important scene from the book, or design a newspaper page that depicted the historical situation in which the book took place. The mainstream students, meanwhile, developed reading skills with skills-oriented basals in a reading lab. On average, three lab instructors had 25 students for 40 minutes at a time.

In essence, those students who could already read reasonably well concentrated on meaning; those who had reading difficulty concentrated on narrowly focused skills. The approach for able readers was to promote critical thinking skills. Built into the curriculum were processes of application, analysis, synthesis, and evaluation. The approach for less able readers was considerably less ambitious. The focus was on word attack skills, vocabulary development, and reading comprehension, as producers of basal materials understand the meaning of the term. That is, from short lists of choices, mainstream students had to "accurately" figure out what writers of curriculum, far removed from the realities of reservation life, meant.

Significant differences clearly marked the two sets of classes. As the talented-and-gifted program instructor, I was given considerable freedom to create curriculum: to stipulate themes, choose reading material, outline interpretive project ideas, identify audiences for student projects, and create evaluation procedures for measuring students' reading and writing progress. In the process, the students and I were able to develop a political discourse that emerged from literature-based analyses of current events, Navajo language, history, and traditional culture, popular culture, understandings of the world, and understandings of the self. Regular literacy program instructors, however, were locked into a "teacher proof" basal program that choreographed the teachers' and students' every move, leaving little room for critical thinking, much less student and teacher empowerment.

I came to Mesa Valley at an opportune time for critically evaluating the secondary school's literacy program. The elementary program had been in place for many years, but the secondary program was still quite new; the community's first group of 12th graders had only graduated the previous Spring. Other teachers and school administrators had the same sense of dissatisfaction with the school's literacy program as I had and recognized the need for change. If nothing else, standardized test scores indicated problems. They showed that the talented-and-gifted students were making excellent progress, but that the mainstream students, as they progressed from one grade level to the next, tended to fall further and further behind. The time was right for abolishing the talented-and-gifted track.

Mesa Valley Secondary's Applied Literacy Program

A team of secondary school administrators and teachers intuitively felt the need for a product-oriented approach. Not only was the approach highly successful in the talented-and-gifted classes, but it was also congruent with a "practice privately and in small groups first, then perform" learning style attributed to Navajos and other Native Americans and well documented in the cultural differences literature (cf. John, 1972; Philips, 1972). The climate of community control and community participation at the school was such that we also felt intuitively the need to create products for viable audiences. The need

245

was to "hook in" not only the students but also their parents and other community members. Because most people in the community spoke only Navajo, inserting the students' first language into instruction was an obvious first requirement.

The effort that has evolved at Mesa Valley Secondary is called the Applied Literacy Program. Starting in 1984, with discretionary funding from the Office of Indian Education, a team of four teachers and one evaluator replaced the talented-and-gifted teacher's slot as well as the three teaching positions in the reading lab. The program specifies a range of products, which develop students' thinking, reading, writing, and speaking abilities in Navajo and English, for a variety of audiences, including elementary students, other secondary-level students and faculty, and most importantly, members of the larger Mesa Valley community. The program's curriculum can be summed up in shorthand: $C = P + A$, or curriculum equals product plus audience. On a quarterly basis, the products constitute elements of a community bilingual newspaper as well as programming material for a low-power community television station. All of the products measure against a model of thinking that ensures cognitively complex activity. Students work within an immediately comprehensible world while project staff members challenge the students to recognize the inherently borderland situation into which they have been born, and to understand skills they need to develop in order to thrive as young Navajo adults in the late 20th century.

The curriculum is organized along three dimensions (see Figure 1). The first dimension consists of four content areas: Navajo Research, English Research, Computers, and Performance. The second dimension, underpinning the first and outlined in a column at the right of the chart, consists of cognitive goals specified for different grade levels. Lifted from Benjamin Bloom (1956) and more contemporary theorists of metacognition and critical thinking (Brown, 1980; Lipman, 1988), knowledge consumption is for grade 7, comprehension and application for grade 8, analysis for grade 9, synthesis and evaluation for grade 10, and metacognition—awareness of the processes of learning—for grades 11 and 12. At the intersection of the content area and the goals for cognitive development, constituting the third dimension, are headings for 9-week learning activities.

In 12th grade, for example, students divide equally into the project's four classes. In Navajo Research, they develop an editorial-style article in Navajo, first articulating research questions, next interviewing at least two experts (with contrasting points of view) on their research topic, then evaluating and synthesizing opinions, and finally writing editorial articles for publication in the bilingual community newspaper. Seniors in English Research follow the same set of procedures, only in English, to develop editorial-style articles for the same newspaper. In Computers, with the Navajo-smart word processors, students learn to use different wordprocessing and page layout programs, which they may encounter at work or in higher education. In Performance, they analyze a topic of critical importance to the individual, the school, the community, or the Navajo Tribe, and prepare comprehensive videotape products to be aired over the community's low-power television station.

All of the students in grades 7 through 12 take the classes. The program is for everyone. It is neither a remedial, pull-out program, nor one merely for talented-and-gifted individuals. At any given point in the academic year, the individual student is involved in one of the four activities for his or her grade level. At the conclusion of the 9-week quarters, the students rotate from one activity to the next. In this way, each grade's four groups take the four class activities, albeit in different order, by the end of the school year (for more details, see McLaughlin, 1990).

Mesa Valley Elementary's Junior Research Program

Similar program development challenges existed in Mesa Valley's Elementary program after I had left secondary teaching to conduct an ethnography of community literacy and reemerged as one of two principals in the elementary school. I inherited a highly successful maintenance bilingual K–6 program that was skills-oriented and driven by criterion-referenced tests, both in English and Navajo, that had been developed entirely at the local level. At the same time, there appeared a pressing need for a comprehensive writing program that aimed to focus less on word-and sentence-based units of meaning than on discourse-level features of texts. In addition, as had been the case at the secondary level previous to the Applied Literacy Program, there were needs to create new functions for English and Navajo writing, promote critical thinking skills in both languages, and encourage students to develop theories of themselves and of the world.

During that first year in elementary, another teacher and I piloted Research classes with fourth graders. The curriculum consisted of a

Figure 1

Mesa Valley Secondary School's Applied Literacy Program

Grade	Navajo Research	English Research	Computers	Performance	Cognitive Strategies
7	*Teach A Story* In Navajo, from texts written after research, students teach a story to elementary classes, and add books to elementary library.	*Teach Item Production* In English, from texts written after interviewing an expert, students teach the production of an item to elementary classes.	*Word Processing I* Students type and edit English and Navajo Research 7th-grade students' products at 15 wpm using Microsoft (MS) Word.	*Video News Bulletin* Students create a periodic bilingual video news bulletin for broadcast on RPCTV; they rotate as crew, reporter, and talent (in E/N).	**Knowledge Consumption** • learn • consume • acquire • master • ascertain • determine
8	*Teach Nonfiction* In Navajo, from texts written after interviewing experts, students teach elementary Navajo classes; books are added to elementary library.	*Teach Pros and Cons* In English, after interviewing experts, students teach and publish in the school newspaper pros and cons of an issue.	*Word Processing II* Students type and edit English and Navajo Research 8th grade students' products at 25 wpm using MS Word.	*Video Character Sketch* Students create a bilingual character sketch for broadcast on RPCTV; they rotate as crew, reporter, and talent (in E/N).	**Comprehension & Application** • interpret • appreciate • expand • utilize • employ • understand
9	*Navajo Feature Writing* Students research and write a feature-style article in Navajo for school newspaper publication.	*English Feature Writing* Students research and write a feature-style article in English for school newspaper publication.	*Word Processing III* Students edit and produce other students' articles using MS Word; align text in columns; learn graphics and SuperPaint.	*Video Feature Program* Students create a bilingual feature program for broadcast on RPCTV; they rotate as crew, reporter, and talent (in E/N).	**Analysis** • scrutinize • contrast • survey • compare • take apart • discover

continued

Figure 1
(continued)

Grade	Navajo Research	English Research	Computers	Performance	Cognitive Strategies
10	*Navajo News Writing* Students research and write news-style articles in Navajo for school newspaper production.	*English News Writing* Students research and write news-style articles in English for school newspaper production.	*Advanced Word Processing* Students edit and produce newspaper articles with MS Word; create tables; retrieve information with MS Works and CompuServe.	*Video Drama* As a group, students learn script-writing and characterization; then write, perform in, and produce a videotaped drama for broadcast on RPCTV (in E/N).	**Synthesis & Evaluation** • arrange • judge • translate • classify • design • rate
11	*Navajo Investigative News Writing* Students research, write, wordprocess, edit, and publish an investigative news-style article in Navajo.	*English Investigative News Writing* Students research, write, wordprocess, edit, and publish an investigative news-style article in English.	*Design and Layout I* Students learn basics of PageMaker; then design and lay out Navajo and English Research 7th and 8th grade students' products.	*Video Production* As a group, students write, perform in, and produce a comprehensive videotaped production, with sound and picture editing, music, and sound effects (in E/N).	**Metacognition** having a complete and effective awareness of each of the above levels of thinking
12	*Navajo Editorial Writing* Students research, write, wordprocess, edit, and publish an editorial-style article in the school newspaper in Navajo.	*English Editorial Writing* Students research, write, wordprocess, edit, and publish an editorial-style article in the school newspaper in English.	*Design and Layout II* Students learn advanced PageMaker, then design and lay out Navajo and English articles for the school newspaper.	*Video Production for Change* As a group, students investigate, critically analyze, then produce a comprehensive video to effect change at the school or community level (in E/N).	**Metacognition** having a complete and effective awareness of each of the above levels of thinking

process of inquiry, writing, and publishing taken straight from secondary's Applied Literacy Program. In essence, there were three steps: the students had to develop research thesis ideas; interview an expert on a self-selected topic; and shape the interview into an article to be published in a school-community newsletter. What has come to be known as the "writing process approach," advocated and detailed by whole language practitioners such as Donald Graves (1983, 1988a, 1988b), Jerome Harste, Kathy G. Short, and Carolyn Burke (1988), and Frank Smith (1984, 1986a), provided centerpiece structures for reorganizing our efforts. In the year following our pilot efforts, we obtained funding from the Office of Bilingual Education and Minority Language Affairs (OBEMLA) for a staff of four teachers. The resulting program, child to the Applied Literacy Program, was called the Junior Research Program.

Similar to its secondary counterpart, the Junior Research Program specifies a range of products to develop students' thinking, reading, writing, and speaking abilities in Navajo and English. On a quarterly basis, the products constitute a variety of books created for parents and other students, a community bilingual newsletter, and a variety of dramatic productions, culminating with public service messages broadcast over the Navajo tribe's 50,000-watt radio station, KTNN. Utilizing the language which students bring with them to the learning situation, staff members challenge the students to think critically about issues affecting them at the levels of community, tribe, country, and world. The curriculum is organized along two dimensions (see Figure 2). The first dimension consists of four content areas: Navajo Writing, English Writing, Computers, and Drama. The second dimension, at the intersection of content areas and grade levels, consists of headings for 9-week learning activities.

In sixth grade, for example, students divide equally into the project's four classes. In Navajo Writing, they develop reports that pertain to a topic of significance at the national or international level. In English Writing, they follow the same set of procedures, only in English, to develop reports. In Computers, with Navajo-smart wordprocessors, sixth graders collate reports and stories written by other students in the program and produce a bilingual community newsletter. In Drama, they analyze topics of critical importance to the individual at the national and international level, and then write and produce dramatic scripts that are aired over the tribe's radio station.

As with the Applied Literacy Program, all of the elementary students in grades 2 through 6 take Junior Research classes. At any given point in the academic year, the individual student is involved in one of the four activities specified for his or her grade level. At the conclusion of 9-week quarters, the students rotate from one activity to the next, taking all four class activities by the end of the school year.

Discussion

The Junior Research and Applied Literacy Programs highlight the efficacy of power as descriptive and prescriptive tools for educational program development. They also show how transformative leadership and roles for transformative intellectuals can proceed. Integral to both programs is the curricular structure I have characterized as C = P + A. In other words, students and teachers work together to produce knowledge for audiences outside of the immediate classroom. The process of knowledge production is developmental in that the programs specify a range of products that increase in cognitive complexity as the students progress into higher grade levels. At the same time, the process is relatively constant. First, the teacher decides which topics to put before the students. Second, individual students decide which topics to explore in considerable depth before, third, shaping their analyses into tangible products in oral or written form for significant audiences. Generally speaking, this three-part sequence is consistent across all the classes in the elementary and secondary programs.

What does change, however, is the curriculum's content. While focusing on social conditions in the family, in the community, and at the levels of tribe, nation, and world, students and teachers are positioned to decide for themselves whose knowledge counts. They are the authors of what gets talked about, analyzed, and produced in the classroom. In so doing, the pedagogical becomes political—in returning to the teachers and students authority for deciding what gets taught; and the political becomes pedagogical—in treating the teachers and students as critical agents, allowing them to analyze existing social conditions, and propounding change.

As the nature of curriculum changes, so does pedagogy and school administration. When students become subjects of the creation of knowledge, the role of the teacher and school administrator evolves from one of omniscient expert-technocrat to one of *moral practitioner*, as William Foster (1989) understands the meaning of the term. In Foster's words, a moral practitioner is someone who encourages the

251

Figure 2
Mesa Valley Elementary School's Junior Research Program

Grade	Navajo Research	English Research	Computers	Drama
Self				
2	*Autobiographies* In Navajo, interpreting children's stories about self; focusing on first lines, leads, characters, and settings; publishing stories about self.	*Autobiographies* In English, interpreting children's stories about self; focusing on first lines, leads, characters, and settings; publishing stories about self.	*Chronicles I* Mastering basic Macintosh computer functions; learning home keys; typing 5 wpm; typing and publishing stories about self.	*Performance Skills* Interpreting children's literature about self; emphasizing characters and settings; performing skits, stressing voice and concentration.
Family-Community				
3	*Fiction I* In Navajo, interpreting children's stories about family-community; focusing on episodes, conflicts, and resolutions; publishing stories about family-community.	*Fiction I* In English, interpreting children's stories about family-community; focusing on episodes, conflicts, and resolutions; publishing stories about family-community.	*Chronicles II* Mastering main menus of Microsoft (MS) Works 2.0; typing 10 wpm; writing, typing, and publishing stories about family-community.	*Performing Stories I* Interpreting children's literature about family-community; emphasizing who, what, and where; performing skits, stressing concentration and voice.
Community-Tribe				
4	*Fiction II* In Navajo, interpreting children's stories about community-tribe; focusing on plot resolutions and endings; publishing stories about community-tribe.	*Fiction II* In English, interpreting children's stories about community-tribe; focusing on plot resolutions and endings; publishing stories about community-tribe.	*Fables* Mastering edit and draw functions of MS Works; typing 15 wpm; publishing and disseminating student-authored fables.	*Performing Stories II* Interpreting children's literature about community-tribe; emphasizing plots and endings; performing skits on community-tribe; stressing acting with whole body.

continued

Figure 2
(continued)

Tribe-U. S.

Grade	Navajo Research	English Research	Computers	Drama
5	*Nonfiction I* In Navajo, understanding current issues effecting tribe-U.S.; developing interview and research skills; publishing issue reports on tribe-U.S. topics.	*Nonfiction I* In English, understanding current issues effecting tribe-U.S.; developing interview and research skills; publishing issue reports on tribe-U.S. topics.	*Newsletter I* Mastering HyperCard clip art functions; doubling initial wpm typing rate; editing, typing, and publishing a school-community elementary newsletter in English and Navajo.	*Performing Scripts* Understanding current issues affecting tribe-U.S.; developing interview and research skills; performing skits about tribe-U.S.; stressing staging.

U. S.-World

Grade	Navajo Research	English Research	Computers	Drama
6	*Nonfiction II* In Navajo, understanding current issues affecting U.S.-world; developing interview and research skills; publishing issue reports on U.S.-world topics.	*Nonfiction II* In English, understanding current issues effecting U.S.-world; developing interview and research skills; publishing issue reports on U.S.-world topics.	*Newsletter II* Mastering main menus of MS Word 4.0; doubling initial wpm typing rate; editing, typing, and publishing a school-community elementary newsletter in English and Navajo.	*Public Service Messages* Understanding current issues affecting U.S.-world; developing interview and research skills; writing and performing messages about U.S.-world for KTNN radio.

critical analysis of power in terms of its relationship to the oppression of different groups in society. To put it in concrete terms, the teacher and administrator's role becomes one of coach, someone to whom learners may turn in order to acquire reading and writing skills, learn about the world, learn about themselves, and ultimately solve problems.

To the degree that language and literacy situations differ from one speech community to the next, the content of effective language and literacy programs must differ. The process of developing model language arts projects such as the ones described here, though, is replicable. The programs' central concern for the politics of knowledge, the politics of oral and written language, the structuring of cognitively complex activity embedded within a process of "products for audiences," and ultimately the empowerment of program students and teachers, such that they develop critical understandings of themselves and of the world, need to be considered in the design of any successful learning program, especially for students of dominated minority background.

The point is one that has been stressed well by Jim Cummins (1986). If school programs for politically disenfranchised, disempowered minority students are to succeed, they must do more than change the school's curriculum or language of instruction. They must position students and teachers alike to recognize how power relations mediate social and school reality and thus reflect people's lived experiences, and permit the development of alternate pedagogical and curricular structures that give students, teachers, and administrators voice—that is, an opportunity to use lived experiences as a basis for acquiring language, literacy, and critical thinking skills. As long as curriculum and pedagogy do no more than shuffle superficial aspects of practices that fail children fundamentally, without taking into account the political nature of all school knowledge, without positioning students to scrutinize and transform what goes on around them, schools will continue to reproduce structural inequities that characterize society in general and that make curriculum, pedagogy, and program development ever problematic, particularly for students of nonmainstream backgrounds.

Conclusion

In this article, I have examined the meanings of power in relation to questions about curriculum, program development, and leadership. I have tried to show how an understanding of power can play a central role in the way teachers and school administrators conceive of their work, both in terms of analyzing curricular and pedagogical challenges they must confront, and developing program solutions, particularly for language minority learners. I have described how two language and literacy programs, both of which employ a "curriculum as products for audiences" process, have allowed for transformative leadership and conditions for students and teachers as transformative intellectuals to take place.

Many times, the calls of critical theorists for transformative leadership and transformative intellectualism amount to obfuscating rhetoric which, in over-intellectualizing what is wrong with mainstream school practices without identifying what teachers and school administrators can do, simply add to the problem. What I have tried to do in this article is pinpoint the efficacy of power as a descriptive and prescriptive tool, and to show how the alternate curricular and pedagogical structures comprising the Applied Literacy and Junior Research Programs not only follow from an understanding of power but also have allowed for important changes to take place. At Mesa Valley School, the C = P + A formulation has allowed for students to use standard and vernacular forms of language in oral and written form in order to analyze social conditions around them; through students' interviews, it has allowed parents and other community members to participate actively in the school; and it has allowed teachers and school administrators to become subjects themselves who engage along with the students in critical dialogue about issues of consequence in the community. Such changes operationalize the important aims of transformative leadership and intellectualism and work to serve language minority learners well.

Summary

The purpose of this chapter has been to examine the meanings of power in relation to questions about leadership, language, school knowledge, and program development for language minority learners. I have suggested that an understanding of power can play a central role in the way educators conceive of their work, both in terms of analyzing curricular challenges and developing program solutions. After discussing power from a critical perspective, I pointed out the utility of power as a descriptive device, as a way of diagnosing curricular challenges that confront Navajo teachers and program developers.

I then tried to make concrete what are often overly abstract formulations in describing how power has been used as a prescriptive notion in order to create English and Navajo literacy programs that specify conditions for student and teacher empowerment.

Acknowledgments

I wish to acknowledge the helpful comments of Denise E. Murray, William Tierney, and Andrew Gitlin.

Discussion Topics and Projects

1. Cultural exclusionists, such as E. D. Hirsch, take an academic-rationalist position in arguing for the formation of a common, national language and culture in schools. Only by acquiring the basic, world knowledge necessary for reading a newspaper competently, grasping implications, and relating new information to unstated contexts, Hirsch argues, can children learn to participate in complex activities with other members of society. School curriculum, thus, should consist of the study of great books, thinkers, ideas, and events, which constitute cultural capital and the currency of knowledge and power. Critical theorists, such as Henry Giroux, hold an opposite view. They urge teachers to bracket standard forms of language and culture with critical understandings of vernacular and popular ways of knowing so as to struggle in the interest of creating a better world. Active participation in society is the goal for the academic rationalists; the transformation of society is the goal for the critical theorists. To which set of values do you subscribe, and why?

2. I have argued that the question for educators of minority and mainstream students alike, as Michael Apple (1990) advises, is not *what* knowledge is most worth, but *whose*. To ask whose knowledge counts is to presume that it is vital to analyze the ideological content of curriculum and to frame its authors' interests and intents. The following questions, from Aronowitz and Giroux (1985), provide starting points for the analysis of curricular texts. Use them to scrutinize a spectrum of school-based learning materials:

a. Who are the authors' sponsors? What are their interests in the issue? Find key phrases, sentences. What images of themselves do they wish to present?

b. Who is the intended audience? What are their interests in the issue? Of what does the author-sponsor wish to persuade them?

c. What content does the author-sponsor focus on? What is omitted? Are biases or prejudices apparent (such as racism, sexism, ageism)?

d. What alternative viewpoints or arguments exist that are not mentioned or acknowledged?

e. What meaning is produced by the interaction of the formal photo/sketches, and written account? (p. 151)

Further Reading

For arguments in favor of cultural exclusionism, see E. D. Hirsch (1987) and Mortimer Adler (1982); for eloquent critiques of cultural exclusionists, see Apple (1987), Aronowitz and Giroux (1985), and Giroux (1988). Working from cultural inclusionism, Cummins (1986) sets forth a comprehensive framework for school practice. For detailed descriptions of program development which works from critical theory and Cummins's frame, see Ruth Gamberg, Winniefred Kwak, Merideth Hutchings, Judy Altheim, and Gail Edwards (1988), Shirley Brice Heath (1983), Christine Sleeter (1991), and Eliot Wigginton (1985, 1989). Instructional orientations and techniques vital to cultural inclusionism can be found in Donald Graves (1983, 1988a, 1988b), Harste et al. (1988), and Smith (1984, 1986a).

11

Unlimited Resources

Tapping into Learners' Language, Culture, and Thought

Denise E. Murray
San José State University, California

The chapters in Part II of this book discuss many differences in language and culture. However, a persistent theme of the book is that these discussions and explanations of differences merely scratch the surface of the cultural, linguistic, and individual differences we may encounter in our classrooms. The particular information in these chapters may help educators as they work with those particular linguistic and cultural groups. However, we must keep in mind that our students, whether children, teens, or adults, bring with them far richer language practices and cultural value systems than we have been able to explore here. In this chapter, then, I want us to think of our students as having *unlimited* resources—ones not discussed here, ones we may not have envisaged, ones that may not have been studied by scholars, or ones that our students may not even be conscious of. Further, I want us to expand the cultural and language theme to include the cognitive abilities our students bring with them. Rather than the more traditional approach to instruction in which the learner is a tabula rasa on which the teacher will write or an empty vessel the teacher will fill, I want us to consider our students as bringing rich resources with them, resources that can be tapped in instruction. Two traditions of scholarship inform the pedagogical suggestions I will discuss here.

Rogerian (or humanistic) approaches to learning focus on the learner being responsible for his/her own learning (see Stevick, 1990, for a discussion of humanism and language teaching); the anthropological method of inquiry known as ethnography views the members of a culture as informants, that is, people with knowledge of the practices of their own culture. With these two approaches to the learner in mind, we can rethink the way we teach, especially the way we teach language. This approach is congruent with the current focus on learner-centered curricula in English as a second language (ESL) instruction (see, e.g., Nunan, 1988).

Although authors of this book value the languages of our students' homes—whether they be nonstandard varieties of English or languages completely unrelated to English—at some point in a person's life, acquisition of a standard language may become necessary—for jobs, for schooling, for participation as a citizen. How can we foster language acquisition, help students become responsible for their own learning, and make use of the knowledge and language our students bring with them to class?

In this chapter, I will give detailed explanations of a number of activities for adult or high school learners of standard English, techniques that focus on the learner as informant, responsible for his/her own learning. By considering learners as informants, we both raise their self-esteem and provide a context in which content rather than form is the focus of instruction and interaction. By having students responsible for their own learning, we empower them. Many of these activities are adaptable to younger children as well as to teen and adult learners. I focus on teens and adults because these are the groups I have taught over the years, using activities such as those I describe below—in adult ESL programs, in college ESL composition classes, and in program's educating future ESL teachers.

In the anthropological sense, our students are informants with a wealth of cultural and linguistic knowledge; however, this knowledge is rarely conscious and rarely articulated in language classrooms. What I am suggesting here is that we create instructional scaffolds (see Applebee, 1984, for a discussion on scaffolding for learners; Johns, this book, also shows the importance of scaffolding) that will help students investigate their own languages and cultures. Scaffolding provides support for students—but only as much support as is needed at any given time, with the scaffold gradually being removed.

Activities

Speech Community

Sociolinguists have varying definitions of the concept of speech community; but for the purposes of students' exploring their own speech communities, I have found John Gumperz's (1972) definition the most useful: a "social group which may be either monolingual or multilingual, held together by frequency of social interactive patterns and set off from the surrounding areas by weaknesses in the lines of communication. Linguistic communities may consist of small groups bound together by face-to-face contact or may cover large regions depending on the level of abstraction we wish to achieve" (p. 219). Thus, a speech community may be an entire nation, or may be members of an association, or of a section of a large city.

I usually start any class with an investigation of the students' speech communities (see Gumperz, 1972, for a discussion on speech community; see Heath, 1983, for the application of ethnography to the classroom). Although my own work has been with nonnative-speaking students learning English or with students in a teacher education program, teachers of African American students (or speakers of other nonstandard varieties) can also use the notion of speech community as a basis for investigating students' uses of language.

To investigate students' speech communities, students whose English is advanced can keep a journal over a period of 2 weeks, jotting down their uses of language. Students with limited English can do the same task in their home language. At the end of the 2-week period, students then fill in a matrix such as the ones that follow (see Figures 1–4 on the following pages). The items on the matrix are chosen from the situations in which the students engaged in language or needed to use a particular language. Thus, for example, in a college writing class, students might include "class discussion in major subject courses" so that they can identify whether they speak in their other college classes, and if not, why not. Similarly, they might include "my children's teachers" if the students are in an adult education program and need to interact with their children's teachers. Some students read and want to read directions or information on warranty or product safety. The items I have used in the samples below are representative of situations various students have identified over the years. Not all classes identify all these situations and some identify others. The categories must come from the students in a particular class. Beginning

ESL students can use pictures (cut from magazines, for example) or drawings to identify the categories in their matrices.

The column "Reasons" is included so that students can think through why they use the particular language they do. Thus, for example, if their primary language is used in talk with family because that is the common shared language, there is no need for us to teach functions in English dealing with family situations. But if a student replies that she uses her primary language when writing notes on the refrigerator for her children (even though they are barely literate in the primary language) because her English is not good enough, we may want to include such situations in our syllabus. Or we may decide that the parent is helping the children acquire literacy in the primary language and want to encourage this practice, knowing that first-language literacy will enhance second-language literacy. Whatever curricular decision we reach, it should be based on firm data of language use *and* consideration of what the students themselves want.

It is also important to separate out oral language from reading and writing because the functions people require for these different channels of communication are rarely the same. For example, a family might discuss the soap operas or their problems at work orally, using the written channel primarily for interactions with schools and other institutions. We need to explore which channels are required for which functions in order to develop appropriate curricula. (See Figures 1, 2, and 3 on the following pages.)

These matrices, which the students complete, provide both learner and teacher with a clearer understanding of the ways in which individual students use both their primary language and English. In class we then discuss situations in which they used English and determine whether they felt their English was adequate for the task. We next discuss situations in which they used their primary language and determine whether they wanted to use English in this situation, but did not have sufficient mastery of that language for it to be appropriate. We are then able to decide on what functions and situations should be in the teaching curriculum, giving students responsibility for their own learning, as advocated by humanistic educators. In this way, we avoid making arbitrary curricular choices or ones based primarily on our intuitions of what students need (as McLaughlin discusses in this book). Using such an approach to syllabus design, for example, would identify the Cambodians' and Mexicanos'[1] need to respond to door-to-door solicitors (as Welaratna and Vasquez suggest in this book).

Sometimes, prior to having students complete the matrices, I have

Figure 1
Language Use Survey: Oral

Talking Situation	Primary/Other English	Either/Both	Reasons
Family			
Friends			
Neighbors			
Shopping			
Doctor			
Dentist			
Post Office			
Teachers			
Social Security			
Getting things repaired			
Interviews			
Class discussion			
Etc.			

them draw speech community networks for each of the languages they speak. This provides them with a visual representation of the journal they have kept for 2 weeks. Quite often they have distinct speech communities for each language, which provides an interesting discussion point for more advanced classes.

A student in one of my teacher education classes adapted this method for her class of beginning adult ESL learners[2]. She had students complete a Student Profile Sheet. (See Figure 4 on p. 265.)

These sheets covered a full page and students were asked to provide seven samples each. She found that students soon got into the spirit of

Figure 2
Language Use Survey: Reading

Reading Situation	Primary/Other English	Either/Both	Reasons
Family/notes			
Friends/notes			
Neighbors/notes			
Service/notes			
School			
Bills			
Products			
Job ads			
Textbooks			
Catalogs			
Enrollment forms			
Etc.			

things: Dialogues began appearing and responses became longer and longer, and, even though they had limited English, they transcribed their observations with amazing clarity, as the examples below testify. Reported uses of English ranged from phatic communication, such as "Have a nice day!" said by a supermarket checker, to dialogues such as:

Cam: Good morning, how are you?

Neighbor: Fine, thanks.

Cam: Your dog came into my backyard. Please keep him at your house. Please repare the fence. Your dog came into my backyard two time.

Figure 3
Language Use Survey: Writing

Writing Situations	Primary/Other English	Either/Both	Reasons
Family/notes			
Friends/notes			
Neighbors/notes			
Service/notes			
School			
Checks			
Papers			
Forms			
Resumes			
Etc.			

Figure 4
Student Profile Sheet

When and where did you use English?

To whom did you speak?   Where?   What happened?

Saturday

Sunday

Neighbor: Yes I will.

Cam: Thank you.

Other students reported their conversations, such as the grandmother who helped her grandchildren with their homework:

I always help them to made homework. . . . Jamie want learned 11–20. I took some number card want she prnounce. If 16 she say sixty. I say sixty is 60 isn't 16. A little while she can say sixteen.

The teacher categorized her students' observations, finding that the category with the largest number was family (22% of uses). For me, this was especially interesting because it was contrary to what I had experienced in my own adult ESL classes. Usually we do not expect our ESL students to be using English with their families. But often English is the only shared language in families with members from different countries or when one member marries a native-English speaker; often grandchildren only use English; often parents help children with their school work. By examining *actual* speech communities and uses of language, we can better design curricula for our students. Thus, we could help Cam with the language needed to make a polite complaint to her neighbor; or we could help others such as the grandmother learn the functions used for U.S. schoolwork.

Cross-Cultural Awareness

Because individuals behave differently in the same situation due to both personal and cultural differences, we need to help them find ways of interacting that are appropriate for them culturally, personally, *and* are appropriate in mainstream U.S. culture. As informants, learners can provide an understanding of their own culture and personal preferences. As instructors, we can provide an understanding of mainstream U.S. practices, as discovered through research (see Wolfson, 1989, for summaries of such research). The following are two ways of comparing and contrasting the students' culture with that of the mainstream.

Role play. Traditionally, role play has required students to take on a new role and thereby demonstrate their proficiency in the target language. Role play can serve quite a different function if we begin instead with what the students *already* know. Let us take the example above of Cam wanting to complain to his neighbor about the neighbor's dog entering his backyard. As a linguistically and cognitively functioning adult, Cam already knows (even if unconsciously) the rules for such a speech event in his own language and culture. He may not be able to articulate this knowledge, but, given the actual situation, he can effectively role play how he would respond. Even if students play the roles as they believe they should be played, rather than as they actually are, we can uncover the culture's values for the particular situation. In a class with a number of Vietnamese students, I would have them role play this situation first *without* using language. While they role play, other members of the class observe nonverbal communication such as use of hands, facial expressions, distance between participants. They write these down or draw diagrams/pictures to illustrate what they have seen. Next, students role play the situation in their primary language, with as many pairs as possible from the same cultural and linguistic background role playing. It is important to stress similar cultural backgrounds as well as linguistic ones. Spanish speakers from Mexico have different cultural values and traditions from Spanish-speaking Argentineans, for example. Ethnic Chinese from Vietnam have different cultural rules from the Chinese from Taiwan. These role plays are either videotaped or audiotaped. Students then translate the language used in the speech event for the rest of the class. The dialogue is put on the overhead by the students or the teacher.

Using these dialogues, first we examine the individual differences among learners from the same cultural background. Then, we identify common behaviors in that culture. I do this with as many linguistic and cultural groups as possible. We then either watch a video of Americans in the same situation or I work with another teacher or aide and role play the situation for the students. We perform the same analysis as we did for the different linguistic and cultural groups. We can now compare and contrast individual and cultural variation in language use, nonverbal cues, and interpersonal relations for this particular situation. From this comparison, we can identify functions and behaviors that can be transferred from the primary language speech event to the U.S. speech event. For more advanced learners, this comparison and contrast can be a discussion or a written paper. For beginning students, I use a matrix on which they can put check marks. A brief sample matrix appears on the following page (see Figure 5).

Figure 5
Speech Event Matrix

Behavior	Primary Language	English
Eye-contact		
Distance between participants		
Use of name in address		
Politeness markers		
Tone of voice		

A useful and more comprehensive rubric for examining the characteristics of these speech events is Dell Hymes's (1986) SPEAKING mnemonic:

Setting: Refers to both physical and psychological environment as to the time and place as well as the cultural definition of the speech act or event.

Participants: Refers to speaker, hearer, occasionally to the audience overhearing the speech act or event.

Ends: Refers to the recognized and expected purpose of the speech act or event.

Act sequence: Refers to the actual sequences of speech acts exchanged between participants.

Key: Refers to the manner and tone in which the event is performed (e.g., joking).

Instrumentalities: Refers to channel of transmission.

Norms: Refers to both norms of interpretation and of interaction, that is, how the event should be understood and what are the culture-based rules of behavior.

Genres: Refers to established categories such as conversation, poem.

Students and teacher can identify how each of these characteristics is present in their speech events. Not all speech events will be defined by all of these features; but they do provide a way for both students and teachers to compare and contrast speech events across and within cultures.

The next step is to identify the extent to which each learner is willing to adapt his or her behavior to fit the U.S. patterns. For many learners, maintaining eye contact between a superior and inferior is too culturally inappropriate for them to be willing to use. Others will find that they can use such behaviors in English because English does not seem as personal and culturally real as does the primary language. It is for this reason that so many people can swear more effectively in a second language than in their first, for which all the cultural taboos operate. The final step is to have students role play the situation in English.

By using this method of role play, I give students the opportunity to explore what they already know and to choose what they will use in the U.S. setting. In this way they can better understand their own difficulties in adapting; but also, they can understand why Americans might react to them in a particular way. If they choose, for example, not to maintain eye contact, they know that many Americans will perceive them as being shifty or even as lying. But they do it with conscious knowledge and by making the decision for themselves. It is not imposed by the teacher, but offered as a choice that carries certain consequences.

Oral life histories.   Another source of cultural knowledge is other members of the students' communities. I have students interview older members of their communities, asking the latter questions about their lives in the home country and their adaptation to the United States, just as Usha Welaratna (this book) did to collect her life histories of Khmer in northern California. Daniel McLaughlin (this book) also has Navajo students interview experts and write articles for publication in the bilingual community newspaper. We prepare in class for these interviews, helping students determine what information they want to discover and what sort of questions they might want to ask. The choice of focus is up to the students. The interviews are usually conducted in the primary language. Students then have the task of summarizing the oral language to report back to the rest of the class. If students work in groups, those with better English proficiency can help those with minimal English. But all contribute knowledge and expertise. We then create a book of life histories for all class members. If the interviewee agrees, we may include photos of the interviewees. Often students want to share these "books" with other members in their community. I also encourage them to write a piece for their local primary-language newspaper, a new and real audience. These life histories provide students with a better understanding of their own community and also an understanding of the communities of other immigrants and refugees. I also collect a life history of an older native-English-speaking person to share with the class. This helps students see the vast patchwork of cultural and linguistic tradition that makes up the United States (see Nichols, this book, for an activity that helps all of us uncover our linguistic and cultural heritage).

Use of Primary Language

Just as our students come to us with different cultural and personal values, they also come with varying competencies in their primary language. Research has shown the advantages of balanced bilingualism (see Collier, 1989, for a summary of such research) and the prevalence of code-switching among bilinguals (see Gumperz, 1982, for a discussion of code-switching), that is, the shift from one language to another within the same speech event. Thus, the use of the primary language in the English language classroom is not a question of laziness (as has been suggested in the past); nor is it an impediment to the acquisition of English. Rather, it is a natural resource that we as teachers can make use of to facilitate learning and build self-esteem. In the previous two sections, I have already indicated several ways of using students' primary language. The following are further suggestions for consciously tapping the language resources our students bring with them to class.

Reading/Writing. Traditional reading exercises consist of teacher-selected texts with end-of-chapter questions that are supposed to determine whether students have understood the passage. Many such texts use questions that require decoding skills only; the student may have very little understanding of the content of the text and still be able to answer the questions. Even if texts include well-designed questions, this task requires students to perform in different ways from the way readers normally respond to a text. Novels are not followed by comprehension questions; newspapers and magazines do not include comprehension questions. When we read, we read for enjoyment or to uncover information that we want to use in some way. We should, as teachers, try to create situations for students that help them read for real purposes, both in English and in their primary language. One way is to use student-produced writing as reading texts for the class. As other students read what a classmate has written, they want to ask more questions, find out why, how, where, and when. The writings might be those collected in the speech community journal or through oral histories or through cultural role plays—some may be in English, some may be in the primary language. Although the ultimate goal may be to encourage reading and writing in English, beginning with the primary language often provides a step into English for many students.

An example of such student writing comes from the language experience approach (see Dixon & Nessel, 1983, for using LEA [the language experience approach] with ESL students), where students audiotape events in their current or past lives. Advanced students can then use these as a basis for writing; for less advanced writers, the teacher can help frame and scaffold the writing for the student. These texts then become the reading material for the class. The readers are interested in getting to know each other better; they have the writer available to ask questions of; and the original writer has a real audience for the piece of writing. I have students draw family trees, identifying the usual biodata such as age, gender, language, and place of birth. Then, I have them choose one member of the family whom they want to introduce to the rest of the class. They then write (or audiotape if they are not yet up to spontaneous writing) about that member, describing him/her physically and his/her character, including some significant events in the person's life. Finally, they say why they chose that family member. Sometimes the original audiotape is made in the primary language; sometimes the class asks questions in the primary language. The choice is left up to the students; however, they are encouraged to share with all class members, even those speaking a different primary language. Thus the teacher, an aide, or a more advanced student from the same class or another class may be called on to act as interpreter. The goal is for students to share information with a real purpose and real audience, unfettered by linguistic limits.

I have suggested some ways of having students use their primary language for writing. Research (Friedlander, 1990) has shown that writers who brainstorm and write outlines in their primary language when the topic is one they experienced in their primary language write more details and have better organized writing than if teachers insist all prewriting be done in English. For such writers, one word in a cluster or brainstormed list will pull up a whole host of connotations and associated events in the primary language, whereas the English vocabulary does not convey such rich connotations for them. Thus, we need to discuss with students which language will better facilitate

271

access to experiences and details for a particular writing assignment. There can be no hard and fast rules. We need to let our students make their own choices.

Grammar.　More advanced students can be encouraged to become minilinguists, collecting language data from their community and analyzing it. In the same way students collected cultural information in the life histories and cultural role plays, students can audiotape dialogues and collect written pieces in their primary language. These can then be the data for a linguistic analysis of features such as word order, verb endings (if any), topic/comment sentence organization, and agreement. Students can write out a word-for-word translation in English, showing how the primary language differs in structure from English. This translation can then be compared with a free translation into conventional English. In this way students discover that they already "know" rules of linguistic structure, those of their primary language. In advanced writing classes, this knowledge can help students understand some of the errors they make in writing English.

Speaking/Listening.　The ability to interact with native speakers in face-to-face encounters depends not only on the cultural and discourse features discussed above, but also on learners' pronunciation. However, nativelike pronunciation need not be the goal for adult learners. We and they must accept that some features of the primary language will probably remain as part of their English speech patterns. Indeed, it is often advantageous to retain some foreign features—Maurice Chevalier and others have capitalized on their foreign accents. If learners have an accent, native speakers do not expect nativelike competence with the culture and may be more forgiving of culturally inappropriate behavior. Our goal as both teachers and students should be for intelligibility. The following activity can help students discover for themselves what is intelligible and what is not in their own speech.

I audiotape the students speaking their primary language. With the class, I analyze some of the distinctive features of the phonology of their languages (e.g., tone in languages such as Vietnamese or Chinese). I then audiotape students speaking English and we identify sounds they are transferring from their primary language. The students then play selections from the English language tapes to native speakers and have them paraphrase what the speaker has said (graduate students in linguistics or teacher education programs are a great source of native speakers for this activity). Even though this is the least context-embedded of interaction situations (but one that occurs in telephone calls), it does help students identify problem areas. Students can then focus on the areas of pronunciation that cause them to be unintelligible and not spend time on features that are unlikely to cause confusion. In a study of the intelligibility of Thai and Japanese speakers of Australian English (Murray, 1983), for example, I found that mispronunciations of /l/ and /r/, traditionally characterized as the most marked features of such speakers, did not lead to confusion. Mispronunciations of fricatives (e.g., /s/, /z/) and the lack of release of word-final plosives (e.g., /d/, /g/) contributed more to lack of intelligibility for these speakers.

Conclusion

It is clear that many strategies exist for building on students' own understandings and for using their communities: self-observation, descriptions of speech communities, community interviews, analysis of culturally relevant speech events, prewriting in the primary language, creating reading texts, and grammar and phonology analyses. Ways of capitalizing on our students' differences are as unlimited as the resources and differences they bring to class. By including the rationale behind the activities suggested, I hope that teachers can create their own activities, building on the wealth of information and understandings all students have.

Summary

Students learning a second language or dialect are not blank slates to be written on by the teacher, nor are they empty vessels to be filled. Whether they are children, teens, or adults, they bring with them to the language classroom, experiences, cultural values, life histories, language, and cognitive ability. By starting with what students bring with them to class, we respect them as whole human beings and also provide a core for syllabus design that motivates and facilitates language acquisition. Activities that capitalize on the resources students bring with them include examining speech communities, collecting life histories, writing about students' own experiences, using the primary language, having students become researchers, and cultural role plays.

Discussion Topics and Projects

1. Following the suggestions given for examining speech communities, examine your own speech community. Who speaks what language, to whom, and when? Draw networks of those interactions that occur most frequently.

2. This task is one teachers can use with ESL or other students; however, as Nichols (this book) explains, it is useful for teachers also to explore their own language heritage. Interview a member of your family or speech community. Find out her/his language experiences. Was s/he literate in more than one language or language variety? What language or language variety was used in the home? In the extended family? In the community? Did s/he find school language easy to acquire? Write up the interview as a newspaper article.

3. This task is also one teachers can use with their ESL or other classes; however, teachers can also benefit from exploring their families. Draw your own family tree, labeling members' characteristics such as gender, age, language. Choose one family member and describe that person for another member of your class. Audiotape your discussion. Jointly write a thumbnail sketch of this family member.

4. Role play a speech event such as returning a sweater to a store because it shrank the first time it was cleaned. Videotape or audiotape the speech event. Analyze the event using Hymes's (1986) SPEAKING mnemonic.

Further Reading

Earl Stevick (1990) has a good discussion of humanism in the language classroom, as well as several books discussing humanistic methods for use in the language classroom. Arthur Applebee (1984) discusses the importance and uses of scaffolding for learners. Shirley Brice Heath (1983) shows how ethnography can be used to facilitate instruction. Carol Dixon and Denise Nessel (1983) have an excellent overview and instructional strategies for the language experience approach to reading and writing. Nessa Wolfson (1989) provides excellent summaries of research on different discourse rules across different language groups.

12

Language in the Attic

Claiming Our Linguistic Heritage

Patricia C. Nichols
San José State University, California

A U.S. Family

The family is gathered after the funeral to eat a meal together, to comfort each other, to share childhood memories. The surviving sister brings down pictures from the attic to divide between the dozen or so cousins sitting around her living room, some of whom are themselves well into the retirement years. As the crinkled black and white photographs are passed around, names and stories accompany them, along with noise and laughter, as one memory prompts another. Soon the oldest cousin is imitating the Swedish accent of the long-departed grandmother sending him to collect his grandfather for a meal and of the grandfather giving him instructions to buy a can of snuff at the market. Only this cousin knows something of those people in the funny clothes, posed rigidly in a few of the oldest photographs: Relatives from the Old County known to him through the stories of his grandparents. In this very U.S. gathering after the funeral of a woman in her eighties, born to Swedish immigrant parents, all those present speak English. Her surviving sister knows Swedish but no longer speaks it; her English is identical to that of her neighbors in the small Massachusetts town where she lived as a child and then brought up her own child.

The woman whose life we were celebrating at this family gathering after her funeral was my husband's mother. Although she had begun school in a small Massachusetts town speaking only Swedish, she quickly learned the English spoken by her playmates. None of the four children born to her can speak Swedish, and only one daughter understands something of it, learned as the "secret" language used between her mother and the aunts when they visited each other. The oldest cousin present, the one who takes such delight in mimicking the accent of the Swedish grandparents, lived with his mother's Swedish parents while he was a child, but even he does not speak Swedish. English is the language of the third generation, and some of them are unaware that Swedish was their parent's home language before they went to school.

This family scene is one that might have innumerable variations, but the pattern would be similar: English has become the primary language for most children of non-English-speaking parents in the United States. Navajo and, to a much lesser extent, Spanish speakers of the southwest are the only sizeable exceptions, according to one recent study (Veltman, 1983). Like the family described above, many families have lost their memory of a non-English-speaking past—at least on the surface. And along with a remembered linguistic heritage, many Americans have lost any understanding of the language problems facing many of their ancestors and the first generation of English-speaking children.

U.S. Classrooms

Most teachers in contemporary U.S. classrooms are monolingual English speakers, but their students may come to them with language backgrounds like that of the Swedish immigrant family described above. One of the most troubling issues for a society that believes in universal education is the difference between the teachers' culture and that of the students. Although the student population in the United States is increasingly of African, Asian, and indigenous North American ancestry (including Latinos in the southwest of mixed Hispanic and Native American heritage), the teacher population is overwhelmingly of European ancestry and will be so for the foreseeable future. The figures for 1989 indicate that 92% of teacher education students were European American; only 4.7% were African American, 1.6% were Hispanic, and 1.5% were Asian (Chira, 1990). At least one third of all schoolchildren will be non-White by the end of this decade, and in some schools in California, that figure is already as high as 90%. What we have is teachers from one cultural background teaching students from very different ones, many of them struggling to learn the language and customs of the public schools. Because so many of these White teachers have forgotten their own linguistic histories, they may have difficulty imagining the problems facing their language minority students. To help activate our imaginations by making the problems more personal, I have designed a set of exercises to help us overcome our own linguistic "amnesia," and by extension to understand more fully what our students are experiencing.

The exercises described below are ones I have used with teachers in workshops and with prospective teachers in college courses. They are designed to bring us into closer touch with our own linguistic heritage and to help us honor the diversity of our shared heritage. Many teachers, even though we ourselves may be from immigrant backgrounds only a generation or two back, seldom reflect on the great changes in language and culture our own ancestors may have experienced. These exercises can be a means of fostering a greater love of language itself and a curiosity about its processes within and among us. They can help us to discover how our own families have developed ways of dealing with linguistic differences and disparate ways of interacting. After I describe these language exercises, I discuss ways (in the section on Classroom Research) in which teachers can engage students in discovering how language is used in home and community, thereby using their linguistic diversity as a resource for the classroom.

Exercises for Language Awareness

Experienced Teachers

The first exercise is suitable for a 10-minute introduction at a conference or a workshop for experienced teachers. It draws on our inherent interest in our own family histories and on our curiosity about our neighbors. I ask everyone to jot down on a scrap of paper the names of their grandparents in a horizontal line across the middle of the page, then above these names to write (if they know them) the names of their great-grandparents. I stress that these should be the names from the family of nurture, which is sometimes different from the family of origin. After they have jotted down as many of the 12 names as they know, I ask them to write beside the names the languages they spoke. Then I ask them to share their findings with a partner. (Many comment on how few of these names they know, and I make an observation about our linguistic "amnesia" as a nation of immigrants.) If there is time, I ask each person to report on the partner's linguistic heritage; if there is not, I ask for a show of hands on how many people had 12 ancestors who spoke English as their primary language. There will be only a few such people in any gathering, a point worth noting. Then I ask for people to call out the languages in their backgrounds, listing them on the board or overhead as they do so. We take a minute or so to comment on the diversity in our group and to compare ourselves to the students we teach. Most of us take a silent moment to honor the memory of unknown ancestors who struggled with a new tongue in a strange land or who met newcomers bringing strange tongues and customs to their homeland.

Undergraduate Students

A second and more detailed two-part exercise is one I use with students who are completing a set of courses leading to a California teaching credential through the university where I teach. Because these prospective teachers are generally younger, they often have backgrounds more similar to the students they will be teaching. But again, the overwhelming majority of these new teachers have spoken English as a primary language all their lives. Some of them will take positions in area schools where the population is as much as 80% language minority. To help ground them in an understanding of the impact language experiences have on one's schooling (and vice versa), I begin by taking them through a "Steppingstones" exercise, based loosely on data-gathering exercises developed by the depth psychologist Ira Progoff (1975).[1] I ask them to think of language as a flowing river, with steppingstones stretching from one bank to the other. Each person goes from one shore to the other by hopping from stone to stone, sometimes making choices between equally attractive stones and other times jumping to the only stone available at that point in the journey. The steppingstones represent major steps taken in their language experience, and I ask them to list no more than 8 to 10 of them, beginning with "I was born into a family that spoke. . . ." and ending with the present. To help them get started, I mention some of the major steppingstones of my own language experience, reminding them that language is used with people and suggesting they think in terms of people they have spoken with most in their families, those friends and mates they have chosen, the colleagues with whom they have worked and studied. I often write along with them, telling them that each time I make a list, the steppingstones are different, depending on what is going on in my life at the moment. A few steppingstones in my own language experience at different times have been the following:

1. I was born into a Scots-Irish family that spoke educated southern American English—to a mother whose father read Greek and Latin and a father whose parents never finished high school.

2. From ages 1½ to 3½, my mother taught school and left me in the daily care of a young woman whose grandmother had been born in Africa.

3. When I went to my segregated college in the fifties, the drama director kept asking me to try out for Black roles in different plays because I was good at Black dialect.

4. When I went up to Massachusetts to work in a Jewish girls' camp one summer, people from New York kept asking me to talk for them.

5. In graduate school in Minnesota, my Old English professor asked me to pronounce the word *cow* aloud. The whole class laughed, and I kept quiet in public for about 3 years.

6. A linguistics professor in California asked what I knew about the Gullah spoken in South Carolina, my home state. I had never heard of it and later learned it was what we called *Geechee* in my part of the state.

7. I taught Chicano students in California during the Vietnam war and watched them get drafted if they failed freshman composition.

8. Sociolinguistics classes in the seventies helped me understand something about Chicano students' problems with academic English as well my own linguistic background. . . .

After about 10 minutes, even though some may be still writing furiously, I ask them to stop and listen to directions for the next part of the exercise: When they have finished their basic list of individual steppingstones, they should read it over silently and allow one of their language experiences to "speak" to them at this time and place. I ask that they star this steppingstone and write a brief focusing statement about it, beginning with the phrase, "It was a time when. . . ." This portion of the exercise can end when they have written this statement, with the entire process requiring about 15 minutes of class time. If there is additional time, they can talk about their selected steppingstones in pairs or groups of three for a few minutes, to get some idea of the language experiences of their classmates and to prod their own memories further. Sharing what they have written about their starred steppingstone with several other classmates is an excellent way of helping them see each other's experiences as resources to explore. If there is limited time, students can simply put the list away for a few days, letting other memories of language in their lives rise to consciousness.

The second stage of this exercise moves beyond personal exploration of language experience to a public sharing of discoveries about language heritage. Once students' personal memories have been tapped, they can more easily recall how these memories are related to experiences shared by others in their immediate family. This is vital for uncovering the linguistic diversity that lies in the background *even for monolingual English speakers*. At a subsequent class (sometimes days or weeks after doing the first part), I ask students to refer to the list of personal steppingstones as a prompt and then to write a narrative of their family language history, reaching as far back as they can. Some moan they know nothing, and I ask them to write *that*, observing that not knowing one's family language history prior to the grandparents' generation is common in the United States, once again taking the opportunity to comment on our national linguistic "amnesia." (Students of Asian ancestry often know far more about their ancestors than those of European ancestry, while students of African ancestry often express a great sense of loss at being cur off from any knowledge of their ancestors' origins.) These narratives usually take about 20 minutes to write, and many students want to write more. Their stories can be used to explore linguistic diversity in two valuable ways: through a panel discussion at a subsequent class meeting or through a written assignment on language heritage and experiences.

For the panel discussions on language background, I collect the narratives, read them, and group them according to common threads in the family histories. These groups differ widely from class to class.

Although a teacher can seldom predict just from its outward appearance what configuration of students will appear in any given class, the process enlightens both students and teacher about the impact that language and attitudes can have on the life choices of people they know well. Following a panel discussion, many students will go back to their families and record the speech of an elderly family member or even, in some cases, study the ancestral language. The panels we have had over the decade I have been using this exercise in California universities include one on German ancestry that displayed a wide range of attitudes toward that language; others on problems encountered by English speakers who moved from one language variety region to another as children; several on Spanish roots in Mexico, Central America, South America, Spain, and the southwest United States, with valuable comments on attitudes associated with different varieties of that language; another on Chinese families who spoke a wide variety of "dialects" or languages as the fortunes of war and politics required them to move to one province or country to another; and a very memorable one on Native American ancestors shared by an African American woman from New York and a White woman from Oklahoma (both Cherokee) and by two Latinas from Central America and Texas (Mayan and Aztec).

The procedures for selecting the panels are simple. At the class meeting prior to the scheduled discussion, I ask the students whom I have chosen to participate (no more than four or five per panel) if they will take part. The focus, I tell them, should be on those aspects of their family history that would be most useful for their classmates. This gives them time to collect their thoughts for an oral presentation and to talk to one another if they choose. A number of participants have used the intervening time to call or talk with older family members for additional information. Occasionally, they come with maps of the ancestral homeland. The discoveries they make are valuable for them and for the class: a journal kept by a Japanese great-grandfather when he immigrated to the United States in the early 1900s, the meanings of words and customs shared by other members of their ethnic group (and not used only by their families), the disparagement of "village" or rural language the world over and the privileging of urban language varieties, the acknowledgment of long-forgotten home languages like Yiddish. After each of the panel members tells his or her family story, I ask if they would like to ask each other any questions, and then we open the floor to questions from the rest of the class. These exchanges are often profoundly insightful about the way language use can be tied up with personal identity, and the open forum gives an opportunity for information exchange that would be inappropriate in most other contexts. Experiences of private pain are suddenly seen as shared social phenomena. For future teachers, this comparison of diverse language experiences on a personal level can be moving and memorable in a way that textbook accounts can never be.[2]

In addition to the oral panel discussion, a written assignment that works especially well is to invite the students to write a story in the voice of one of their ancestors, imagining details about which they have no actual knowledge. These fictional pieces are especially appropriate for classes where the curriculum is literature-based. Students and colleagues have written moving narratives through the voice of a grandfather whose family was killed in the Holocaust, a grandmother who immigrated alone as an 18-year-old from the Azores to America, a grandmother who was widowed as a bride and had to give up a child for adoption so that her second husband from a traditional Japanese family would not be burdened with the care of a child not his own. These narratives are sometimes funny, sometimes searingly painful.

Both the spoken and written explorations of language history help students come to believe that "we belong to a larger community that extends backwards before our birth and most likely forwards after our death."[3]

Teachers-in-Training

A second appropriate use for the Steppingstones material and family language histories is in the methods classes for English or Language Arts, where there is far less cultural diversity among the students than in the classes for undergraduates. Most students in these methods classes will have become aware that they will be teaching students very different from themselves. The exercise described here can be introduced as a means of exploring the collective diversity present within the class so that imaginations can be stretched to encompass their future classrooms.

For my methods students in English, after I take them through the first stage of the Steppingstones exercise described above, I ask them to write a paper for distribution to the class, which either expands on a selected personal experience or summarizes their family's language history. Asking them to discuss an initial draft of the paper in small groups, I use this assignment to illustrate different parts of the writing process as well as the importance of encouraging students to select meaningful topics for their compositions. When the typed revisions are completed and given to me, I reproduce them in a class booklet and give each class member a copy. I ask that they read all of these final papers and write about them in a journal that they keep for this class. After they have done so, we discuss the papers again in small groups and as a class, focusing on the diversity of experiences with language even within a mostly monocultural and monolingual group.

To help them make connections between themselves and their future students, I lead a discussion on experiences within the class that might help them identify with experiences of language minority students. In one such class of 20 students, only two of whom were from minority backgrounds, several helpful experiences were identified. One of these teachers-in-training had lived abroad as a child and was able to tell us what it actually felt like to be the only English speaker in a Spanish-speaking classroom at age 7: "The first day was terrifying." Another had traveled as a young adult, finding that the Italian learned in her college classes was far from adequate: "I felt stupid or perceived as stupid more than once." Yet another had a German mother, who sent her to Saturday school to learn that language; although she begrudged the lost Saturdays as a child, she could tell us now how proud she was to be able to talk with her German relatives on recent summer visits. A sensitive older student was able to comment on the functions of language that characterized her home: The long silences used by her father's mother (who regarded talking "as an interruption of her work") and the warm talkativeness of her own mother (who believed that "if you don't talk to children they will not learn.") Others told of experiences with speech therapy, with being teased about accent as a teenager, with class distinctions based on language use, and—heartbreakingly—with a grandfather who had returned a child's letter with corrections in red pen. The remembered pain of receiving such a response to his letter was related eloquently by this teacher-in-training, giving us an inside view of the effects of the red pen: "I wish he had sent me a letter that he had written. Maybe he did, but I was so bewildered by receiving my corrected letter that this is all that stands out now."

One common thread that ran through the papers from this class was the love of language, the lifelong involvement with reading and writing for most of them. One young woman recalled a specific period of her life when reading was almost as important as the air she breathed, helping her to cope with the break-up of a family. Others remembered writing copiously in journals, composing poems, taking imaginary journeys to Middle Earth, and just being exhilarated by understanding words on paper. Because these teachers-in-training would work with many youngsters who had *not* had such experiences with "words on paper," memories of the contexts in which they themselves had such experiences were important reality checks for them. They could ask themselves and each other how best to create classroom environments and assignments that might lead to delight with writing, to incorporate words on paper into daily lives and future ways of being for their students.

Evelyn Dandy (this book) reflects on the rich verbal experiences in many student homes and communities and describes ways in which teachers can honor the language students bring with them, expanding on them as a bridge to different language functions. As Dandy observes, some of the most important and exciting encounters with language for many students will have been in oral form. To lure them into adventures with written texts, a teacher must ensure that written words are just as exciting and familiar as those they have learned in the songs, chants, and stories of their communities.

My experiences with language minority students and with teacher education suggest that the texts of the European culture celebrated by E. D. Hirsch (1987) sometimes will not be the appropriate choices for early literacy. Rather, written examples of stories children have heard in oral versions will be a more suitable introduction to the link between spoken and written language. During a discussion of Rudolfo Anaya's (1972) *Bless Me, Ultima* in a college literature class I was teaching, several Chicano students spoke of how important the story of "La Llorona" (The Weeping Woman) had been to them as children. One student had been told the story in English, several others in Spanish. As one young woman told us of how her mother had warned her against going near the river because the "weeping woman" might snatch her up, her voice trembled with remembered fear. None of the non-Hispanics had ever heard of the story, a central one in Hispanic culture of the southwestern United States and one that Anaya refers to briefly in his novel. The importance of having that story discussed in a university setting was later affirmed by another student in the class, herself a teacher-in-training who was always searching for literature that would appeal to linguistically diverse students. For the benefit of us all, she unearthed a literary version of "La Llorona" by Anaya himself, written in 1984, which turns the simple folktale into a stunning portrayal of cross-cultural tension. In his retelling, the weeping woman becomes Malinche, the indigenous woman who served as interpreter for the Spanish adventurer, Cortes. Malinche drowns the children born to her and her Spanish mate, rather than let their father take them with him back to Spain, and her cries of grief can be heard today along rivers of the southwest. Because the young woman who uncovered Anaya's text for our literature class was herself of mixed Chicano and Spanish heritage, we might suspect that these "words on paper" have helped her to imagine the kinds of language and culture contact her ancestors would have experienced. She will surely understand the importance of putting similar texts in the hands of her language minority students.

Classroom Research into Teaching and Learning

Reversing the usual order of presenting a study and then discussing implications for teaching, I have chosen here to present the teaching activities first, then discuss their implications for further research. My own experience as a teacher and as a sociolinguist has convinced me that it is the grounded daily experiences with active learners and language users that feeds the cycle of research. When I first began to study the language of African American children over a decade ago, I made my most important discoveries by observing their language in the classroom, on the playground, and in their homes and churches (Nichols, 1977). From these observations made as a participant in a variety of social situations, I learned what questions to ask, what research might be most valuable for these children and their teachers. The collaborative research I have recently done at the university level has been informed most by the classes I have taught in developmental English, classes which have allowed me to observe language minority students using English in an academic setting (see Murray, Nichols, & Heisch, this book). The research projects that I will describe here are grounded in such classroom and community contexts.

Readers and Cultural Diversity

Although the impact of childhood stories seen for the first time in print can be dramatic for individuals, as we have seen for the discussion of

"La Llorona" above, there is little evidence as yet of what impact such stories might have on large groups of students. Over the past two decades, classroom teachers and researchers have found the use of students' own language to be a valuable tool in promoting the acquisition of literacy. In an approach to the teaching of reading known as Language Experience, the teacher elicits key words from the children themselves, words that have meaning and value in their everyday experience and with their help, creates stories for them to read. (See Cullinan, 1974, for applications of this approach to the language variety used by many African American children.) Elsewhere I have discussed the historical importance of texts that link with reader's own lives in the acquisition of literacy across cultures (Nichols, 1988).

The impact of such materials on our contemporary students' lives, however, has not yet been examined systematically. We know little about how our culturally diverse students respond to stories that Hirsch (1987) includes in his discussion of the background necessary for common cultural literacy—those stories of Scandinavian heroes, of Greek and Roman gods, of English kings, of rebellious adolescent males at private boarding schools. How do our students interpret frequent allusions to the creation story of Genesis, when their family background may be Buddhist? Or Steinbeck's portrayal of the valiant "American" survivors of the dustbowl in Oklahoma, when their ancestors may have been Native Americans or Chicanos on California farms, displaced by these migrants? We have mostly only anecdotal evidence that written references to stories one has heard in childhood can have a powerful effect as children become participants in literacy communities. An individual teacher might compare the attendance record of classes in which culturally diverse literature is used with those where traditional works of European perspective predominate. A school system might examine its dropout rate when curricular changes are made to include multicultural literature along with traditional texts. These are questions to investigate, the answers to which could inform our teaching as we continue to inhabit classrooms where the teacher is literate in a culture that is different from that of so many of the students.

Beginning Readers

One striking example of just how beginning readers do more than read words on a page as they tackle the problems of symbol and meaning shows us how firmly embedded the act of reading is in its social context. The dynamic picture of a first-grade reader named Michael (Lovell & Barone, 1990) challenges our stereotypic image of the solitary reader alone with his book behind a closed door in a quiet room. Michael's teacher had her first-grade class keep a journal for a book the class was reading together. In their journal they were to enter their guesses about how the story would develop and their responses to the chapters they were reading. She and Jonathan Lovell, the university researcher, kept notes of their observations on other activities Michael participated in beyond the reading activity. Between their observations and the child's journal, Lovell and Barone have pieced together a compelling picture of how words on paper became integrated into this child's social activities, allowing him to participate on a new level with his classmates as a "magician" with secrets to be shared. Through the writings and pictures drawn by Michael himself, these classroom researchers provide a striking example of how the words on paper come alive in this child's daily life and are integrated into on-going activities, which in turn provide further incentive to explore the lessons to be learned, the people to be met in books, then to be shared with one's peers. For Michael, and for readers of any age, reading had become an experience to be shared in many dimensions of his life—not just as a solitary encounter between himself and the words on the page. For the teacher who witnesses this process, providing just the right books for a particular student and a forum for sharing discoveries made through them becomes an on-going enterprise, one worth exploring with other teachers as frontline researchers in living laboratories.

The question facing teachers from the majority culture, who will be teaching many more students of minority cultures, is how to choose good selections which encompass the cultural perspectives represented by all of their students. Lovell and Barone have provided a paradigm for examining the acquisition of literacy in very young children within a classroom setting. Similar case studies, using a variety of reading texts, would help us understand how children across a wide range of cultural and linguistic backgrounds integrate their reading with social activities going on around them.

Student Researchers and Writers

Shirley Brice Heath (1983) has described uses of reading and writing in communities of the Carolina piedmont, showing us how very different the norms for literacy may be for home and school. Heath suggests that by engaging such students themselves in directed study of how language is used in their homes and communities, teachers can build on the competencies the children bring with them to the classroom and thus help them to move more rapidly into acquisition of the kinds of literacy required by the schools. In a more recent essay (1987), she describes classrooms across the country in which students go into their own communities and homes, taking notes on the ways in which people use language for writing, reading, and talking: recording speech events like sermons, songs, riddles, and jokes and bringing these collections back into the classroom for study of the form and functions of language. Heath suggests that in the process of doing such research, the teacher and students will become "members of a classroom learning community—an oral and literate community learning together" (p. 105). Denise E. Murray (this book) provides further suggestions for such community-classroom research.

A detailed description of a yearlong collaboration between Heath and a high school English teacher gives some idea of the great potential represented by involving both teacher and student in an investigation of language use (Heath & Branscombe, 1985). Through the words of the students themselves, these teacher-researchers introduce us to high school students in Alabama who blossomed as writers, in correspondence with upperclassmen in their own school and with Heath and her daughter in California. One key factor for these beginning writers, who had done virtually no writing in their earlier special education classes, was the necessity to make their thoughts clear in writing to correspondents they knew only through writing. Heath and Branscombe demonstrate the kinds of negotiated understandings that developed through words on paper between 9th and 11th graders and then between 9th graders and a university professor and a teenager they had never met. Students themselves helped these researchers analyze their own letters, examining the development of their rhetorical skills, their adherence to the conventions of the letter as a genre, the expansion of their vocabulary, and the growing sense of themselves as writers over the year's time.

Teachers and students sometimes find, after analyzing audiotaped oral stories and comparing them with pieces they have written, that cultural groups (or individual students) show preferences for different organization in both storytelling and in writing (Nichols, 1989). Such discoveries can lead to experimentation with newly recognized narrative devices, descriptive detail, reported conversation—ones used by real speakers and writers rather than by anonymous "models" presented in textbooks. In classrooms where diversity is the norm, students can learn new modes of writing from each other, building on the oral traditions of their homes and communities. In the process, we may find our national repertoire expanding, as children in our increasingly diverse classrooms share their cultural traditions and expand our common cultural literacy.

Conclusion

The exciting possibility of employing literacy as a bridge between and across cultures is a real one if the teaching and research activities described above are pursued. As Mary Louise Pratt (1987) has so eloquently reminded us, modern linguistic communities are largely imagined or invisible ones, no longer characterized by the intimate and frequent face-to-face interaction once found in rural villages. In today's world, and certainly in today's schools, we are interacting with each other from very different cultural and linguistic bases, across communities of the imagination, as were members of the Swedish-American family at the funeral gathering. For many members of that family, the rules for how to use language were quite different from those of the ancestors from the Old Country, peering out at us from the crinkled photographs brought down from the attic. My husband's mother, born to Swedish immigrant parents, married a non-Swede, as did her sister and her three brothers. These children of Swedish immigrants, by their choice of mates, ensured that their own children's homes would be English-speaking. In such homes, even though both parents were of European ancestry, there were probably important differences in the ways they used English, ways that were learned in the ancestral homes. In many other American homes in the United States, even though English is the common language, there are significant differences in language use between parents from different cultural traditions. If we think back to our personal Steppingstones of language experience, many of us can remember the silent eloquence and dry wit of one side of the family and the laughing, noisy, constant talk of the other side. How many of our parents had the same kind of baby talk, told the same kinds of jokes, even knew the same fairy tales?

Most of us know families of mixed cultures, either in our own backgrounds or in some of our friends'. One of my favorite illustrations of how these mixed traditions can become part of our common culture comes from Leslie Silko's (1981) book, *Storyteller*, which some have called a Native American version of *Roots*. Silko describes a tall Hopi basket that contained hundreds of photographs taken since the first camera came to the Laguna pueblo of New Mexico in the 1890s. In one of the pictures from this basket, her white-haired grandmother is sitting at a table reading a children's storybook to Silko's two little sisters. Silko tells us that the photographs from this basket bring back memories of the stories she heard growing up in Laguna; for each photograph there is a cluster of stories. Like Tayo in her (1977) novel, *Ceremony*, Silko is of mixed racial heritage. Through a literary creation, she is able to portray the tension between both parts of Tayo's heritage, as well as the European world he must come to terms with. The children in our classrooms today may also have had diverse sets of caretakers, lived in numerous geographical locations, and made many friends of backgrounds different from their own. If Pratt is right in her characterization of our modern linguistic communities, the most interesting question for us to examine is how we develop ways of bridging our disparate ways of interacting, within families, within geographic communities, within classrooms. Finding the answers to this question is perhaps the most significant enterprise of our time.

There should be no question that we are a nation characterized by linguistic contact. We remember the contact between the Native Americans and Spanish in the southwest, Russians in the northwest, French along the Mississippi River, and English along the Atlantic; that between the Africans and the Europeans along the east coast and the Mississippi; that between the Chinese and the Europeans on the railroad beds that spanned the continent. All along we have been working out ways of speaking with each other across and through our differences. What we have not done yet is tell each other the stories of how this has been done, in ways that can help us build and throw across bridges for the future. The chapters that make up this book, and the teaching and research they will influence, are efforts toward that end.

Summary

This chapter has presented teaching activities for experienced and prospective teachers, designed to help us gain access to our own memories of linguistic diversity. Only through understanding the linguistic and cultural diversity hidden away in our family attics can we begin to understand how best to use the diversity of our students as a resource for the classroom. It also describes research grounded in classroom and community contexts, in which teachers and researchers collaborate with students and communities to understand the linguistic practices and values students bring with them to school. It contends that understanding how successive generations have interacted across and through their diversity is one of the most important questions facing us as both teachers and researchers.

Acknowledgments

My thanks to Evelyn Baker Dandy, Neal Lerner, Denise E. Murray, and Keith Walters for their comments on ealier drafts of this chapter. A California State University grant for Academic Program Improvement during the academic year 1986–1987 funded the development of several of the language exercises described here. My thanks to Allison Heisch and John Lamendella, corecipients of this grant, who helped develop these exercises in classes and workshops.

Discussion Topics and Projects

1. Examine the linguistic and cultural backgrounds present in the town or city in which you live, taking care to examine evidence for cultural groups that lived there prior to European contact. What evidence can you find that people from these cultural groups still live in the area? How many languages are now spoken in your town or city? (U.S. Census Bureau records will be a valuable resource here.)

2. Interview older residents of your community about their memories of the community. Ask for permission to audio- or videotape them, and give them a copy of the tape when you return for a follow-up interview. Compare the interviews of speakers from different ethnic groups and try to describe how they organize their stories about the past. Interview an older member of your own family on a similar topic and compare his or her stories with those you have collected from your community. What are the differences and similarities?

3. Ask a group of young adults to describe how they learned to read and to list their favorite books as children. How many have you read from their lists? What seems to characterize their selections? How do their stories of learning to read compare with yours?

4. After a holiday or important shared event (hurricane, earthquake, snowstorm), record children telling stories of what happened to them. Transcribe these stories and let the children read them to each other. Compare the structure of these stories with those in their classroom textbooks. Are there any significant differences?

Further Reading

Only in the last decade or so have we begun to pay attention to the total range of language and literature that exists in the United States, which is after all a "nation of immigrants." An excellent nontechnical introduction to the languages and varieties of English spoken from colonial times to the present is *Language in the USA*, edited by Charles A. Ferguson and Shirley Brice Heath (1981). This volume, however, does not contain a description of Chicano English, a very important variety of English spoken throughout the southwest. *Chicano English: An Ethnic Contact Dialect*, edited by Joyce Penfield and Jacob Ornstein-

Galicia (1985), gives an excellent, though somewhat technical, description of its structure and uses. A source of information on recent literature from a variety of cultures within the United States is *MELUS*, a journal published by the Society for the Study of the Multiethnic Literature of the United States and available through University Microfilms International, 100 North Zeeb Road, Ann Arbor, MI 48106–1346. It is probably the most up-to-date source of information for new works and for anthologies of earlier works suitable for use in public schools. An excellent source for audiotapes of authors reading their own works is The American Audio Prose Library, P.O. Box 842, Columbia, MO 65205. Since 1981, this literary arts organization has been recording authors like Alice Walker, Rudolfo Anaya, Ernest Gaines, Maxine Hong Kingston, James Baldwin, and N. Scott Momaday reading from their works and talking about how and why they wrote as they did. One of my favorite tapes is of Alice Walker reading her short story "1955," which gives a Black woman's perspective on Elvis Presley's musical career and cultural limitations.

A useful collection of articles on how language of the classroom differs from that used in many communities is the volume edited by Courtney B. Cazden, Vera P. John, and Dell Hymes's (1972), *Functions of Language in the Classroom*. Two of the articles are especially enlightening for teachers from mainstream cultural backgrounds: Stephen Boggs' description of Hawaiian children's perception of questions and narratives and Susan Philips' evocative picture of how children of the Warm Spring Indian Reservation in central Oregon use language in community and classroom. The much acclaimed volume by Shirley Brice Heath (1983), *Ways with Words*, describes an African American and a White community of the Carolina piedmont, both of which have different uses of language from those expected in the schools. Written for teachers in a narrative style, this book outlines ways that teachers can build on children's home language, thus expanding rather than replacing the language of the home. Two other books that enlarge on this theme for different social settings are Sarah Freedman's (1985) *The Acquisition of Written Language* and Judith Langer's (1987) *Language, Literacy, and Culture: Issues of Society and Schooling*.

Endnotes

Chapter 1 *Walters*

1. Citing Haugen (1966) as justification, Hirsch equates *grapholects* with "written languages" although Haugen and Hirsch use the term in different ways. In fact, most of Hirsch's uses of the phrase *standard grapholect* seem to mean "the conventions associated with standard written English when used in academic, formal, or public contexts." From his discussion (p. 82), one assumes that, for Hirsch, the standard grapholect includes matters of lexis, syntax, spelling, and usage.

2. A sampling of articles criticizing Hirsch and his program include those by Armstrong (1988), Buckley (1988), Hovey (1988), Menocal (1988), Moglen (1988), and Sledd and Sledd (1988b). See also Graff's (1988) discussion of "educational fundamentalism" of which, he contends, Hirsch is merely a part.

3. Hirsch uses the term "*mono*literacy" (p. 92), by implication a reference to his own project, as part of his argument against any sort of "multiliteracy," multilingualism, or linguistic pluralism. Hirsch's use of terms like "bilingualism" (e.g., pp. 232–233, note 41) is exceedingly idiosyncratic.

4. Many of the writers who have been labeled as subscribing to a Great Leap theory of literacy or its tenets vociferously reject that characterization (e.g., Farrell, 1984; Goody, 1987; Ong, 1988) although their critics continue to find evidence of such beliefs in the works of these researchers (e.g., Daniell, 1986; Walters, 1990). The situation is reminiscent of the reception of Basil Bernstein's work in this country in the late 1960s. Bernstein and many of his supporters contended that no negative criticism was intended in his characterization of "restricted codes" as they contrasted with "elaborated" ones. Many of his critics, however, continued to argue that just such a negative evaluation was implied, if not intended, largely because of the kinds of dichotomies and the

kinds of language Bernstein had used in describing the two codes, their characteristics, and their users.

5. According to Ogbu's taxonomy, Mormons and the Amish are autonomous minorities; recent immigrants are members of a voluntary minority; and African Americans, Native Americans, and American-born Mexican Americans as groups constitute castelike minorities.

One can argue that perhaps the major criteria Judge Charles Joiner used in his 1979 ruling in favor of the plaintiffs in Martin Luther King Junior Elementary School Children et al. v. Ann Arbor School District Board (Joiner, 1981) and against the School Board were, first, the failure of their teachers to recognize the children's home language, a dialect of Black English, as a variety distinct from Standard English, and, second, their failure to take this fact into account when attempting to teach the children to read Standard English. As Judge Joiner understood the state of then current knowledge and applied it in his ruling, teachers' attitudes about students' language influenced not only student achievement but also student attitudes and ultimately the likelihood of student success in school and in life. One might interpret Judge Joiner's ruling to mean that we as teachers have a legal responsibility to educate ourselves about linguistic differences and to use that knowledge as we teach.

Chapter 2   *Soter*

1. Names of students are pseudonyms.

2. A critical factor to determine when we assign writing tasks such as personal narratives to students from other cultural backgrounds is whether they have experienced the genre in a different form or whether that genre exists at all in their own culture. Additionally, what evaluative criteria is the instructor bringing to the task of reading personal narratives written by novices and what criteria would these students use to evaluate personal narratives in their own cultural contexts? Mixed signals are again given when we assign students personal narrative writing that will be formally graded.

Chapter 3   *Murray, Nichols, and Heisch*

1. Where they differ from a student's native-language patterns, English rhetorical patterns might be presented as an addition rather than a substitute.

Chapter 4 *Dandy*

1. For thorough coverage of African American culture and contributions, as well as detailed lesson plans for all grade levels, see the Portland, Oregon public schools' (1990) *African-American Baseline Essays*. Write to Portland Public Schools, District 1, Multnomah County, Portland, OR 97227.

2. For a discussion of the similarities across the diaspora, see the *Story of English* series segment (Cran & McCrum, 1986), "Next Year's Words: A look into the Future." Write to Films Incorporated, 5547 N. Ravenswood, Chicago, IL 60640–1199.

3. Silently read each line of the following Biblical verses, repeating each highlighted word aloud. In the silent reading, you are taking the part of the speaker issuing the call. In the oral reading, you are the listener giving the response:

> In the beginning was the *Word*
> And the word was with *God*
> And the word was *God.* (John 1:1, emphasis mine)

4. The National Broadcasting Company (NBC) has recently aired a new television situation comedy that has a fun-loving, innocent rapper as the star: "Fresh Prince of Bel Air." It will be interesting to follow the progress of a show that portrays obvious language differences within the African American community.

5. For an in-depth discussion, see William Labov (1972) for examples of rhymes categorized by complex syntactic structures with strict discourse rules.

Chapter 5 *Vasquez*

1. *Mexicano* is a self-ascribed label used by members of the four families described in this field study. In contrast to the term *Mexican American* used by Mexican-origin individuals who have been in the United States one of more generations, Mexicano implies a stronger, more recent connection to Mexico. See José Limon (1981) for an analytical description of the uses of *Chicano, Mexicano,* and *Mexican American* among the populations of south Texas.

2. The concept of knowledge used in this chapter is interchangeable with the notion of information as the act, fact, or state of knowing, "acquired in any manner; facts; data; learning; lore" (*Websters,* 1976). Knowledge here is not

restricted to canonical knowledge (i.e., the accumulated body of knowledge recognized by scholars as the official authority).

3. The ethnographic study informing this work included 7 months of extensive field work in the east side of Lincoln City. It focused on the connection of oral language activities in the daily life of four families to literacy-related activities conventionally conceptualized as print-initiated oral language. Audiotapes and subsequent verbatim transcriptions of selected language samples; collection of print related materials; and personal field notes of observations informed the analysis. Three patterns of language use were identified that used a text—oral or written—as the basis of the discussion. Oral strategies sharing analytic characteristics of literate behaviors (Heath & Hoffman, 1986) were found across the three patterns without restriction to print. Thus, it was found that the boundaries between oral and written language, at least in the level of malleability, were blurred and oftentimes nonexistent.

4. The conceptual boundaries of Extensions apply to a Mexican immigrant setting. Further research is necessary to determine the nature of Extensions in nonimmigrant settings and whether they contain the linguistic and cultural resources available to the four families of the study.

5. Physical boundaries such as railroad tracks and thoroughfares (see Camarillo, 1979, and Shannon, 1987, for details on the markers that set off a Mexicano community, commonly called a *barrio*) did not distinguish this Mexicano community. Instead, it was demarcated by interaction patterns established between individuals who shared a similar structural and familial background.

6. Pseudonyms are used for names of people and places.

7. Nearly all the data are in Spanish.

8. I gained entry to the community as *la maestra* [the teacher] of two daughters of the Orozco and Cristobal families. The preadolescent girls had been participants in the Stanford Interactive Reading and Writing Project for which I had served as a research assistant.

Chapter 7 *Casanave*

1. I use this term rather loosely, as did the students in the program although arguments as to its meaning were presented to students early in the year.

2. Giroux (1988), for one, has made this argument in the field of education.

Chapter 8   *Johns*

1. There seem to be a number of reasons for faculty refusal to provide explicit grading criteria for students. In this case, it appeared that the instructor had never listed the criteria for himself and didn't want to think about doing so for the students. When I asked him to be more explicit about what he would consider during grading, he responded curtly, "Don't be ridiculous, Ann. They ought to know how to write a paper like this."

2. This preference for content and organization over sentence structure, mechanics, and grammar is common to academic faculty who administer essay examinations, as Brent Bridgeman and Sybil Carlson (1983) found when conducting research for the development of the Educational Testing Service's (ETS) Test of Written English (TWE).

3. See Vande Kopple (1985) and Brandt (1990) for discussions of these "messages of involvement" (Brandt, 1990, pp. 63–64).

4. Since this paper was written, Tic has negotiated a truce with her family. She has agreed to marry the chosen older Lao and to continue to assist her brother-in-law at the swap meets. In return, she will be permitted to complete her BA in accounting. She appears to be busy, happy, and doing well in her classes.

5. See Brinton, Snow, and Wesche (1989) for a discussion of adjunct models.

Chapter 9   *Lucas*

1. Schemata or frames are the organized bodies of experience and information that we use to help us interpret and understand the objects and events of the world as we encounter them. With relation to texts, schema theory holds that "the text itself does not carry meaning. Rather, a text provides clues to enable readers and listeners to construct meaning from existing knowledge—the text activates and builds on [and expands] existing schemata" (Pearson-Casanave, 1984, p. 334).

2. Names of students are pseudonyms.

3. The teachers used an excerpt from Hellman's *An Unfinished Woman* as an example of reflective autobiographical writing and as an inspiration to the students, who were themselves learning to write.

4. One of the journal assignments, adapted from Ira Progoff (1975), was to make a list of important events, or steppingstones, in their lives starting from their childhoods and going to the present. Then, the next assignment was to pick one of those events and describe it in detail. See Nichols (this book) for an adaptation of this task to language experiences.

5. For discussion of this phenomenon in first and second language learning, see, for example, Carrell (1987), K. Goodman, Brooks, Smith, Meredith, and Y. M. Goodman (1987), Heath (1983), Krashen and Biber (1988), Langer (1984), Langer and Applebee (1986), Michaels (1981), and Smith (1986b).

Chapter 11 *Murray*

1. I am here using "Mexicano" as used by Vasquez (this book).

2. I wish to thank Nancy Rubio for allowing me to use her Student Profile Sheet and some of her students' observations.

Chapter 12 *Nichols*

1. Tamara Lucas (this book) describes another use of Progoff's (1975) technique for individual assignments. The writing of her students indicates what a powerful prewriting exercise this technique can be.

2. A 30-minute videotape of two panel discussions by participants of Italian and of Filipino descent is available from San José State University (SJSU), San José, CA 95192, entitled "Linguistic Heritage Panel," catalog number TM 00538. Contact the producer, Bob Reynolds, at SJSU Instructional Resource Center for further information.

3. I am indebted to my colleague, Jonathan Lovell, for this observation.

References

Abrahams, R. D. (1963). *Deep down in the jungle*. Chicago: Aldine.

Abrahams, R. D. (1972). Talking my talk: Black English and social segmentation in Black communities. *The Florida FL Reporter, 10*, 29–35.

Abrahams, R. D. (1976). *Talking Black*. Rowley, MA: Newbury House.

Abrahams, R. D., & Gay, G. (1975). Talking Black in the classrooms. In P. Stoller (Ed.), *Black American English: Its background and its usage in the schools and in literature* (pp. 158–167). New York: Dell.

Ackerman, J. M. (1991). Reading, writing, and knowing: The role of disciplinary knowledge in comprehension and composing. *Research in the Teaching of English, 25*, 133–178.

Adams, M. J., & Collins, A. (1979). A schema-theoretic view of reading. In R. O. Freedle (Ed.), *New directions in discourse processing* (pp. 1–22). Norwood, NJ: Ablex.

African-American baseline essays and *African-American lesson plans* (1990). Portland, OR: Portland Public Schools. (Available from Portland Public Schools, District 1, Multnomah County, Portland, OR 97227, Tel. 503–249–2000)

Alder, M. (1982). *The Paideia proposal: An educational manifesto*. New York: Macmillan.

Allexsaht-Snider, M. (1989). *Language, culture, and schooling: Family Literacy Project at Morgan Elementary School*. Unpublished manuscript. University of California Graduate School of Education, Santa Barbara.

Alleyne, M. C. (1980). *Comparative Afro-American*. Ann Arbor, MI: Karoma.

Altick, R. D. (1957). *The English common reader*. Chicago: University of Chicago Press.

Alvarez, L., & Koller, A. (1986). *American tongues* [videotape]. New York: New Day Films. (Available from New Day Films, 853 Broadway, Suite 1210, New York, NY 10003, Tel. 212–645–8210)

Alvarez, L. P. (1986). *Home and school contexts for language learning: A case study of two Mexican-American bilingual preschoolers*. Unpublished doctoral dissertation, Stanford University, Stanford, CA.

Anaya, R. (1972). *Bless me Ultima*. Berkeley, CA: Quinto Sol.

Anaya, R. A. (1984). *The legend of la llorona*. Berkeley, CA: Tonatiuh-Quinto Sol.

Apple, M. W. (1982). *Education and power: Reproduction and contradiction in education*. New York: Routledge.

Apple, M. W. (1987). *Teachers and texts: A political economy of class and gender relations in education*. New York: Routledge.

Apple, M. W. (1990). *Ideology and curriculum*. (2nd ed.). New York: Routledge.

Applebee, A. N. (1981). *Writing in the secondary school: English and the content areas*. Urbana, IL: National Council of Teachers of English.

Applebee, A. N. (1984). *Contexts for learning to write*. Norwood, NJ: Ablex.

Armstrong, P. B. (1988). Pluralistic literacy, *Profession 88*, pp. 29–32.

Aronowitz, S., & Giroux, H. A. (1985). *Education under siege: The conservative, liberal, and radical debate over schooling*. North Hadley, MA: Bergin & Garvey.

Asante, M. K. (1987). *The Afrocentric idea*. Philadelphia, PA: Temple University Press.

Ballard, B., & Clanchy, J. (n.d.) *Assessment by misconception: Cultural influences and intellectual traditions*. Unpublished monograph. Canberra: Australia National University.

Barber, E. G. (1985). *Foreign student flows: Their significance for American higher education* (Institute for International Education Research Report No. 7). New York: Institute for International Education.

Bartholomae, D. (1985). Inventing the university. In M. Rose (Ed.), *When a writer can't write* (pp. 134–65). New York: Guildford Press.

Bartlett, F. C. (1932). *Remembering: A study in experimental and social psychology*. Cambridge: Cambridge University Press.

Baugh, A. C., & Cable, T. (1978). *A history of the English language*. (3rd ed.). Englewood Cliffs, NJ: Prentice Hall.

Bazerman, C. (1981). What written knowledge does: Three examples of academic discourse. *Philosophy of the Social Sciences, 11*, 361–387.

Bazerman, C. (1987). Codifying the social scientific style: The APA Publication Manual as behaviorist rhetoric. In J. S. Nelson, A. Megill, & D. N. McCloskey (Eds.), *The rhetoric of the human sciences: Language and argument in scholarship and public affairs* (pp. 125–144). Madison: University of Wisconsin Press.

Bazerman, C. (1988). *Shaping written knowledge: The genre and activity of the experimental article in science*. Madison: University of Wisconsin Press.

Becker, H. S., & Carper, J. W. (1956). The development of identification with an occupation. *The American Journal of Sociology, 61*, 289–298.

Becker, H. S., Geer, B., & Hughes, E. C. (1961). *Boys in white: Student culture in medical school*. New Brunswick, NJ: Transaction Books.

Benesch, S. (Ed.). (1988). *Ending remediation: Linking ESL and content in higher education*. Washington, DC: TESOL.

Benson, M. J. (1991). University ESL reading: A content analysis. *English for Specific Purposes, 10,* 75–88.

Bereiter, C., & Scardamalia, M. (1982). From conversation to composition: The role of instruction in a developmental process. In R. Glaser (Ed.), *Advances in instructional psychology* (Vol. 2, pp. 1–64). Hillsdale, NJ: Lawrence Erlbaum.

Berger, P. L., & Luckmann, T. (1967). *The social construction of reality: A treatise in the sociology of knowledge.* New York: Anchor Books.

Berkenkotter, C., Huckin, T., & Ackerman, J. (1988). Conventions, conversations, and the writer: Case study of a student in a rhetoric Ph.D. Program. *Research in the Teaching of English, 22,* 9–45.

Bernhardt, S. A. (1988). Text revisions by basic writers: From impromptu first draft to take-home revision. *Research in the Teaching of English, 22,* 266–280.

Bernstein, B. (1973). *Class, codes and control: Vol. 1. Theoretical studies toward a sociology of language.* London: Routledge & Kegan Paul.

Bizzell, P. (1982). College composition: Initiation into the academic discourse community. *Curriculum Inquiry, 12,* 191–207.

Bizzell, P. (1987). Language and literacy. In T. Enos (Ed.), *A sourcebook for basic writing teachers* (pp. 125–137). New York: Random House.

Bizzell, P. (1990). Beyond anti-foundationalism to rhetorical authority: Problems defining "cultural literacy." *College English, 52,* 661–675.

Bloom, B. (1956). *Taxonomy of education objectives: Handbook 1. Cognitive domain.* New York: McKay.

Bowles, S., & Gintes, H. (1976). *Schooling in capitalist America: Educational reform and the contradictions of economic life.* New York: Basic Books.

Bransford, J. D., & McCarrell, N. S. (1974). A sketch of a cognitive approach to comprehension: Some thought about understanding what it means to comprehend. In W. B. Weimer & D. S. Palermo (Eds.), *Cognition and the symbolic processes* (pp. 189–229). Hillsdale, NJ: Lawrence Erlbaum.

Brandt, D. (1990). *Literacy as involvement: The acts of writers, readers, and texts.* Carbondale: Southern Illinois University Press.

Bridgeman, B., & Carlson, S. B. (1983). *Survey of academic tasks required of graduate and undergraduate foreign students* (Research Report No. 83–18). Princeton, NJ: Educational Testing Service.

Brinton, D. M., Snow, M. A., & Wesche, M. B. (1989). *Content-based second language instruction.* New York: Newbury House.

Brinton, D. M. (1990). *You have a chance also: ESL students at the university.* Paper presented at the 21st Annual CATESOL Conference, Los Angeles, CA.

Britton, J. (1970). *Language and learning.* London: Allen Lane/ Penguin.

Britton, J., Burgess, T., Martin, N., McLeod, A., & Rosen, H. (1975). *The development of writing abilities (11–18).* London: Macmillan.

References

Broadhead, R. S. (1983). *The private lives and professional identity of medical students.* New Brunswick, NJ: Transaction Books.

Broudy, H. S. (1977). Types of knowledge and purposes of education. In R. C. Anderson, R. J. Spiro, & W. E. Montague (Eds.), *Schooling and the acquisition of knowledge* (pp. 1–17). Hillsdale, NJ: Lawrence Erlbaum.

Browder, A. T. (1991). *My first trip to Africa.* Washington, DC: Institute for Karmic Guidance.

Brown, A. (1980). Metacognitive development and reading. In R. Spiro, B. Bruce, & W. Beaver (Eds.), *Theoretical issues in reading comprehension* (pp. 453–482). Hillsdale, NJ: Lawrence Erlbaum.

Brown, P., & Levinson, S. C. (1987). *Politeness: Some universals in language usage.* Cambridge: Cambridge University Press.

Brown, G., & Yule, G. (1983). *Discourse analysis.* Cambridge: Cambridge University Press.

Brown, R. (1973). *A first language: The early stages.* Cambridge, MA: Harvard University Press.

Brown, R. (1986). Testing Black student writers. In K. L. Greenberg, H. S. Wiener, & R. A. Donovan (Eds.), *Writing assessment: Issues and strategies* (pp. 98–108). New York: Longman.

Brown, R., & Bellugi, U. (1964). Three processes in the acquisition of syntax. *Harvard Educational Review, 34,* 133–151.

Bruffee, K. A. (1983). Writing and reading as collaborative or social acts. In J. N. Hays, P. A. Roth, J. R. Ramsey, & R. D. Foulke (Eds.), *The writer's mind: Writing as a mode of thinking* (pp. 159–169). Urbana, IL: National Council of Teachers of English.

Bruner, J. S. (1978). The role of dialogue in language acquisition. In A. Sinclair et al. (Eds.), *The child's conception of language* (pp. 241–256). New York: Springer-Verlag.

Buckley, W. K. (1988). The good, the bad, and the ugly in Amerika's Akademia. *Profession 88,* pp. 46–52.

Burling, R. (1973). *English in Black and White.* New York: Holt, Rinehart and Winston.

California Tomorrow. (1988). *Crossing the schoolhouse border: Immigrant students and the California public schools.* (California Tomorrow Policy Research Report). San Francisco: California Tomorrow Immigrant Students Project.

Camarillo, A. (1979). *Chicanos in a changing society: From Mexican pueblos to American barrios in Santa Barbara and Southern California. 1848–1930.* Cambridge, MA: Harvard University Press.

Candlin, C. N. (1989). Language, culture and curriculum. In C. N. Candlin & T. F. McNamara (Eds.), *Language learning and community* (pp. 1–24). Sydney, Australia: National Centre for English Language Teaching and Research.

Carey, L., Flower, L., Hayes, J. R., Schriver, K. A., & Haas, C. (1989). *Differences in writer's initial task representations.* (Technical Report No. 35).

Berkeley: University of California, Berkeley, Center for the Study of Writing.

Carrell, P. L. (1983). Three components of background knowledge in reading comprehension. *Language Learning, 33,* 183–207.

Carrell, P. L. (1984). Evidence for a formal schema in second language comprehension. *Language Learning, 34,* 87–112.

Carrell, P. L. (1987). Content and formal schemata in ESL reading. *TESOL Quarterly, 21,* 461–481.

Carrell, P. L., & Eisterhold, J. C. (1983). Schema theory and ESL reading. *TESOL Quarterly, 17,* 553–574.

Carrell, P. L., Pharis, B. G., & Liberto, J. C. (1989). Metacognitive strategy training for ESL reading. *TESOL Quarterly, 23,* 647–678.

Carson, J. G., Chose, N. D., & Gibson, S. U. (1990). *Literacy demands of the undergraduate curriculum.* Paper presented at the 24th Annual TESOL Convention, San Francisco, CA.

Casanave, C. P. (1990). *The role of writing in socializing graduate students into an academic discipline in the social sciences.* Unpublished doctoral dissertation, Stanford University, Stanford, CA.

Cazden, C. B., John, V. P., & Hymes, D. (Eds.). (1972). *Functions of language in the classroom.* New York: Teachers College Press.

Chandler, D. P. (1983). *A history of Cambodia.* Boulder, CO: Westview Press.

Chhim, S. H. (1987). *Introduction to Cambodian culture.* Sacramento: Bilingual Education Office, California State Department of Education.

Chin, E. (1991). *Learning to write the news.* Unpublished doctoral dissertation, Stanford University, Stanford, CA.

Chira, S. (1990, August 27–29). Tomorrow's teachers (3-part series). *The New York Times,* pp. A1, 13; A1, 12; B8.

Cintron, R. (1989). *The use of oral and written language in the homes of three Mexicano families.* Unpublished doctoral dissertation, University of Illinois at Chicago.

Collier, V. (1989). How long? A synthesis of research on academic achievement in a second language. *TESOL Quarterly, 23,* 509–531.

Conklin, N. F., & Lourie, M. A. (1983). *A host of tongues: Language communities in the United States.* New York: Free Press.

Connor, U., & Johns, A. M. (Eds.). (1990). *Coherence in writing: Research and pedagogical perspectives.* Alexandria, VA: TESOL.

Cook-Gumperz, J. (1986). The social construction of literacy. In J. Cook-Gumperz (Ed.), *The Social construction of literacy* (pp. 1–15). Cambridge: Cambridge University Press.

Cook-Gumperz, J. (1987). Caught in a web of words: Some considerations on language socialization and language Acquisition. In J. Cook-Gumperz, W. Corsaro, & J. Streeck (Eds.), *Children's worlds, children's language* (pp. 89–108). New York: Mouton de Gruyter.

Cooke, B. G. (1980). Nonverbal communication among Afro-Americans: An initial classification. In R. Jones (Ed.), *Black psychology* (2nd ed.) (pp. 139–160). New York: Harper & Row.

Cooper, G. (1977). *Black stylistic features in student compositions.* Paper presented at the 67th Annual Meeting of the National Council of Teachers of English, New York.

Couch, R. (1978). *Valid philosophies of composition.* Paper presented at the Annual Meeting of the Southwest Regional Conference on English in the Two-Year College, Denver, CO.

Cran, W. (Producer), & McCrum, R. (Series writer). (1986). Next year's words: A look into the future. In *The Story of English* (Videocassette, Series 0834–9009). Chicago: BBC/MacNeil-Lehrer Productions. (Available from Mac-Neil-Lehrer Films, 5547 N. Ravenswood, Chicago, IL 60640–1199)

Cronnell, B. (1984). Black-English influences in the writing of third and sixth grade Black students. *Journal of Educational Research, 77,* 223–236.

Cullinan, B. E. (Ed.). (1974). *Black dialects and reading.* Urbana, IL: National Council of Teachers of English.

Cummins, J. (1982, February). Tests, achievement and bilingual students. *FOCUS, 9.* Arlington, VA: National Clearinghouse for Bilingual Education Occasional Papers.

Cummins, J. (1986). Empowering minority students: A framework for intervention. *Harvard Educational Review, 56,* 18–36.

Cummins, J., & Swain, M. (1986). *Bilingualism in education.* London: Longman.

Dandy, E. B. (1990). Consequences of ignoring specific dialect differences. *Thresholds in Education, 16,* 11–13.

Dandy, E. B. (Ed.). (1991). *Black communications: Breaking down the barriers.* Chicago: African American Images.

Dandy, E. B. (in press). Language and the Afrocentric curriculum: The affirmative. In O. Taylor (Ed.), *SENGA:Language and the black child* (special ed.). New Orleans, LA: Megasin Publications.

Daniell, B. (1986). Against the Great Leap theory of literacy. *Pre/Text, 7,* 181–194.

de Castell, S., & Luke, A. (1988). Defining "literacy" in North American schools. In E. R. Kington, B. M. Kroll, & M. Rose (Eds.), *Perspectives on literacy* (pp. 159–74). Carbondale: Southern Illinois University Press.

Delgado-Gaitan, C. (1983). *Learning how: Rules for knowing and doing for Mexican children at home, play, and school.* Unpublished doctoral dissertation, Stanford University, Stanford, CA.

Delgado-Gaitan, C. (1989). *Literacy for empowerment: The role of Mexican parents in their children's education.* Manuscript submitted for publication.

Delpit, L. D. (1988). The silenced dialogue: Power and pedagogy in educating other people's children. *Harvard Educational Review, 58,* 43–61.

Demarest, D. (1969). *I obey the rules and remain a fool.* Paper presented at the Annual Convention of the National Council of Teachers of English, Washington, DC. (ERIC Document No. ED039233)

DeStefano, J. (1972). Productive language differences in fifth grade Black students' syntactic forms. *Elementary English, 49*, 522–555.

Dewalt, M. W., & Troxell, B. K. (1989). Old Order Mennonite one-room school: A case study. *Anthropology and Education Quarterly, 20*, 308–326.

Díaz, S., Moll, L. C., & Mehan, H. (1986). Sociocultural resources in instruction: A context-specific approach. In California State Department of Education (Ed.), *Beyond language: Social and cultural factors in schooling language minority students* (pp. 187–230). Los Angeles: California State University, Evaluation, Dissemination and Assessment Center.

Dixon, C. N., & Nessel, D. (1983). *Language experience approach to reading (and writing).* Hayward, CA: Alemany Press.

Dulay, H., Burt, M., & Krashen, S. (1982). *Language two.* New York: Oxford University Press.

Dyson, A. (1984). Learning to write/learning to do school: Emergent writers' interpretations of school literacy tasks. *Research in the Teaching of English, 18*, 233–264.

Ebihara, M. M. (1968). *Svay, a Khmer village in Cambodia.* Unpublished doctoral dissertation, Columbia University, New York.

Ebihara, M. M. (1987). The Khmer. In D. Haines (Ed.), *Refugees in the United States.* Westport, CT: Greenwood Press.

Edmonds, I.G. (1970). *The Khmers of Cambodia: The Story of a Mysterious People.* New York: Bobbs-Merrill.

Ellis, R. (1986). *Understanding second language acquisition.* Oxford: Oxford University Press.

Erickson, F. (1986). Qualitative research on teaching. In M. C. Wittrock (Ed.), *Handbook of research on teaching* (3rd ed.). New York: Macmillan.

Erickson, F. (1988). School literacy, reasoning and civility: An anthropologist's perspective. In E. R. Kintgen, B. M. Kroll, & M. Rose (Eds.), *Perspective on literacy* (pp. 205–226). Carbondale: Southern Illinois University Press.

Farr, M. (in press). Lyrical learning and literacy practices among Mexicanos in Chicago. In B. Moss (Ed.), *Literacy across communities.* Norwood, NJ: Ablex.

Farr, M., & Janda, M. (1985). Basic writing students: Investigating oral and written language. *Research in the Teaching of English, 19*, 62–83.

Farr, M., & Daniels, H. (1986). *Language diversity and writing instruction.* Urbana, IL: Institute for Urban and Minority Education, National Council of Teachers of English.

Farrell, T. J. (1983). IQ and Standard English. *College Composition and Communication, 34*, 470–487.

Farrell, T. J. (1984). Reply by Thomas J. Farrell. *College Composition and Communication, 35*, 469–478.

References

Ferreiro, E., & Teberosky, A. (1982). *Literacy before schooling.* Exeter, NH: Heinemann.

Ferguson, C. A. (1985). The study of religious discourse. In D. Tannen & J. E. Alatis (Eds.), *Georgetown University Round Table of Languages and Linguistics, 1984.* (pp. 205–213). Washington, DC: Georgetown University Press.

Ferguson, C. A., & Heath, S. B. (Eds.). (1981). *Language in the USA.* New York: Cambridge University Press.

Finegan, E. (1980). *Attitudes toward English usage: The history of a war of words.* New York: Teachers College Press.

Fishman, A. (1988). *Amish literacy: What and how it means.* Portsmouth, NH: Heinemann.

Flores, M. F., & Díaz, S. (1991). *Whole language development of literacy among bilingual students.* Paper presented at the Literacy Roundtable, Santa Barbara, CA.

Flower, L. (1981). *Problem-solving strategies for writing.* New York: Harcourt Brace.

Foster, H. L. (1986). *Ribbin', jivin' & playin' the dozens: The persistent dilemma in our schools* (2nd ed.). Cambridge, MA: Ballinger.

Foster, W. (1989). The administrator as transformative intellectual. *Peabody Journal of Education, 66,* 5–18.

Fowler, A. (1982). *Kinds of literature: An introduction to the theory of genres and modes.* Cambridge, MA: Harvard University Press.

Fowler, R. J. (1985). The composing processes of Black student writers. In C. K. Brooks (Ed.), *Tapping potential: English Language Arts for the Black learner* (pp. 182–186). Urbana, IL: National Council of Teachers of English.

Fox, R. C. (1957). Training for uncertainty. In R. K. Merton, G. Reader, & P. L. Kendall (Eds.), *The student-physician: Introductory studies in the sociology of medical education* (pp. 207–241). Cambridge, MA: Harvard University Press.

Frake, C. O. (1977). Plying frames can be dangerous: Some reflections on methodology in cognitive anthropology. *The Quarterly Newsletter of the Institute for Comparative Human Development, The Rockefeller University, 1,* 1–7.

Freedman, S. (1985). *The acquisition of written language.* Norwood, NJ: Ablex.

Freire, P., & Macedo, D. (1987). *Literacy: reading the word and the world.* Cambridge, MA: Bergin & Garvey.

Friedlander, A. (1990). Composing in ESL: Effects of a first language on writing in English as a second language. In B. Kroll (Ed.), *Second language writing* (pp. 109–125). Cambridge: Cambridge University Press.

Frost, R. (1917). *North of Boston.* (2nd ed.) New York: Henry Holt & Co. (Originally published 1914)

Fulwiler, T. (Ed.). (1987). *The journal book.* Portsmouth, NH: Boynton/Cook.

Gamberg, R., Kwak, W., Hitchings, M., Altheim, J., & Edwards, G. (1988).

Learning and loving it: Theme studies in the classroom. Portsmouth, NH: Heinemann.

Gardner, R. (1980). On the validity of affective variables in second language acquisition: Conceptual, contextual and statistical considerations. *Language Learning, 30,* 255–270.

Gardner, R., & Lambert, W. (1967). *Attitudes and motivation in second language learning.* Rowley, MA: Newbury House.

Geertz, C. (1973). *The interpretation of cultures: Selected essays.* New York: Basic Books.

Geertz, C. (1983). *Local knowledge: Further essays in interpretive anthropology.* New York: Basic Books.

Gilbert, G. N. (1976). The transformation of research findings into scientific knowledge. *Social Studies of Science, 6,* 281–306.

Giroux, H. A. (1981). *Ideology, culture, and the process of schooling.* Philadelphia, PA: Temple University Press.

Giroux, H. A. (1988). *Teachers as intellectuals: Toward a critical pedagogy of learning.* Grandby, MA: Bergin & Garvey.

Giroux, H. A., & McLaren, P. (1986). Teacher education and the politics of engagement: The case for democratic schooling. *Harvard Educational Review, 56,* 213–238.

Gitlin, A., & Smyth, J. (1989). *Teacher evaluation: Educative alternatives.* London: Falmer Press.

Goddard, I. (1990, September 29). Time to retire an Indian place-name hoax. [Letter to the editor]. *New York Times,* p. 14.

Goldman, S. R., & Trueba, H. T. (Eds.) (1987). *Becoming literate in English as a second language.* Norwood, NJ: Ablex.

Goodman, K. (Ed.). (1967). Reading: A psychological guessing game. *Journal of the Reading Specialist, 6,* 126–135.

Goodman, K. (Ed.). (1973 [1967]). *The psycholinguistic nature of the reading process.* Detroit, MI: Wayne State University.

Goodman, K., Brooks Smith, E., Meredith, R., & Goodman, Y. M. (1987). *Language and thinking in school: A whole-language curriculum.* (3rd ed.). New York: Richard C. Owen.

Goody, J. (1987). *The interface between the oral and the written.* Cambridge: Cambridge University Press.

Goody, J., & Watt, I. (1968). The consequences of literacy. In J. Goody (Ed.), *Literacy in traditional societies* (pp. 27–68). Cambridge: Cambridge University Press. (Originally published in 1963)

Graff, G. (1988). Teach the conflicts: An alternative to educational fundamentalism. In B. J. Craige (Ed.), *Literature, language, and politics* (pp. 99–109). Athens, GA: The University of Georgia Press.

Grant, M. C. (1987). A study of Black students' perceptions of the strategies used to complete critical writing tasks at the college level. *Dissertation Abstracts International*, 47, 04, SECA, PP1223.

Graves, D. (1983). *Writing: Teachers and children at work.* Portsmouth, NH: Heinemann.

Graves, D. (1988a). *Experiment with fiction.* Portsmouth, NH: Heinemann.

Graves, D. (1988b). *Investigate nonfiction.* Portsmouth, NH: Heinemann.

Gray, B. (1975). Dialect interference in writing: A tripartite analysis. *Journal of Basic Writing, 1*, 14–22.

Gray, C. P. (1989). Stop the violence. *Strictly Hip-Hop Magazine*, p. 2.

Green, R., & Griffore, R. (1980). The impact of standardized testing on minority students. *Journal of Negro Education, 49*, 238–252.

Guerra, J. (1990). *Literacy learning and use among Mexican immigrant families.* Unpublished doctoral dissertation, University of Illinois at Chicago.

Gumperz, J. (1972). The speech community. In P. P. Giglioli (Ed.), *Language and social context* (pp. 219–231). Baltimore, MD: Penguin Books.

Gumperz, J. (1982). *Discourse strategies.* Cambridge: Cambridge University Press.

Gutierrez, C. D. (1987). The composing processes of four college-aged ethnic minority basic writers: A cognitive, sociocultural analysis. *Dissertation Abstracts International, 49*, 03, SECA, PP449.

Hale-Benson, J. E. (1986). *Black children: Their roots, culture and learning styles* (rev. ed.). Baltimore, MD: Johns Hopkins.

Haley, A. *Roots.* (1976). New York: Doubleday.

Halliday, M. A. K. (1975). *Learning how to mean.* London: Edward Arnold.

Halliday, M. A. K. (1978). *Language as social semiotic.* London: Edward Arnold.

Halliday, M. A. K. (1981). Linguistic function and literary style: An inquiry into the language of William Golding's "The inheritors." In D. C. Freeman (Ed.), *Essays in modern stylistics.* London: Methuen.

Hannerz, U. (1977). Growing up male. In D. Wilkinson & R. Taylor (Ed.), *The Black Male in America* (pp. 33–59). Chicago: Nelson Hall.

Hansen, J., & Stansfield, C. (1981). The relationship of field-dependent-independent cognitive styles to foreign language achievement. *Language Learning, 31*, 349–367.

Hansen, K. (1988). Rhetoric and epistemology in the social sciences: A contrast of two representative texts. In D. A. Jolliffe (Ed.), *Writing in academic disciplines* (pp. 167–210). Norwood, NJ: Ablex.

Hare, N., & Hare, J. (1985). *Bringing the black boy to manhood.* San Francisco: Black Think Tank.

Harris, J. (1989). The idea of community in the study of writing. *College Composition and Communication, 40*, 11-22.

Harste, J., Short, K., & Burke, C. (1988). *Creating classrooms for authors: The reading-writing connection.* Portsmouth, NH: Heinemann.

Hatch, E. (1983). *Psycholinguistics: A second language perspective*. Rowley, MA: Newbury House.

Haugen, E. (1966). Linguistics and language planning. In W. Bright (Ed.), *Sociolinguistics* (pp. 50–71). The Hague: Mouton.

Heath, S. B. (1980). The functions and uses of literacy. *Journal of Communication, 30*, 123–133.

Heath, S. B. (1982). What no bedtime story means: Narrative skills at home and school. *Language in Society, 11*, 49–76.

Heath, S. B. (1983). *Ways with words: Language, life and work in communities and classrooms*. Cambridge: Cambridge University Press.

Heath, S. B. (1986). Sociocultural contexts of language development. In California State Department of Education (Ed.), *Beyond language: Social and cultural factors in schooling language minority students* (pp. 143–186). Los Angeles: California State University, Evaluation, Dissemination and Assessment Center.

Heath, S. B. (1987). The literate essay: Using ethnography to explode myths. In J. A. Langer (Ed.), *Language, literacy, and culture: Issues of society and schooling* (pp. 89–107). Norwood, NJ: Ablex.

Heath, S. B. (1989). Oral and literate traditions among black Americans living in poverty. *American Psychologist, 44*, 45–56.

Heath, S. B. (1990). The children of Trackton's children: Spoken and written language in social change. In J. W. Stigler et al. (Eds.), *Cultural psychology: Essays on comparative human development* (pp. 496–519). Cambridge: Cambridge University Press.

Heath, S. B., & Branscombe, A. (1985). "Intelligent writing" in an audience community: Teacher, students, and researcher. In S. W. Freedman (Ed.), *The acquisition of written language: Response and revision* (pp. 3–32). Norwood, NJ: Ablex.

Heath, S. B., & Hoffman, D. M. (1986). *Interactive reading and writing in elementary classrooms* [Guidebook for inside learners (film)]. (Available from S. B. Heath, Stanford University.)

Hellman, L. (1974). *An unfinished woman*. New York: Bantam Books.

Hernandez-Chavez, E., & Curtis, J. K. (1984). The graphic sense hypothesis or "you can't read firecrackers." In C. Rivera (Ed.), *Placement procedures in bilingual education: Education and policy issues* (pp. 121–151). Clevedon, England: Multilingual Matters.

Herrington, A. (1985). Writing in academic settings: A study of the contexts for writing in two college chemical engineering courses. *Research in the Teaching of English, 19*, 331–361.

Herskovits, M. (1941). *The myth of negro past*. Boston: Beacon Press.

Hill, H. D. (1989). *Effective strategies for teaching minority students*. Bloomington, IL: National Educational Service.

Hilliard, A. G. (1985). Kemetic concepts of education. In I. Van Sertima (Ed.),

311

Nile Valley civilizations (153–162). New Brunswick, NJ: Journal of African Civilizations.

Hildyard, A., & Olson, D. (1982). On the comprehension and memory of oral vs. written discourse. In D. Tannen (Ed.), *Spoken and written language: Exploring orality and literacy* (pp. 19–34). Norwood, NJ: Ablex.

Hinds, J. (1987). Reader versus writer responsibility: A new typology. In U. Connor & R. B. Kaplan (Eds.), *Writing across languages: Analysis of L2 text* (pp. 141–153). Reading, MA: Addison-Wesley.

Hirsch, E. D., Jr. (1987). *Cultural literacy: What every American needs to know.* Boston: Houghton Mifflin.

Hirsch, E. D., Jr. (1988). *Cultural literacy: What every American needs to know with an updated appendix, What literate Americans know.* In E. D. Hirsch, Jr., J. F. Kett, & J. Trefil. New York: Vintage Books/Random House.

Hirsch, E. D., Jr., Kett, J. F., & Trefil, J. (1988). *The dictionary of cultural literacy.* Boston: Houghton Mifflin.

Holm, W. (1971). *Some aspects of Navajo orthography.* Unpublished doctoral dissertation, University of New Mexico, Alburquerque, NM.

Hoover, M. R. (1985). Ethnology of black communications. *Journal of Black Reading/Language Education, 2,* 2–4.

Horowitz, D. (1986a). What professors actually require: Academic tasks for the ESL classroom. *TESOL Quarterly, 20,* 141–144.

Horowitz, D. (1986b). Process, not product: Less than meets the eye. *TESOL Quarterly, 20,* 445–462.

Hovey, K. A. (1988). The Great Books versus America: Reassessing The closing of the American mind. *Profession 88,* pp. 40–45.

Howard, R. (1974). A note on *S/Z.* In R. Barthes, *S/Z.* (R. Miller, Trans.). New York: Hill & Wang.

Hymes, D. (1980). *What is ethnography? Language in education: Ethnolinguistic essays.* (Series 1). Washington, DC: Center for Applied Linguistics.

Hymes, D. (1986). Models of the interaction of language and social life. In J. J. Gumperz & D. Hymes, (Eds.), *Directions in sociolinguistics: The ethnography of communication* (pp. 35–71). Oxford: Basil Blackwell.

Jeremiah, M. A. (1987). Writing Blacks or Blacks writing. *The Western Journal of Black Studies, 11,* 111–114.

John, V. (1972). Styles of learning—styles of teaching. In C. Cazden, V. John, & D. Hymes (Eds.), *Functions of language in the classroom* (pp. 331–343). New York: Teachers College Press.

Johns, A. M. (1990). *Advanced culture shock: Student perspectives on "equivalent" high school and university classes.* Unpublished manuscript. San Diego State University, San Diego, CA.

Johns, A. M. (1991a). Faculty assessment of student literacy skills: Implications for ESL/EFL writing assessment. L. Hamp-Lyons, (Ed.), *Assessing second language writing in academic contexts.* New York: Ablex.

Johns, A. M. (1991b). Interpreting an English competency examination: The frustrations of an ESL science student. *Written Communication, 8*, 379–401.

Johnson, J. (1990). *The endangered black male: The new bald eagle*. Paper presented at a Conference on Male Involvement in Responsible Decision-Making, Atlanta, GA.

Johnson, S. (1963). Preface to the Dictionary. In J. C. Gray (Ed.), *Words, words, words about dictionaries* (pp. 129–144). San Francisco: Chandler Publishing. (Originally published 1755)

Johnson, D. M., & Roen, D. H. (Eds.) (1989). *Richness in writing*. New York: Longman.

Johnson, P. (1981). Effects on reading comprehension of language complexity and cultural background of a text. *TESOL Quarterly, 15*, 169–182.

Johnson, P. (1982). Effects on reading comprehension of building background knowledge. *TESOL Quarterly, 16*, 503–516.

Joiner, C. A. (1981). Memorandum opinion and order. In G. Smitherman (Ed.), *Black English and the education of black children and youth: Proceedings of the National Invitational Symposium on the King Decision (February 21–23 1980)* (pp. 336–358). Detroit, MI: Wayne State University.

Jolliffe, D. A. (Ed.). (1988). *Writing in academic disciplines: Vol. 2. Advances in writing research*. Norwood, NJ: Ablex.

Kaplan, R. B. (1966). Cultural thought patterns in intercultural education. *Language Learning, 16*, 1–20.

King, M., & McKenzie, M. (1988). Research Currents: Literary discourse from the child's perspective. *Language Arts, 65*, 304–314.

Kintgen, E. R., Kroll, B. M., & Rose, M. (Eds.), *Perspective on literacy*. Carbondale, IL: Southern Illinois University Press.

Knoblauch, C. H., & Brannon, L. (1984). *Rhetorical traditions and the teaching of writing*. Upper Montclair, NJ: Boynton/Cook.

Kochman, T. (1981). *Black and white styles in conflict*. Chicago: University of Chicago Press.

Krashen, S., & Biber, D. (1988). *On course: Bilingual education's success in California*. Sacramento: California Association of Bilingual Education.

Kroll, B. (1979). A survey of writing needs of foreign and American college freshmen. *ELT Journal, 33*, 219–226.

Kroll, B. (Ed.) (1990). *Second language writing*. New York: Cambridge University Press.

Kucer, S. B. (1987). The cognitive base of reading and writing. In J. R. Squire (Ed.), *The dynamics of language learning: Research in reading and English* (pp. 27–51). Urbana, IL: ERIC Clearinghouse of Reading and Communication Skills.

Kuhn, T. S. (1970). *The structure of scientific revolutions*. (2nd ed.). Chicago: University of Chicago Press.

References

Kunjufu, J. (1986). *Countering the conspiracy to destroy black boys* (Vols. 1 & 2). Chicago: African American Images.

Kunjufu, J. (1987). *Lessons from history—A celebration in blackness—elementary or high school edition.* Chicago: African American Images.

Kunjufu, J. (1988). *To be popular or smart: The Black peer group.* Chicago: African American Images.

Labov, W., & Waletsky, J. (1967). Narrative analysis: Oral version of personal experience. In J. Helm (Ed.), *Essays on the verbal and visual arts: Proceedings of the 1966 Annual Spring Meeting of the American Ethnological Society* (pp. 12–44). Seattle: University of Washington Press.

Labov, W. (1969). The logic of nonstandard English. *Monograph Series on Languages and Linguistics* (No. 22). Washington, DC: Georgetown University Press.

Labov, W. (1972). Rules for ritual insults. In T. Kochman (Ed.), *Rappin' and stylin' out* (pp. 265–314). Urbana, IL: University of Illinois Press.

Laine, C. H., & Fagan, E. R. (1980). The preparation of English teachers: Has it been a decade of change? *English Education, 11,* 199–208.

Langer, J. A. (1984). The effects of available information on responses to school writing tasks. *Research in the Teaching of English, 18,* 27–44.

Langer, J. A. (Ed.), *Language, literacy, and culture: Issues of society and schooling.* Norwood, NJ: Ablex.

Langer, J. A. (1987). A sociocognitive perspective on literacy. In J. A. Langer (Ed.), *Language, literacy, and culture: Issues of society and schooling* (pp. 1–38). Norwood, NJ: Ablex.

Langer, J. A., & Applebee, A. N. (1986). Reading and writing instruction: Toward a theory of teaching and learning. In E. Z. Rothkopf (Ed.), *Review of Research in Education* (pp. 171–194). Washington, DC: American Educational Research Association.

Lave, J., Murtagh, M., & de la Rocha, O. (1984). The dialectic of arithmetic in grocery shopping. In B. Rogoff & J. Lave (Eds.), *Everyday cognition: Its development in social context* (pp. 67–94). Cambridge, MA: Harvard University Press.

Lemke, J. (1988). Genres, semantics, and classroom education. *Linguistics and Education, 1,* 81–99.

Le Page, R. B. (1978). Projection, focussing, diffusion. *Society for Caribbean Linguistics,* Occasional Paper, 9.

Le Page, R. B., & Tabouret-Keller, A. (1985). *Acts of identity: Creole-based approaches to language and ethnicity.* Cambridge: Cambridge University Press.

Lévy-Bruhl, L. (1985). *How natives think.* (L. A. Clare, Trans.). Princeton, NJ: Princeton University Press. (Originally published as Les fonctions mentales dans les sociétés inférieures, 1910; original English version published, 1926)

Limon, J. E. (1982). The folk performance of "Chicano" and the cultural limits of political ideology. In L. Elías-Olivares & J. Amastnc (Eds.), *Spanish in the United States: Sociolinguistic aspects.* Cambridge: Cambridge University Press.

Linn, M. (1975). *Stylistic variation in Black English Vernacular and the teaching of college composition.* (ERIC Document No. ED211984)

Lipman, M. (1988). Critical thinking—What can it be? *Educational Leadership, 46,* 38–43.

Lortie, D. C. (1959). Laymen to lawmen: Law school, careers, and professional socialization. *Harvard Educational Review, 29,* 352–369.

Lortie, D. C. (1975). *School-teacher: A sociological study.* Chicago: University of Chicago Press.

Lourie, M. A., & Conklin, N. F. (Eds.) (1978). *A pluralistic nation: The language issue in the United States.* Rowley, MA: Newbury House.

Lovell, J., & Barone, D. (1990). Michael the show and tell magician: A journey through literature to self. *Language Arts, 67,* 134–143.

Lucas, T. (1990). Personal journal writing as a classroom genre. In J. K. Peyton (Ed.), *Students and teachers writing together: Perspectives on journal writing* (pp. 99–123). Alexandria, VA: TESOL.

Lunsford, A., Moglen, H., & Slevin, J. (1990). *The right to literacy.* New York: Modern Language Association.

McCarthy, L. P. (1987). A stranger in strange lands: A college student writing across the curriculum. *Research in the Teaching of English, 21,* 233–265.

McGoarty, M. (1986). Educators' responses to sociocultural diversity: Implications for practice. In California State Department of Education (Eds.), *Beyond language: Social and cultural factors in schooling language minority students* (pp. 299–343). Los Angeles: California State University, Evaluation, Dissemination and Assessment Center.

McKay, S. L., & Wong, S. C. (1988). *Language diversity: Problem or resource? A social and educational perspective on language minorities in the United States.* Cambridge, MA: Newbury House.

McLaughlin, B. (1987). *Theories of second-language learning.* London: Edward Arnold.

McLaughlin, D. (1989). The sociolinguistics of Navajo literacy. *Anthropology and Education Quarterly, 20,* 275–90.

McLaughlin, D. (1990). Curriculum for cultural politics: Language program development in a Navajo setting. In C. D. Martin & R. Blomeyer (Eds.), *Case studies in computer assisted instruction* (pp. 151–164). London: Falmer Press.

McLaughlin, D. (1992). *When literacy empowers: An ethnography of English and Navajo print.* Albuquerque: University of New Mexico Press.

McLean, S. V. (1990). Early childhood teachers in multicultural settings. *The Educational Forum, 54,* 197–204.

MacDonald, M. (1987). *Angkor and the Khmers.* Oxford: Oxford University Press.

References

Maxwell, M. M. (1985). Some functions and uses of literacy in the deaf community. *Language in Society, 14,* 205–221.

Maxwell, M. M. (in press). Conversational literacy in the deaf community. In B. J. Moss (Ed.), *Literacy across communities.* Norwood, NJ: Ablex.

May, S. (1986). *Cambodian witness.* New York: Random House.

Mehan, H. (1980). The competent student. *Anthropology and Education Quarterly, 11,* 131–151.

Mellix, B. (1989). From outside in. In R. Atwan (Ed.), *Our times: Readings from recent periodicals* (pp. 171–179). New York: St. Martin's Press.

MELUS. (1974–   ) Ann Arbor, MI: The Society for the Study of the Multiethnic Literature of the United States.

Menocal, M. R. (1988). We can't dance together. *Profession 88,* pp. 53–58.

Merton, R. K. (1957). Some preliminaries to a sociology of medical education. In R. K. Merton, G. G. Reader, & P. L. Kendall (Eds.), *The student-physician: Introductory studies in the sociology of medical education* (pp. 3–80). Cambridge, MA: Harvard University Press.

Merton, R. K., Reader, G. G., & Kendall, P. L. (1957). *The student-physician: Introductory studies in the sociology of medical education.* Cambridge, MA: Harvard University Press.

Michaels, S. (1981). "Sharing time": Children's narrative styles and differential access to literacy. *Language in Society, 10,* 423–442.

Michaels, S. (1986). Narrative presentations: An oral preparation for literacy with first graders. In J. Cook-Gumperz (Ed.), *The social construction of literacy* (pp. 95–116). Cambridge: Cambridge University Press.

Moglen, H. (1988). Allan Bloom and E. D. Hirsch: Educational reform as tragedy. *Profession 88,* pp. 59–64.

Moll, L. C., Vélez-Ibáñez, C., Greenberg, J., Whitmore, K., Saavedra, E., Dworin, J., & Andrade, R. (1990). *Community knowledge and classroom practice: Combining resources for literacy instruction.* Tucson: University of Arizona, College of Education and Bureau of Applied Research in Anthropology.

Moran, M. (1984). Vocabulary development. In M. Moran & R. F. Lunsford (Eds.), *Research in composition and rhetoric* (pp. 347–370). Westport, CT: Greenwood Press.

Morrow, D. H. (1989). Black American English style shifting and writing error. *Research in the Teaching of English, 22,* 326–343.

Moss, B. (in press). Literacy events in three Black churches. In B. Moss (Ed.), *Literacy across communities.* Norwood, NJ: Ablex.

Moss, B., & Walters, K. (in press). Rethinking diversity: Axes of difference in the writing classroom. In L. Odell (Ed.). *Issues in composing theory.* Carbondale: Southern Illinois University Press.

Muller, T., & Espensade, T. (1985). *The fourth wave.* Washington, DC: The Urban Institute Press.

Murphy, A. (1989). Transference and resistance in the basic writing classroom. *College Composition and Communication, 40,* 175–187.

Murray, D. (1985). *A writer teaches writing.* Boston: Houghton Mifflin.

Murray, D. E. (1983). Diagnostic testing of the intelligibility of Thai and Japanese speakers of English as a foreign language. In C. Campbell, V. Flashner, T. Hudson, & J. Lubin (Eds.), *Proceedings of the Los Angeles Second Language Research Forum,* (Vol. 2: pp. 226–236). Los Angeles: University of California, Los Angeles, Department of English.

Murray, D. E. (1990). Literacies as sociocultural phenomena. *Prospect, 6,* 55–62.

Murray, D. E., & Nichols, P. C. (1992). Literacy practices and their effect on academic writing: Vietnamese case studies. In F. Dubin & N. Kuhlman (Eds.), *Cross-cultural literacy: Global perspectives on reading and writing* (pp. 175–187). New York: Prentice Hall.

Mussen, P. H., Conger, J. J., & Kagan. J. (1956). *Child development and personality* (4th ed.). New York: Harper & Row.

Naiman, N., Frohlich, M., Stern, H., & Todesco, A. (1978). *The good language learner.* Unpublished manuscript. Ontario Institute for Studies in Education, Toronto, Canada.

Nelson, J. (1990). This was an easy assignment: Examining how students interpret academic writing tasks. *Research in the Teaching of English, 24,* 362–396.

Nelson-Barber, S., & Meier, T. (1990). Multicultural context a key factor in teaching. *Academic Connections,* pp. 1–5, 9–11.

Nembhard, J. P. (1983). A perspective on teaching Black dialect speaking students to write Standard English. *Journal of Negro Education, 52,* 75–82.

Ngor, H. (1987). *A Cambodian odyssey.* New York: Macmillan.

Nichols, P. C. (1977). A sociolinguistic perspective on reading and Black children. *Language Arts, 54,* 150–157.

Nichols, P. C. (1988). English as a bridge between cultures: Scotland, Carolina, and California. *The CATESOL Journal, 1,* 5–16.

Nichols, P. C. (1989). Storytelling in Carolina: Continuities and contrasts. *Anthropology and Education Quarterly, 20,* 232–245.

Nobles, W. W. (1980). African philosophy: Foundation for Black psychology. In R. J. Jones (Ed.), *Black psychology* (2nd ed.) (pp. 23–36). New York: Harper & Row.

Noonan-Wagner, D. (1980). *Black writers in the classroom: A question of language experience.* Paper presented at the Annual Meeting of the Conference on College Composition and Communication, Washington, DC.

North, S. M. (1986). Writing in a philosophy class: Three case studies. *Research in the Teaching of English, 20,* 225–262.

Nunan, D. (1988). *The learner-centred curriculum: A study in second language teaching.* Cambridge: Cambridge University Press.

Ogbu, J. (1987a). Opportunity, structure, cultural boundaries and literacy. In J. Langer (Ed.), *Language, literacy and culture* (pp. 149–77). Norwood, NJ: Ablex.

Ogbu, J. (1987b). Variability in minority school performance: A problem in search of an explanation. *Anthropology and Education Quarterly, 18*, 312–334.

Olson, D. R. (1977a). From utterance to text: The bias of language and speech in writing. *Harvard Educational Review, 47*, 257–281.

Olson, D. R. (1977b). The languages of instruction: The literate bias of schooling. In R. C. Anderson, R. J. Spiro, & W. E. Montague (Eds.), *Schooling and the acquisition of knowledge* (pp. 65–89). Hillsdale, NJ: Lawrence Erlbaum.

Olson, D. R. (1980). On the language and authority of textbooks, *Journal of Communication, 30*, 186–196.

Ong, W. J. (1982). *Orality and literacy: The technologizing of the word.* London: Metheun.

Ong, W. J. (1988). A comment about "Arguing about literacy." *College English, 50*, 700–701.

Ouk, M., Huffman, F. E., & Lewis, J. (1988). *Handbook for teaching Khmer-speaking students.* Folsom/Cordova, CA: Folsom Cordova Unified School District.

Pattison, R. (1982). *On literacy.* Oxford: Oxford University Press.

Pearson-Casanave, C. R. (1984). Communicative pre-reading activities: Schema theory in action. *TESOL Quarterly, 18*, 334–336.

Penfield, J., & Ornstein-Galicia, J. (Eds.). (1985). *Chicano English: An ethnic contact dialect.* Amsterdam, Netherlands: J. Benjamins.

Perfetti, C. A. (1987). Language, speech, and print: Some assymetries in the acquisition of literacy. In R. Horowitz & S. J. Samuels (Eds.). *Comprehending oral and written language* (pp. 355–369). San Diego, CA: Academic.

Petrosky, A. R. (1982). From story to essay: Reading and writing. *College Composition and Communication, 33*, 19–36.

Peyton, J. K. (Ed.). (1990). *Students and teachers writing together: Perspectives on journal writing.* Alexandria, VA: TESOL.

Peyton, J. K., & Reed, L. (1990). *Dialogue journal writing with nonnative English speakers: A handbook for teachers.* Alexandria, VA: TESOL.

Philips, S. (1972). Participant structures and communicative competence. In C. Cazden, V. John, & D. Hymes (Eds.), *Functions of language in the classroom* (pp. 370–394). New York: Teachers College Press.

Pike, P. (1987). *Wordbuster reading rap.* Chicago: Pike Unlimited.

Pine, G. J., & Hilliard, A. G. (1990). Rx for racism: Imperatives for America's schools. *Phi Delta Kappan, 71*, 593–600.

Popper, K. R. (1979). *Objective knowledge: An evaluatory approach* (rev. ed.). Oxford: Clarendon Press. (Original work published 1972)

Pratt, M. L. (1987). Linguistic utopias. In N. Fabb, D. Attridge, A. Durant, & C.

MacCabe (Eds.), *The linguistics of writing* (pp. 48–66). Manchester, England: Manchester University Press.

Prior, P. (1991). Contextualizing writing and response in a graduate seminar. *Written Communication, 8,* 267–310.

Progoff, I. (1975). *At a journal workshop.* New York: Dialogue House.

Raimes, A. (1983). Anguish as a second language? Remedies for composition teachers. In A. Freedman, I. Pringle, & J. Yalden (Eds.), *Learning to write: First language/ second language* (pp. 258–272). Harlow, England: Longman.

Raimes, A. (1985a). *Key questions about writing.* Paper presented in a Round-table Discussion at the 21st Annual TESOL Convention, Miami, FL.

Raimes, A. (1985b). What unskilled ESL students do as they write, *TESOL Quarterly, 19,* 229–258.

Rogoff, B., & Gardner, W. (1984). Adult guidance of cognitive development. In B. Rogoff & J. Lave (Eds.), *Everyday cognition: Its development in social context* (pp. 95–116). Cambridge, MA: Harvard University Press.

Rosen, B. C., & Bates, A. P. (1976). The structure of socialization in graduate school. In R. M. Pavalko (Ed.), *Sociology of education: A book of readings* (2nd ed.) (pp. 154–167). Itasca, NY: F. E. Peacock.

Rosenblatt, L. M. (1978). *The reader, the text, the poem: The transactional theory of the literary work.* Carbondale: Southern Illinois University Press.

Rosenblatt, L. M. (1988). Writing and reading: The transactional theory. *Reader, 20,* 7–31.

Ross, R. (1990). *Cambodia: A country study.* Washington, DC: Government Printing Office.

Rumelhart, D. E. (1980). Schemata: The building blocks of cognition. In R. J. Spiro, B. C. Bruce, & W. F. Brewer (Eds.), *Theoretical issues in reading and comprehension* (pp. 33–58). Hillsdale, NJ: Lawrence Erlbaum.

Santos, T. (1988). Professors' reactions to the academic writing of nonnative-speaking students. *TESOL Quarterly, 22,* 69–90.

Saville-Troike, M. (1989). *The ethnography of communication.* New York: Basil Blackwell.

Schank, R. C., & Abelson, R. P. (1977). *Scripts, plans, goals, and understanding: An inquiry into human knowledge structures.* Hillsdale, NJ: Lawrence Erlbaum.

Schultz, D. A. (1977). Coming up as a boy in the ghetto. In D. Wilkinson & R. Taylor (Eds.), *The Black male in America* (pp. 11–17). Chicago: Nelson Hall.

Schuman, J. (1978). The acculturation model of second language acquisition. In R. Gingras (Ed.), *Second language acquisition and foreign language teaching* (pp. 27–50). Arlington, VA: Center for Applied Linguistics.

Scollon, R., & Scollon, S. B. K. (1981). *Narrative, literacy and face in interethnic communication.* Norwood, NJ: Ablex.

Scott, H. J. (1979). *Minimum-competency testing: The newest obstruction to the education of Black and other disadvantaged Americans.* Princeton, NJ: ERIC

Clearinghouse on Tests, Measurements and Evaluation/Educational Testing Service. (ETS Archives Microfiche No. 1906)

Scott, H. J. (1981). Black language and communication skills: Recycling the issues. In G. Smitherman (Ed.), *Black English and the education of Black children and youth*. Detroit, MI: Harlo Press.

Scribner, S., & Cole, M. (1981). *The psychology of literacy*. Cambridge, MA: Harvard University Press.

Shamos, M. (1988, July/August). The lesson every child need not learn: Scientific literacy for all is an empty goal. *The Sciences*, pp. 14–20.

Shannon, S. M. (1987). *English in el barrio: A sociolinguistic study of second language contact*. Unpublished doctoral dissertation, Stanford University, Stanford, CA.

Shawcross, W. (1979). *Sideshow: Kissinger, Nixon and the destruction of Cambodia*. New York: Simon and Schuster.

Shuman, A. (1986). *Storytelling rights: The uses of oral and written texts by urban adolescents*. Cambridge: Cambridge University Press.

Shih, M. (1986). Content-based approaches to teaching acdemic writing. *TESOL Quarterly, 20*, 617–648.

Silko, L. M. (1977). *Ceremony*. New York: Viking/ Penguin.

Silko, L. M. (1981). *Storyteller*. New York: Seaver Books.

Simonson, R., & Walker, S. (1988). *Multicultural literacy: Opening the American mind*. St. Paul, MN: Graywood Press.

Skehan, P. (1989). *Individual differences in second-language learning*. London: Edward Arnold.

Slavin, R. E. (1987). *Cooperative learning: Student teams*. (2nd ed.). Washington, DC: National Educational Association.

Sledd, J. (1984). Dialectology in the service of Big Brother. *College English, 33*, 439–456.

Sledd, A., & Sledd, J. (1988a). Hirsch's use of his sources in Cultural Literacy: A critique. *Profession 88*, pp. 33–39.

Sledd, A., & Sledd, J. (1988b). Success as failure and failure as success: The cultural literacy of E. D. Hirsch, Jr. *Written Communication, 6*, 364–389.

Sleeter, C. (1991). *Empowerment through multicultural education*. Albany: State University of New York Press.

Smith, E. A. (1974). *The evolution and continuing presence of the African oral tradition in Black America*. Unpublished doctoral dissertation, University of California, Irvine.

Smith, F. (1984). *Joining the literacy club*. Victoria, Canada: Abel Press.

Smith, F. (1986a). *Insult to intelligence: The bureaucratic invasion of our classrooms*. Portsmouth, NH: Heinemann.

Smith, F. (1986b). *Understanding reading* (3rd ed.). Hillsdale, NJ: Lawrence Erlbaum.

Smitherman, G. (1969). *A comparison of the oral and written styles of a group of inner-city Black students.* Unpublished doctoral dissertation, University of Michigan, Ann Arbor. (ERIC Document No. ED049205)

Smitherman, G. (1977). *Talkin' and testifyin'.* Boston: Houghton Mifflin.

Smitherman, G. (1983). *Black student writers, storks and familiar places: What can we learn from the National Assessment of Educational Progress?* Unpublished manuscript. Detroit, MI: Wayne State University, Department of Black Studies.

Smith-Hefner, N.J. (1990). Language and identity in the education of Boston-area Khmer. *Anthropology and Education Quarterly, 21,* 250–268.

Snow, C., & Hoefnagel-Höhle, M. (1978). Age differences in second language acquisition. In E. Hatch (Ed.), *Second language acquisition: A book of readings* (pp. 333–344). Rowley, MA: Newbury House.

Soter, A. O. (1990). The English teacher and the non-English-speaking student: Facing the multicultural/multilingual challenge. In G. Hawisher & A. O. Soter (Eds.), *On literacy and its teaching: Issues in English education* (pp. 224–242). Albany: State University of New York Press.

Spack, R. (1988). Initiating ESL students into the academic discourse community: How far should we go? *TESOL Quarterly, 22,* 29–51.

Spolsky, B., & Irvine, P. (1982). Sociolinguistic aspects of the acceptance of literacy in the vernacular. In F. Barkin, E. Brandt, & J. Ornstein-Galicia (Eds.), *Bilingualism and language contact: Spanish, English, and Native American Languages* (pp. 73–79). New York: Teachers College Press.

Sprotte, N. (1990, December). Personal communication with the Director of Admissions, San Diego State University, San Diego, CA.

Stanford, G. (Ed.). (1979). *Classroom practices in teaching English, 1979–1980: How to handle the paper load.* Urbana, IL: National Council of Teachers of English.

Staton, J., Shuy, R., Peyton, J. K., & Reed, L. (1988). *Dialogue journal communication: Classroom, linguistic, social and cognitive views.* Norwood, NJ: Ablex.

Steinberg, B. D. (1959). *Cambodia.* New Haven, CT: Human Relations Area Files.

Sternglass, M. (1973). *Similarities and differences in nonstandard features in the compositions of Black and White college students in freshman remedial writing classes.* Unpublished doctoral dissertation, University of Pittsburgh, Pittsburgh, PA. (ERIC Document No. ED092941)

Stevick, E. (1990). *Humanism in language teaching: A critical perspective.* Oxford: Oxford University Press.

Street, B. (1984). *Literacy in theory and practice.* Cambridge: Cambridge University Press.

Strong, M. (1983). Social styles and second language acquisition of Spanish-speaking kindergartners. *TESOL Quarterly, 17,* 241–258.

Stubbs, M. (1980). *Language and literacy: The sociolinguistics of reading and writing.* London: Routledge & Kegan Paul.

Stubbs, M. (1990). Language in education. In N. E. Collinge (Ed.). *An encyclopedia of language* (pp. 551–589). London: Routledge.

Swales, J. M. (1990). *Genre analysis: English in academic and research settings.* New York: Cambrige University Press.

Swales, J. M., & Horowitz, D. M. (1988). *Genre-based approaches to ESL and ESP materials.* Paper presented at the 22nd Annual TESOL Convention, Chicago, IL.

Sy, J. H. (1989). Theophile Obenga: At the forefront of Egypto-Nubian and Black African renaissance in philosophy. In I. Van Sertima (Ed.), *Egypt Revisited* (2nd ed.) (pp. 277–285). New Brunswick, NJ: Journal of African Civilizations.

Tamez, J. D. (1989). *"Es que somos muy burros": Attitudes toward English education among Mexican adult undocumented workers.* Unpublished master's thesis, University of Texas at Austin.

Tannen, D. (1979). What's in a frame? Surface evidence for underlying expectations. In R. Freedle (Ed.), *New directions in discourse processing* (pp. 137–181). Norwood, NJ: Ablex.

Tannen, D. (1982). The oral/literate continuum in discourse. In D. Tannen (Ed.), *Spoken and written language: Exploring orality and literacy* (pp. 1–16). Norwood, NJ: Ablex.

Tarynor, N. K. (1976). *The impact of the African tradition on African christianity.* (self-published ed.) Ann Arbor, MI: Xerox University Microfilms.

Taylor, O. (1987). *Cross-cultural communication—An essential dimension of effective education.* Washington, DC: Mid-Atlantic Center for Race Equity.

Thomas, R. (1989). Oral tradition and written record in Classical Athens. Cambridge: Cambridge University Press.

Thompson, R. F. (1981). *Flash of the spirit: African and Afro-American art and philosophy.* New York: Random House.

Tierney, W. G. (1989). *Curriculum landscapes, democratic vistas: Transformative leadership in higher education.* New York: Praeger.

Tierney, W. G., & Foster, W. (1989). Editor's introduction: Educational leadership and the struggle for mind. *Peabody Journal of Education, 66,* 1–4.

Tollefson, W. (1991). *Planning language: Planning inequality.* London: Longman.

Trueba, H. T. (1984). The forms, functions and values of literacy: Reading for survival in a barrio as a student. *NABE Journal, 9,* 21–38.

Trueba, H. T. (Ed.) (1987). *Success or failure? Learning and the language minority student.* Cambridge, MA: Newbury House.

Trueba, H. T. (1988). Culturally based explanations of minority students' academic achievement. *Anthropology and Education Quarterly, 19,* 270–287.

Trueba, H. T. (1989). *Raising silent voices: Educating the linguistic minorities for the 21st century.* Cambridge, MA: Newbury House.

Trudgill, P. (1975). *Accent, dialect, and the school*. London: Edward Arnold.

Trudgill, P. (1983a). Standard and non-standard dialects of English in the United Kingdom: Attitudes and policies. In *On dialect: Social and geographic perspectives* (pp. 186–200). New York: New York University Press.

Trudgill, P. (1983b). Sociolinguistics and linguistic value judgements: Correctness, adequacy and aesthetics. In *On dialect: Social and geographic perspectives* (pp. 201–225). New York: New York University Press.

Turner, L. D. (1949). *Africanisms in the Gullah dialect*. Chicago: University of Chicago Press.

Vande Kopple, W. (1985). Some exploratory discourse on metadiscourse. *College Composition and Communication, 36*, 82–93.

Vanett, L., & Jurich, D. (1990a). A context for collaboration: Teachers and students writing together. In J. K. Peyton (Ed.), *Students and teachers writing together: Perspectives in journal writing* (pp. 49–62). Alexandria, VA: TESOL.

Vanett, L., & Jurich, D. (1990b). The missing link: Connecting journal writing to academic writing. In J. K. Peyton (Ed.), *Students and teachers writing together: Perspectives in journal writing* (pp. 21–33). Alexandria, VA: TESOL.

Van Sertima, I. (1989). *Blacks in science: Ancient and modern*. New Brunswick, NJ: Journal of African Civilizations.

Vasquez, O. A. (1989). *Connect oral language strategies to literacy: An ethnographic study among four Mexican immigrant families*. Unpublished doctoral dissertation, Stanford University, Stanford, CA.

Vasquez, O. A., Pease-Alvarez, L. P., & Shannon, S. M. (forthcoming). *Language learning and language socialization in a Mexican immigrant community*.

Vass, W. K. (1979). *Bantu speaking heritage of the United States*. Los Angeles: University of California, Center for Afro-American Studies.

Vélez-Ibañez, C. G. (1988). Networks of exchange among Mexicans in the U.S. and Mexico: Local level mediating responses to national and international transformations. *Urban Anthropology and Studies of Cultural Systems and World Economic Development, 17*, 27–52.

Veltman, C. (1983). *Language shift in the United States*. Berlin: Mouton.

Vygotsky, L. S. (1962). *Thought and language*. Cambridge, MA: Harvard University Press.

Vygotsky, L. S. (1978). Mind in society: The development of higher psychological processes. (M. Cole, V. John-Steiner, S. Scribner, & E. Souberman, Eds.). Cambridge, MA: Harvard University Press.

Vygotsky, L. S. (1986). *Thought and language* (A. Kozulin, Trans. & Ed.). Cambridge, MA: The MIT Press.

Walters, K. (1989). *Language, logic, and how the natives think*. Paper presented at the Conference on College Composition and Communication, Seattle, WA.

Walters, K. (1990). Language, logic, and literacy. In A. Lunsford, H. Moglen,

References

& J. Slevin (Eds.), *The right to literacy* (pp. 173–188). New York: Modern Language Association.

Walters, K. (in press). Writing and education. In H. Günther & O. Ludwig (Eds.) *Schrift und Schriftlichkeit/Writing and its uses.* Berlin: Walter de Gruyter.

Walters, K., Daniell, B., & Trachsel, M. (1987). Formal and functional approaches to literacy. *Language Arts, 64,* 855–868.

Walters, K. et al. (in press). English only? Literate traditions in the ethnic communities of Columbus, Ohio. In B. Moss (Ed.), *Literacy across communities.* Norwood, NJ: Ablex.

Weinstein-Shr, G. (in press). From mountaintops to city streets: Literacy in Philadelphia's Hmong community. In B. Moss (Ed.), *Literacy across communities.* Norwood, NJ: Ablex.

Welaratna, U. (1988). Cambodian refugees: Factors affecting their assimilation and English language instruction. *The CATESOL Journal, 1,* 17–27.

Welaratna, U. (1989). *Cambodian refugees in California: After the holocaust.* Unpublished master's thesis, San José State University, San José, CA.

Welaratna, U. (1990). Visits with a Cambodian refugee family. *San José Studies, 16,* 86–96.

Welaratna, U. (in press). *Images of freedom: Voices from the Cambodian holocaust.* Stanford, CA: Stanford University Press.

Wells, G. (1981). *Learning through interaction: The study of language development.* Cambridge: Cambridge University Press.

Wigginton, E. (1985). *Sometimes a shining moment: The Foxfire experience.* New York: Doubleday.

Wigginton, E. (1989). Foxfire grows up. *Harvard Educational Review, 59,* 24–49.

Williams, R. (1989a). Culture is ordinary. In R. Gable (Ed.), *Resources of hope: Culture, democracy, socialism* (pp. 3–18). London: Verso. (Originally published 1958)

Williams, R. (1989b). The idea of a common culture. In R. Gable (Ed.), *Resources of hope: Culture, democracy, socialism* (pp. 32–38). London: Verso. (Originally published 1968)

Williams, W. C. (1946). *Paterson.* (Book 1) New York: New Directions.

Witte, S., Trachsel, M., & Walters, K. (1986). Literacy and the direct assessment of writing: A diachronic perspective. In K. L. Greenberg, H. S. Wiener, & R. A. Donovan, (Eds.), *Writing assessment: Issues and strategies* (pp. 13–34). New York: Longman.

Wolfson, N. 1989. *Perspectives: Sociolinguistics and TESOL.* Cambridge, MA: Newbury House.

Wolfram, W. (1991). *Dialects and American English.* Englewood Cliffs: NJ: Prentice Hall.

Wolfram, W., & Whiteman, M. W. (1971). *The role of dialect interference in composition.* Washington, DC: Center for Applied Linguistics. (ERIC Document No. ED 045 971)

Woolf, V. (1948). *The common reader*. (First and second series combined in one volume). New York: Harcourt, Brace and Company. (Originally published in 1925 (first series) and 1932 (second series))

Yathay, P. (1987). *Stay alive, my son*. New York: Simon and Schuster.

Ya'ari, E., & Friedman, E. (1991, February). Curses in verses. *The Atlantic*, pp. 22–26.

Young, R. W. (1977). A history of written Navajo. In J. Fishman (Ed.), *Advances in the creation and revision of writing systems* (pp. 459–470). The Hague: Mouton.

Zamel, V. (1983). The composing processes of advanced ESL students: Six case studies. *TESOL Quarterly, 17*, 165–175.

Zamel, V. (1985). Responding to student writing. *TESOL Quarterly, 19*, 79–101.

Zamel, V. (1987). Recent research on writing pedagogy. *TESOL Quarterly, 21*, 697–716.

Zikopoulos, M. (1987). *Open doors: 1986/1987: Report on international educational exchange*. New York: Institute of International Education.

Also available from TESOL

A World of Books:
An Annotated Reading List for ESL/EFL Students
Dorothy S. Brown

Children and ESL: Integrating Perspectives
Pat Rigg and D. Scott Enright, Editors

Coherence in Writing:
Research and Pedagogical Perspectives
Ulla Connor and Ann M. Johns, Editors

Current Perspectives on Pronunciation:
Practices Anchored in Theory
Joan Morely, Editor

Dialogue Journal Writing with Nonnative English Speakers:
A Handbook for Teachers
Joy Kreeft Peyton and Leslee Reed

Dialogue Journal Writing with Nonnative English Speakers:
An Instructional Packet for Teachers and Workshop Leaders
Joy Kreeft Peyton and Jana Staton

Directory of Professional Preparation Programs
in TESOL in the United States, 1992–1994

Ending Remediation: Linking ESL
and Content in Higher Education
Sarah Benesch, Editor

Research in Reading in English as a Second Language
Joanne Devine, Patricia L. Carrell,
and David E. Eskey, Editors

Reviews of English Language Proficiency Tests
J. Charles Alderson, Karl J. Krahnke,
and Charles W. Stansfield, Editors

Selected Articles from the TESOL Newsletter: 1966–1983
John F. Haskell, Editor

Students and Teachers Writing Together:
Perspectives on Journal Writing
Joy Kreeft Peyton, Editor

Video in Second Language Teaching:
Using, Selecting, and Producing Video for the Classroom
Susan Stempleski and Paul Arcario, Editors

For more information, contact

Teachers of English to Speakers of Other Languages, Inc.
1600 Cameron Street, Suite 300
Alexandria, Virginia 22314 USA
Tel 703-836-0774 • Fax 703-836-7864